Landscape Plants for the Gulf and South Atlantic Coasts

UNIVERSITY PRESS OF FLORIDA / STATE UNIVERSITY SYSTEM

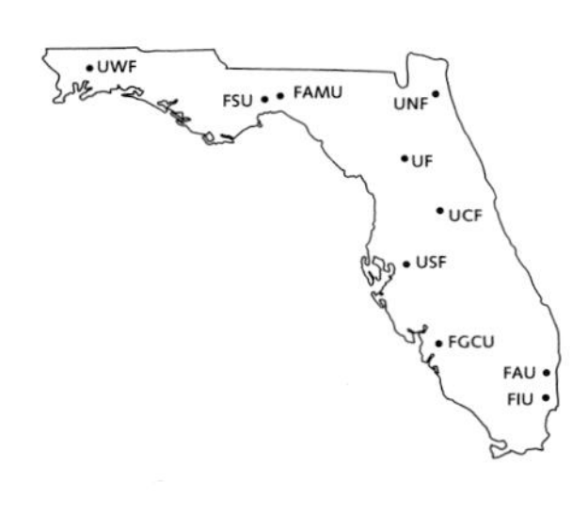

Florida A&M University, Tallahassee
Florida Atlantic University, Boca Raton
Florida Gulf Coast University, Ft. Myers
Florida International University, Miami
Florida State University, Tallahassee
University of Central Florida, Orlando
University of Florida, Gainesville
University of North Florida, Jacksonville
University of South Florida, Tampa
University of West Florida, Pensacola

Landscape Plants for the Gulf and South Atlantic Coasts

Selection, Establishment, and Maintenance

Robert J. Black and Edward F. Gilman

University Press of Florida
Gainesville · Tallahassee · Tampa · Boca Raton
Pensacola · Orlando · Miami · Jacksonville · Ft. Myers

09 08 07 06 05 04 6 5 4 3 2 1

Library of Congress Cataloging-in-Publication Data
Black, Robert J. (Robert John), 1942-
Landscape plants for the Gulf and South Atlantic Coasts: selection, establishment, and maintenance / Robert J. Black and Edward F. Gilman.
p. cm.
Includes bibliographical references (p.).
ISBN 0-8130-2722-5 (pbk.: alk. paper)
1. Landscape plants—Gulf Coast (U.S.) 2. Landscape plants—Atlantic Coast (U.S.)
3. Coastal plants—Gulf Coast (U.S.) 4. Coastal plants—Atlantic Coast (U.S.) I. Gilman, Edward F. II. Title.
SB407.B57 2004
635.9'0976—dc22 2004042558

The University Press of Florida is the scholarly publishing agency for the State University System of Florida, comprising Florida A&M University, Florida Atlantic University, Florida Gulf Coast University, Florida International University, Florida State University, University of Central Florida, University of Florida, University of North Florida, University of South Florida, and University of West Florida.

University Press of Florida
15 Northwest 15th Street
Gainesville, FL 32611-2079
http://www.upf.com

Contents

Figures

Tables

Preface

More than 70 percent of our nation's population lives along a coast. Expanding urbanization along these coastlines has resulted in increased construction of individual residences, condominiums, and commercial establishments. This surge in construction has produced a great need and demand for landscaping to solve aesthetic and functional design problems. Unfortunately, there are many environmental stresses present in these areas that predispose plants to decline and eventually to die.

Perhaps the most common cause of stress is salinity. Yet it should be understood that the specific salt tolerance of a given plant is related to its ability to withstand not only salinity but also a number of other environmental stresses. Coastal soils are generally alkaline and sandy. Alkaline soils may lock up vital mineral nutrients (for example, iron and manganese) needed for plant growth, and sandy soils lack the capacity to retain water and nutrients. Plant damage can also result from high-velocity winds and frequently heavy surf.

The purpose of this book is to assist gardeners of the Gulf and south Atlantic coasts in the selection and maintenance of plants adapted to their sites.

Acknowledgments

A number of people have provided assistance to us throughout the writing of this book. We wish to thank Bart Schutzman and Bijan Dehgan for their help with plant names, and Ken Langeland for his assistance in identifying invasive plant species that appear in this book. For their help with editing and typing, we would also like to thank Priscilla DelCarpio and Heather Randall. We extend a special thanks to Gary Knox and Tom MacCubbin for reviewing this book. Many other people have contributed, in various ways and sometimes unwittingly. They, too, have our deep appreciation. Without them, it would have been difficult if not impossible to produce this book at all. We also thank Horticopia, Inc., Purcellville, Virginia, for providing the initial data for many plants described in this book.

Chapter 1

Salt and Related Plant Problems

Injury to plants can occur when winds carrying salt spray deposit salts on leaves, when coastal soils are inundated with saline or brackish water during catastrophic storm events such as hurricanes, when plants are overfertilized, or when plants are irrigated with saline water.

Much of the water used to irrigate landscape plants comes from municipal or private wells. Intrusion of salt water into these previously nonsaline wells can occur along the coast. Saltwater intrusion occurs when water use is more rapid than the recharge rate, allowing the water table to fall and salt water to flow down into the aquifer. Wells can also be contaminated with salt from above when flooded with saline storm water. High levels of salt can also be found in some reclaimed wastewater used to irrigate landscape plants.

Measuring Salinity

Soil and irrigation water salinity is determined by using an instrument that measures the electrical conductivity (EC) of a soil or water solution. The saltier the solution, the greater its conductivity. Electrical conductivity is recorded in units of Siemans per meter (S/m) or in mhos per centimeter (mhos/cm). Generally, EC is reported in tenths of Siemans or Decisiemans per meter (dS/m), which are equal to millimhos per centimeter (mmhos/cm). Salinity is sometimes reported in parts per million (ppm) or milligrams per liter (mg/L) of total dissolved salts. There is a direct relation between the unit's dS/m and ppm. Each individual salt solution varies from 550 to 700 ppm for every 1 dS/m. For example, a sodium chloride solution of 1 dS/m is equal to 640 ppm soluble salts. Therefore, dS/m or mmhos/cm are the preferred units to express salinity because they can be read directly from an electrical conductivity meter. To accurately convert these units to ppm requires knowing the identities and concentrations of each salt present in the sample.

Effects of Excess Salts on Plants

Excessive concentrations of salts can damage plants by causing water to move out of plant cells through a process called osmosis. As a result, plants suffer from a "physiological drought" condition, since normal water uptake is impaired. In addition, a plant may accumulate chloride or sodium ions, components of salt that can eventually reach damaging or toxic levels in the plant. Also, excessive sodium destroys soil structure and is an antagonistic ion that will displace potassium on the soil complex and can limit the availability of iron, manganese, and phosphorus in soils.

Injury caused by high salt concentrations in the soil around the roots of plants may be expressed by wilting of plants even when adequate water is available. Other symptoms of high soil salinity are an overall reduction in growth (stunting), the burning of margins or tips of leaves followed by defoliation, stem dieback, and death of salt-sensitive species.

High salt levels in the soil can be beneficial to some plants. They can promote growth in salt-loving plants, which are called halophytes, and can increase the yield or quality of some crops. Cotton yields have been shown to increase when plants are grown in moderately saline soils. Also, moderate salinity can enhance tomato fruit quality and citrus freeze tolerance.

The plant response to soil salinity depends on soil properties, irrigation water quality, irrigation management, and weather. Because sandy soils hold less water and nutrients, and clay or organic soils hold more water and nutrients, the severity of injury to plants exposed to the same level of salt is usually greater for plants growing in sandy soils than for those growing in clay or organic soils.

Saline irrigation water can increase the level of salt in the soil and can dry on plant leaves causing damage similar to that caused by ocean salt spray. When saline irrigation is used, provide excellent drainage and excess irrigation to leach excess salts. Table 1.1 presents soluble salt levels at various salt indices for soil and water. Note that although EC is a good indicator of total salt content, it does not indicate the composition of salts in a soil. The relative abundance of an individual salt can still lead to plant injury, even though total salinity may be low.

Weather can have an effect on the response of plants to soil salinity. Leaf burn caused by sodium or chloride is more severe during hot, dry weather. Also, hot, dry weather can increase evaporative water loss from the soil and the plant, resulting in higher levels of salt in the soil.

Salt injury from oceanic spray can add to the challenge of growing plants near the gulf or ocean. Potentially, the biggest problem is related to soil salinity, yet injuries from spray reduce the ornamental value of landscape plantings. Salt-spray injury is characterized by scorched, dry, often burned-looking foliage. Injury symptoms are generally more severe on the ocean-facing portions of plants. As injury progresses, salt-sensitive plants can become completely defoliated. The physiological basis of this injury has been attributed to the caustic nature of salt particles

Table 1.1. Salt index as related to soluble salt levels in soils and irrigation water*

	Soil Type				Irrigation Water	
	Sandy		Organic			
Salt Index	dS/m	ppm	dS/m	ppm	dS/m	ppm
Low	<0.25	<175	<0.50	<350	<0.25	<175
Low to medium	0.25–0.50	175–350	0.50–1.00	350–700	0.25–0.75	175–525
Medium to high	0.50–1.00	350–700	1.00–1.75	700–1,225	0.75–2.00	525–1,400
High to very high	1.00–1.50	700–1,050	1.75–2.75	1,225–1,925	2.00–3.00	1,400–2,100
Excessive	>1.50	>1,050	>2.75	>1,925	>3.00	>2,100

*Modified from information presented in: Waters, W. E.; J. E. Hesmith, C. M. Geraldson and S. S. Woltz, 1972. The interpretations of soluble salt tests and soil analysis by different procedures. Bradenton AREC Mimeo Report GC-1972-4.

deposited on leaf surfaces. Further, the abrasive action of windblown sand particles magnifies this problem. Full sun and winds of high velocities contribute to increased evapotranspiration rates. Following penetration of salt ions through epidermal tissues, a number of physiological problems may occur. Salt ions often cause direct membrane damage to cellular components, and/or metabolic processes may be altered, often leading to an accumulation of toxic substances.

Salt-Tolerant Plants

The physiological basis for salt tolerance in plants is complex and at best is vaguely understood. Morphological features such as thick, waxy cuticles and epidermal hairs and trichomes that limit penetration have been associated with resistance. Other plants have the ability to "detoxify" salt ions once absorbed, while a few species have salt glands for excretion of damaging ions.

Plants installed within about one-eighth of a mile of saltwater coastlines should possess some degree of salt tolerance. Those planted near brackish water estuaries do not need to be as salt tolerant as those planted near the coast. On the other hand, those exposed to direct spray along dunes should be highly salt tolerant. Salt-tolerant plants are often deformed by direct exposure to salty air, but they survive and grow. Foliage on salt-sensitive plants is severely damaged, so these plants become deformed and grow poorly when exposed to salty air.

The best recommendation for alleviating problems associated with salt-spray injury is to use plants that are salt tolerant. Many native plants that are already growing at the site possess a high degree of resistance and should be protected, or incorporated into new or existing landscapes. The Plant Selection Guide (page 62) in this book indicates the degree of salt tolerance of some common landscape plants. Barriers such as fences or plantings of salt-tolerant screens can reduce the injury to more sensitive plants. Frequent spraying of the foliage with nonsaline water will also minimize the problems.

Chapter 2

Selecting the Appropriate Plant for Your Landscape

To obtain the most satisfactory landscape effects, plants should be adapted to the environment in which they are being planted. In general, the central and northern portions of the coastal southern United States are subject to frequent heavy frosts and freezes, whereas portions of southern Florida rarely experience frosts. Because of such differences in winter temperatures, comparatively few plants are adapted for use throughout this region.

There are no clear lines of demarcation between the major climatic zones in the southern states. However, the coastal areas can be roughly divided into northern (hardiness zone 8), central (hardiness zone 9), and southern zones (hardiness zones 10 and 11). A given landscape or portion of it may be a few degrees warmer or cooler than the rest of the climatic zone because of the site's proximity to a lake, estuary, or coast, its elevation, or its air drainage. ("Air drainage" refers to the phenomenon of cold air moving down a slope to settle in the lowest area in the landscape.) As a consequence of such variables, a landscape may accommodate plants that are not usually recommended for its hardiness zone. The hardiness map (Figure 2.1) can be used as a guide to selecting plants that will survive the cold temperatures expected in your area. It also can be used to indicate how far south a plant will grow. The hardiness ranges given for each plant in this book indicate the coldest (smallest zone number) and warmest (largest zone number) areas of a region where that plant will grow well. For example, firebrush grows well in zones 9A through 11 (the Florida Keys).

Based on response to cold temperatures, plants may be classified as "tender," "semihardy," or "hardy" in each of the climatic zones. A plant considered hardy in hardiness zone 9A might be considered tender in hardiness zone 8A. Some semihardy plants grown in zone 9B can be successfully grown in warmer parts of zone 9A. Plants located in regions colder than indicated by their hardiness range may be killed to the ground some years, but they often come back from the roots in the

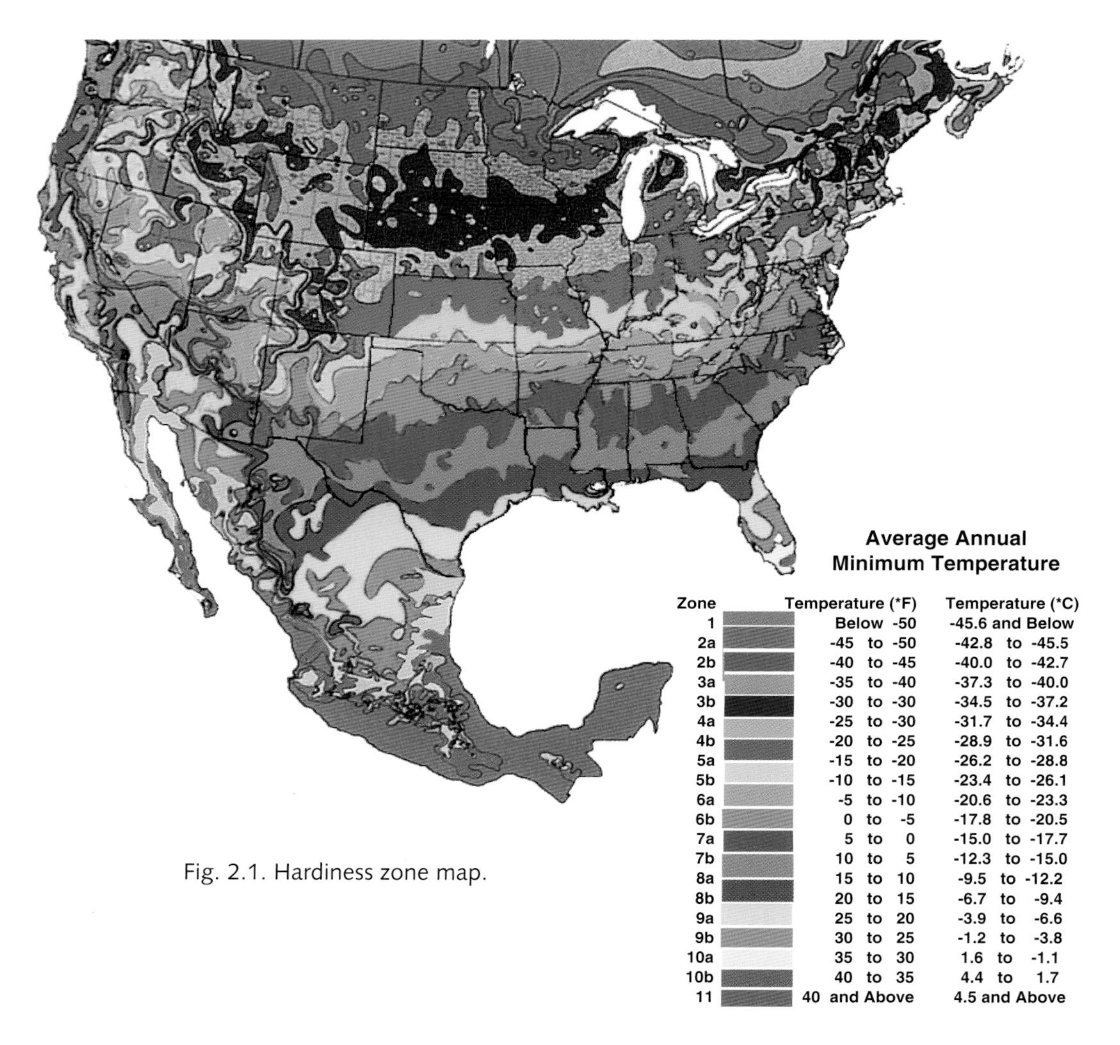

Fig. 2.1. Hardiness zone map.

spring. For example, princess-flower (*Tibouchina* sp.) will be killed to the ground in most winters in zone 9A, but new growth emerges in the spring. Because they are subject to this dieback, these plants will not reach their mature size, but might be grown as perennials reaching 4 to 6 feet tall each year.

Tender plants are confined largely to zones 10A, 10B, and 11, but a few species are adapted to the warmest parts of zone 9B. Semihardy and tender plants will normally survive lower temperatures when mature, or if they have been previously conditioned by several weeks of cool or cold temperatures prior to a freeze. At the other extreme, some plants require specific periods of cool or cold temperatures to induce dormancy required for proper growth and flowering in the next season.

Consider Environmental and Other Factors

Before heading to a nursery, study the environmental conditions of your landscape site. The time you spend doing this now will pay dividends in healthy plants, lower maintenance costs, and fewer plant replacements in the future. Plants have different requirements, and the success of a planting depends on how well you select plants that match the light level, soil, and other characteristics of the site. These characteristics can differ greatly within the same landscape. In a landscape that contains large trees, light levels can vary in different areas of the site from full sun exposure to dense shade. In some landscapes, soil can vary from well-drained sand to poorly drained clay.

Many plants are well adapted to a wide range of soil types, soil moisture conditions, and pH ranges, but most grow best in slightly acid to neutral soils (pH of 5.5 to 7). If your soil pH is above 7.5, choose plants tolerant of alkaline soil. If you ignore this advice, you risk poor plant performance and increasing maintenance costs due to pH-induced nutrient deficiencies.

Although some plants tolerate dry, sandy soils and some tolerate poorly drained soils, most grow best in moist, well-drained soils. Most plants adapted to well-drained soils do not grow well if soils remain wet. Plants adapted to moist or wet soils usually grow poorly in dry, sandy locations. Those adapted to flooding or poorly drained soils are the best choices for areas of the yard where water accumulates. If you dig a planting hole and it fills with water, or water runs into the bottom of the hole from the sides, be sure that the plant you place there tolerates wet soil.

Some people prefer to plant only native plants in their yard. Fortunately, many garden centers and nurseries offer these plants. The Plant Selection Guide in this book indicates which plants are native to the southeastern United States. Frequently, undue emphasis is given to plants that have striking characteristics such as an unusual color. Although plants producing striking effects may be put to good use in the landscape, they should be used sparingly, and their location should be carefully chosen for aesthetic reasons.

Determine Plant Sizes and Numbers

Choose the appropriate mature plant size for the site. Although a plant may look small in the nursery, it can rapidly outgrow its allotted area after a few years. Consider its final mature height and spread, as well as the length of time it will take to reach that size. Often, dwarf varieties of plants are good choices for sites next to buildings, driveways, and roads. These plants do not need frequent pruning, and because dwarf plants stay small, they will not have to be replaced for outgrowing their space. Unfortunately, most people choose large-maturing plants inadvertently. Because these grow the fastest in the nursery, they can be purchased in a large size for a relatively low price. Nevertheless, you will pay many, many times the original cost of the plant when you have to prune it to keep it in bounds. Most homeowners and landscape designers could construct more efficient landscapes by increasing the use of low-growing plants and ground covers, and using less of those that require pruning to keep them at the desired height.

Unless planting a hedge, base the number of plants you need on the mature spread of the plant, the space to be planted, the growth rate, and the planting density you desire. In areas where you want a mass effect, such as for a hedge, plants can be planted close together. In most other instances, space them far enough apart to allow each to develop its full form or shape. This provides a softer effect in the landscape, reduces the need for pruning, and can minimize disease problems by providing good air circulation within the plant canopy.

Examine Plants at the Nursery

After deciding the kind and number of plants you need, you are ready to shop for reasonably priced, good quality plants. Healthy ones establish faster and have fewer problems than plants in poor health. That is why it is so important that you examine them very closely and look for healthy, vigorous ones.

A plant kept in its container too long is often larger than others and has roots wrapping around the inside of the container. It is likely to grow slowly once it is planted. Therefore, when choosing among plants in a given container size, it is often best to choose the moderately sized plants, not the largest ones.

Avoid plants that are infested with lace bugs, spider mites, whiteflies, or scales. These pests suck juices from leaves and stems and can seriously damage a plant. They can also spread to the other plants in your landscape. Some of these pests are very small and are only visible through a magnifying lens. You can easily detect their damage to plant foliage, which often manifests itself as flecking or spotting on the upper sides of leaves. Spotted leaves also can be a symptom of a leaf-spot disease. Except when it attacks Indian hawthorn, red-tip photinia, and some other plants, this disease is not usually serious, but you are better off buying disease-free plants. Avoid purchasing plants with weeds in the root-ball because they can rapidly spread throughout the landscape.

For help in determining what to look for in a quality plant, make use of the American Standard for Nursery Stock (American National Standards Institute ANSI Z60.1, Washington, D.C.—http://hort.ufl.edu/woody/planting/american standard.htm) or the Florida Grades and Standards for Nursery Plants (http://hort.ufl.edu/woody/planting/floridagradesandstandards.htm).

Inspect for Mechanical Injury

Inspect plants closely, and do not purchase any with scars or open wounds along their stems. Large wounds are unsightly and expose the plant to a higher incidence of decay.

Do not buy plants with many broken branches or torn leaves. A plant with a few small, broken twigs is acceptable, if they can be removed without destroying the plant's shape. Removal of large branches results in large holes in the plant's canopy, and it could take years for the plant to regain its natural shape.

Examine grafted plants, such as gardenia and citrus, to determine if the graft union has closed properly. The union is typically close to the ground and should be smooth and clean. There should be no suckers on the stem below the graft union.

Check for Cold Injury

Stems and roots may be damaged on tender plants that were left unprotected from frost or freezing temperatures. Obvious symptoms of cold injury are brown leaves, split bark, dead branches, and brown roots. Some plants may not express symptoms of cold injury until they are stressed by warmer weather in the spring or summer. Therefore, if you are buying plants after an unusually cold winter, you should closely inspect their roots and stems in the spring or summer for signs of root injury or split bark.

Study Condition and Shape of Canopy

Select specimens with uniform canopies filled with healthy, vigorous leaves of normal size, shape, color, and texture. Young plants or those spaced too closely together in the nursery may not develop a uniform canopy until placed in the landscape for several years. Avoid plants with leaves of abnormal size or excessively yellowed leaves unless the plant naturally has variegated or multicolored foliage. Large, high-quality shade trees have one sturdy stem with plenty of uniformly distributed branches forming a well-balanced plant. Unevenly spaced branches or branches clustered together on the main stem usually result in weak or leggy plants, and they should be avoided. Small-maturing ornamental trees like crape myrtle can have several stems, but main stems should not touch each other.

Examine the Root System

Inspecting the belowground portions of nursery stock is important because the plant's ultimate survival depends largely on the health of its root system. For this reason, buy your plants from a nursery that allows customers to examine the roots of the plants. Small plants purchased from nurseries usually come in containers. Large trees can be purchased balled and burlapped or in containers. Inspect the roots of a container-grown plant by laying it on its side and sliding the container off the root-ball. If you find it difficult to remove the container, the plant may be root-bound (Figure 2.2). Root-bound plants have a mass of roots circling the outside surface of the root-ball. This root mass can be so dense that it prevents roots from penetrating the soil after planting. Circling roots can also girdle the plant as it grows and eventually kill it. Be sure there are no roots circling close to the trunk because

Fig. 2.2. Root-bound plant.

Fig. 2.3. Recently repotted plant.

these could stress or kill the plant. On the other hand, if the root-ball falls apart (Figure 2.3) when you remove the container, it could have been repotted recently, or the root system may be inadequate or unhealthy. You could be buying a container of potting media with very few roots.

Examine the roots on the surface of the root-ball. Do not buy a plant with dark brown or black roots that are mushy (Figure 2.4). Heat stress, freezing temperatures, overwatering, or drought probably killed these roots. Poke your finger down into the rooting medium next to the main trunk to look and feel for bent or circling roots. These can prevent plants from becoming properly established and can lead to premature plant death. Also, the topmost root emerging from the trunk should be located within the top 2 inches of the soil surface.

Roots should be distributed throughout the container medium. They should not protrude outside the container or penetrate the ground (Figure 2.5). If you try to pick up a container plant and find it is fastened to the ground by escaping roots, move to another plant. The root-ball should also be free of weeds (Figure 2.6). Weeds will slow the establishment of a plant and may spread into the surrounding

Fig. 2.4. Plants with black roots on root-ball.

landscape. The root-ball should be moist, not dry, and you should see some white, yellow, or light brown roots on the sides of the root-ball when you slip it from the container.

The root-balls of plants that are balled and burlapped should be moist, with the soil firmly held around the roots by burlap that has been tightly secured with pins, twine, wire, or a wire basket. The stem of the plant should be sturdy in the root-ball. A loose or droopy root-ball indicates that the plant was treated roughly, resulting in poor plant establishment and growth in the landscape.

Fig. 2.5. Plant with escaping roots

Fig. 2.6. Plant with obvious weed problem.

Chapter 3

Planting

Plants can be installed throughout the year in warm climates where soil does not freeze for extended periods (hardiness zones 7 through 11). Soil temperatures are usually warm enough for some root growth in winter, so plants that are planted in the fall can establish roots into the landscape soil before warm summer temperatures draw moisture from the plants and cause stress. This could give them an edge over plants installed in the spring, which will have few roots out into the landscape soil when warm temperatures arrive soon after planting.

Handling and Preparing Root-Balls for Planting

If plants are to survive and become established in a landscape, they have to be planted correctly. The procedures for planting container-grown and balled and burlapped plants are essentially the same. Root-balls in containers are more resistant to rough handling than those that are balled and burlapped. A balled and burlapped plant should be handled carefully, because shifting of soil inside the root-ball may break roots and leave cracks in the root-ball. A cracked root-ball will dry out quickly and require more water.

Before planting a container-grown plant, slip the container off the root-ball. The root-ball should remain intact and be somewhat pliant, or flexible. If the plant is root-bound or has many circling roots around the outside, you should slice the sides of the root-ball with pruning shears, a serrated knife, or a utility knife (Figure 3.1). Make three or four evenly spaced slices, each one going from the top to the bottom of the root-ball, 1 to 2 inches deep. Any circling roots that remain should be pulled away from the root-ball. Recent studies show that although this kind of pruning does not increase root growth after planting, slicing root-balls (whether root-bound or not) does enhance the distribution of regenerated roots in the surrounding landscape soil. Instead of occurring almost exclusively from the bottom

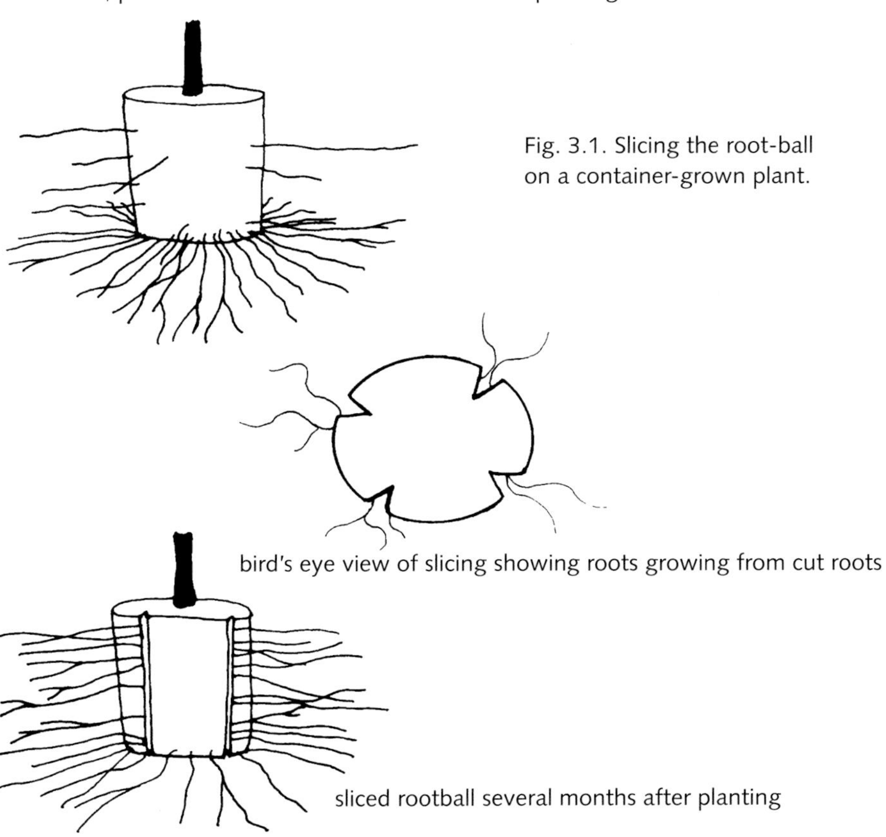

Fig. 3.1. Slicing the root-ball on a container-grown plant.

of the root-ball, root generation occurs along the slice from the top to the bottom of the root-ball.

When planting a balled and burlapped shrub or tree, it is important to know whether the root-ball is wrapped in natural or synthetic burlap. You can determine which type is used by holding a lit match to a small portion of the burlap. As a rule, natural burlap will burn; synthetic burlap will melt. Because synthetic burlap does not decompose in the soil and can girdle roots, it must be entirely removed after the plant is placed in the planting hole. To remove it, cut the string and ties from around the trunk, pull the burlap away from the sides of the root-ball, and remove the burlap from the hole. Natural burlap decomposes readily in the soil and can be left along the sides and bottom of the root-ball, but it should be removed from the top of the root-ball where it is subject to drying out. Dry burlap repels water, making it difficult to rewet the root-ball. **Always remove nylon twine used to hold burlap around the plant stem. Nylon twine does not rot and will eventually girdle the stem if left in place.**

Wire baskets and wire wrapping are frequently used to help hold a balled and burlapped root-ball of a large tree intact during shipping and handling. Trees that are stored after being dug with a tree spade are also placed in wire baskets. Placement in a wire basket is an effective means of keeping roots in contact with soil until planting. Although there are no documented reports of wire baskets strangling trees, some horticulturists remove the top layer or two of wire from the basket at the time of planting. Also, if the burlap inside the basket is synthetic, cut it away from the root-ball.

Digging and Filling the Planting Hole

Begin planting by digging the planting hole about two times the diameter of the root-ball (Figure 3.2). The planting hole should never be dug any deeper than the height of the root-ball. Disturbing the soil beneath the plant may cause it to settle too deep in the soil. Gently place the plant straight upright in the hole, making sure that the root flare—the point where the topmost root emerges from the trunk—is a couple inches higher than the surface of the surrounding soil. In compacted or poorly drained soil, the top quarter to top third of the root-ball should be planted above the soil surface, with soil then placed around the exposed sides of the root-ball to provide an adequate volume of well-drained soil for root development (Figure 3.3).

After placing the root-ball into the planting hole, backfill the bottom half of the planting hole with loose, unamended soil. Mixing amendments such as organic matter or other soil conditioners into the backfill soil provides no benefit. Tamp the soil lightly to settle it around the root-ball, but not so heavily as to compact the soil. Finish filling the hole and gently tamp again. Instead of tamping lightly with your feet, you can settle the soil by inserting a hose of briskly running water into the

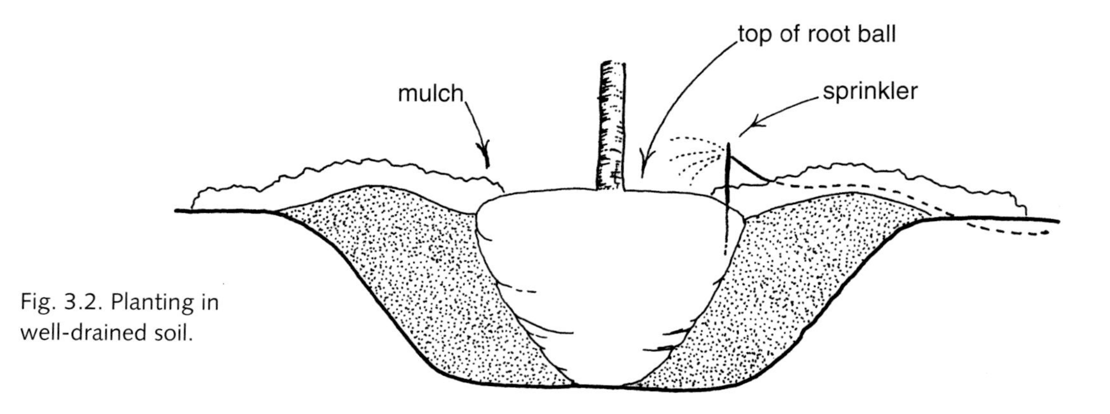

Fig. 3.2. Planting in well-drained soil.

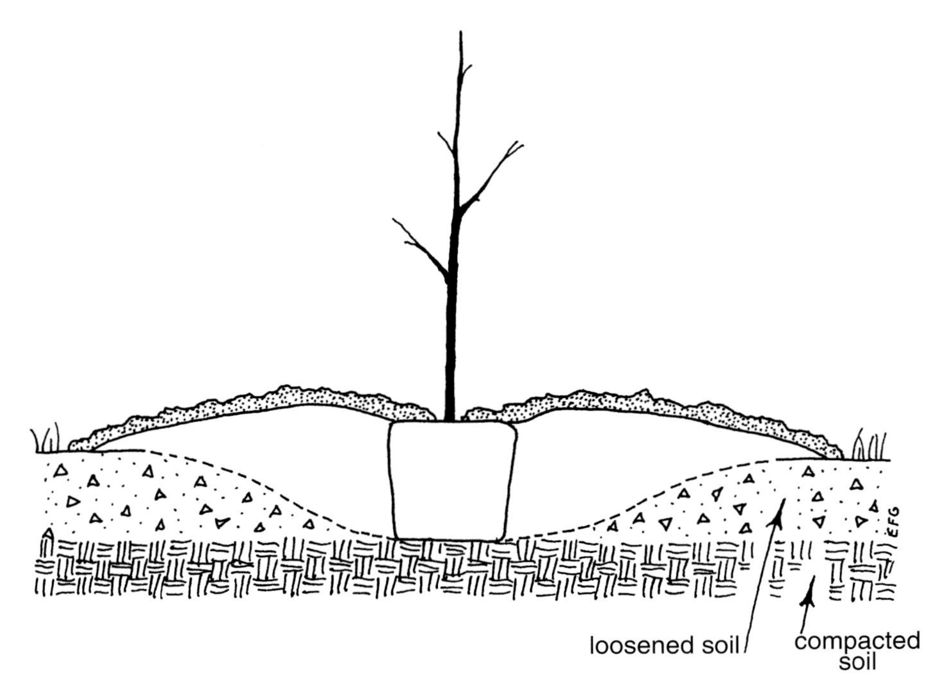

Fig. 3.3. Planting in compacted or poorly drained soil. Keep mulch away from trunk.

backfill soil and running it up and down in that soil all the way around the hole. Never place soil over the top of the root-ball because it can prevent water from reaching the roots in the root-ball, which can kill the plant. Planting too deeply and placing soil over the top of the root-ball are among the leading causes of plant decline in many landscapes. Sometimes the effects of planting too deeply might not be seen for several years.

After planting the tree and settling the soil, construct a 2- to 3-inch-high soil or mulch berm (also called a "water ring") around the outer edge of the root-ball to hold irrigation water during the first growing season (Figures 3.2–3.3). Never construct a berm or ring more than 3 inches high because it will bury the roots too deep and can lead to poor growth or plant mortality. By the end of the first growing season, remove the berm by pulling it away from the plant. Many roots will have grown well beyond the berm by then. Soil and mulch should never be pushed in against the trunk because it can bury the trunk, causing it to rot.

Planting in Beds

If no trees or mature shrubs are in the vicinity, prepare the bed for a group or row of plants by spading or tilling the entire bed to a depth of 8 to 12 inches. If existing shrubs or trees are present nearby, keep spading or tilling activities outside their drip lines (circular area directly beneath the branch tips of a tree canopy) to avoid injuring their roots. Do not spade or till within the drip line of a tree; simply dig a hole for each plant, being careful not to cut or injure tree roots more than 1 inch in diameter.

There may be some benefit to amending the soil in the entire bed with peat, compost, or other soil amendments. Some researchers have found greater root growth in amended beds. If using soil amendments, spade or till 3 to 6 inches of organic matter such as compost into the top 6 to 12 inches of soil in the entire bed prior to planting (Figures 3.4–3.5). Then, dig a hole for each plant and backfill with the amended bed soil.

Fig. 3.4. Spade or till organic matter and fertilizer into the bed to a depth of 6 to 12 inches.

Fig. 3.5. Level the soil in the bed with a garden rake.

Mulching

Mulches (Table 3.1) enhance root growth, reduce soil temperature fluctuations, prevent packing and crusting of the soil, minimize runoff and soil erosion, conserve moisture, help control weeds, and add to the beauty of the landscape by providing a cover of uniform color and an interesting texture to the surface. Mulch newly situated plants with a 3-inch layer of organic or inorganic material. Keep the mulch 4 to 6 inches away from the stems of the plants. When placed against the stem, the high-moisture environment of the mulch increases the chances of stem rot, which can result in plant death. Avoid applying a thick layer of finely textured mulches over the root-ball, as it can restrict the movement of water into the root-ball.

When mulching individual shrubs and trees planted in lawns, cover an area at least three times larger than the planting hole. This will help the plant to establish more quickly by reducing competition from turfgrass. When mulching a shrub bed, cover the entire area of the bed. For trees, apply mulch in a circle at least 2 to 3 feet in diameter for each inch of trunk diameter (Table 3.2). Maintain or increase the size of the circle of mulch as the tree grows until the tree is fully established.

Table 3.1. Mulches

Mulch type	Color	Longevity	Weed Control	Notes
pine bark chips	dark brown	medium to long	good	acid-forming
pine needles	light brown	short	fair	acid-forming
cypress	light tan	long	very good	acid-forming (not recommended)
hardwood chips	brown/gray	medium to long	good	acid-forming
pine wood chips	tan	medium	good	acid-forming
oak leaves	dark brown	short	fair to good	acid-forming (can blow around)
grass clippings	green	very short	good	mats down (not recommended)
yard debris	light brown	medium	fair	recycles yard waste (highly recommended)

Table 3.2. Minimum diameter of mulch circles for establishing trees*

Trunk diameter (in inches)	Mulch circle diameter (in feet)
1	4
2	4
3	6
4	8

*A larger area will help even more. Keep mulch free of weeds.

Planting Palms

When planting palms, the hole should be wide enough to easily accept the root-ball and provide about 12 inches of room for new growth from the ball. The hole should only be deep enough to situate the topmost root at the soil surface. Planting too deeply will cause root suffocation, nutritional deficiencies, root-rot disease, and perhaps even loss of the palm. The decline of palms planted too deeply may take several years to become apparent, especially in very well-drained soils, and at that point it can only be reversed by removing the backfill from the suffocated root initiation zone or by replanting the palm.

All air pockets should be tamped out of the backfill as the planting hole is filled. A 3- to 4-inch-high berm of soil or mulch should be mounded up at the periphery of the root-ball to retain water during irrigation. The initial irrigation should be deep and thorough; filling the planting hole with water up to the berm two or three times may be necessary to fully wet and settle the soil at the time of planting.

Chapter 4

Establishing Plants

Shrubs and Ground Covers

Strive to maintain constant moisture in the root-balls of shrubs and ground covers, but avoid keeping them saturated. If planting during the warm part of the year, water the root-balls every day for the first few weeks after planting. Gradually decrease the frequency of irrigation to every other day and then to every third day until plants are established. Plants that are planted in cooler seasons can be watered less often. There is usually no need to water the soil outside the root-ball because this soil dries slowly until roots grow into it.

If provided with regular irrigation, 1-gallon plants become established about three to six months after planting, and 7-gallon plants take about a year. Watering under the canopy weekly through the second year after planting can help maintain vigorous growth. To encourage fast growth, you might consider this irrigation strategy until the plants are close to the desired size, and then eliminate irrigation to slow down growth. In most landscapes, well-established plants do not need to be watered except during drought or perhaps occasionally in the dry season.

Shrubs and ground covers can benefit from a small amount of slow-release fertilizer applied to the top of the root-ball four to six weeks after planting, but it is not needed for survival.

Trees

Even the healthiest trees planted in the most ideal circumstances need a substantial amount of time, care, and most particularly, proper irrigation to become established in the landscape (Table 4.1). During the establishment period, roots are expanding out into the landscape soil, and shoots and trunk grow more slowly than

Table 4.1. Length of tree establishment period with optimum irrigation*

Trunk diameter of nursery stock	Establishment period (in months)		
	North Florida	Central Florida	South Florida
Less than 2"	4–8	3–6	2–4
2" to 4"	8–15	6–12	5–9
Over 4"**	15+	12+	10+

*See Table 4.2 for optimum irrigation schedule.
**For each additional inch of trunk diameter, trees in north Florida require about 4 more months for establishment. Trees in central Florida require 3 months and in south Florida 2 months per additional inch.

they did before transplanting (Figure 4.1). Once shoot and trunk growth rates match the rates before planting, the tree is considered established. An established tree has developed a root system substantial enough to keep it alive without supplemental irrigation. Trees transplanted from containers take longer to establish and therefore may require supplemental irrigation for a longer period than do field-grown trees. Research indicates that establishment time for container-grown trees can be an additional one to two months *per inch of trunk diameter.* If supplemental irrigation is halted too soon, the mortality rate for container-grown trees will be higher than for hardened off field-grown trees.

Establishment occurs more rapidly in warm climates and when irrigation is supplied in correct quantity and frequency. Frequent irrigation benefits the transplanted tree more than large volumes of water that are applied infrequently. In well-drained soil, apply water to the root-ball every day for the first several weeks when planting during the growing season. Irrigation conducted according to the schedule in Table 4.2 will provide for the most rapid establishment. In poorly drained soil, a set irrigation schedule may be impractical. Instead, monitor the site for changes in moisture levels caused by rainfall or possibly runoff from adjacent irrigation. Essentially, the root-balls of newly planted trees must not be allowed to dry out nor remain too wet. It is easy to kill trees that have been planted into poorly drained sites.

The best way to determine how much irrigation to apply to container-grown trees after planting into well-drained soil is to ask the nursery operator how much was applied in the nursery just prior to purchase. Apply this amount or slightly more directly to the root-ball. There is no need to wet the surrounding soil at this time because it will be wetted by water draining from the container root-ball and by rainfall. Container-grown trees planted into poorly drained soil may need a smaller volume of irrigation than they received in the nursery.

As a rule of thumb for field-grown trees, 1½ to 3 gallons of water per inch of trunk diameter applied each time the tree is irrigated during the growing season

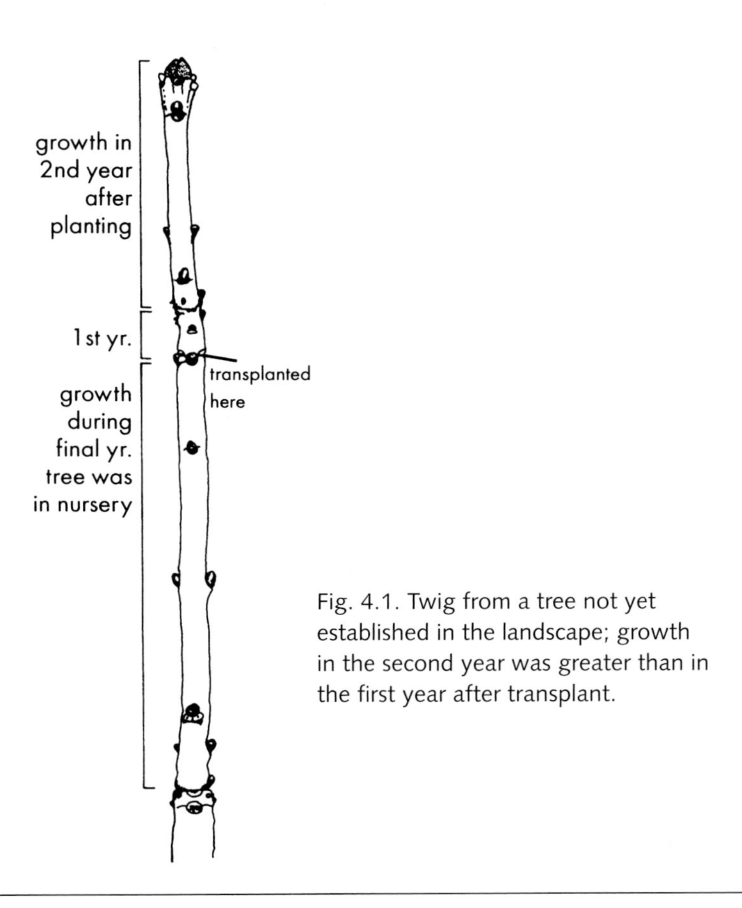

Fig. 4.1. Twig from a tree not yet established in the landscape; growth in the second year was greater than in the first year after transplant.

Table 4.2. Irrigation schedule for quickly establishing trees in well-drained sites during the growing season*

Trunk diameter of tree	North Florida	Central/South Florida
Under 2"	Daily for 1 month, then 3 times a week for 2 months, then weekly until established.	Daily for 1 month, then 3 times a week for 3 months, then weekly until established.
2" to 4"	Daily for 1–2 months, then 3 times a week for 3 months, then weekly until established.	Daily for 2 months, then 3 times a week for 4 months, then weekly until established.
Over 4"	Daily for 2 months, then 3 times a week for 4 months, then weekly until established.	Daily for 2–3 months, then 3 times a week for 5 months, then weekly until established.

*Frequency of irrigation may be slightly reduced for hardened-off field-grown trees. Frequency may also be reduced when planting in the cooler months or in poorly drained soils. Apply 1½–3 gallons per inch of trunk diameter at each irrigation. Trees often survive without the daily irrigation but will grow more slowly. See Table 4.1 for establishment times.

should be enough to maintain adequate root growth. For example, a tree with a 2-inch trunk diameter needs about 3 to 6 gallons each time it is irrigated. Trees planted during the cooler months may need less water, depending on the weather and soil drainage.

Palms

The root-ball and surrounding backfill should remain evenly moist but never saturated during the first four to six months after installation. Supplementary irrigation is necessary unless adequate rainfall is received during this time. Newly transplanted specimen-sized palms should not be expected to produce a great deal of new top growth during the first year after transplanting; much of the palm's energy reserves will (and should) be channeled into root growth. Drenching the root zone two to four times during the first few months with a fungicide labeled for landscape use on soilborne root fungal pathogens is recommended for high-value palms. A light (that is, one-third of recommended rate) surface application of a slow-release "palm special" granular fertilizer can be broadcasted on and slightly beyond the root-ball three to four months after transplanting. A foliar spray of soluble micronutrients (iron, manganese, zinc, copper, boron, molybdenum, and chlorine) may be beneficial during this period, since root absorption activity is limited. Macronutrients (nitrogen, phosphorous, potassium, and magnesium) are negligibly absorbed through the leaves and are typically not applied as a foliar feed. When the appearance of new leaves indicates that establishment has been successful, a regular fertilization program at an optimum of three to four times per year can begin.

Staking and Wood Supports

In addition to requiring special irrigation, some trees in the establishment period may need to be staked. There are two types of staking, each used for a different purpose. **Anchor staking** prevents a newly planted tree from tilting in the planting hole when the wind blows. Such tilting will cause root-ball movement and can break roots and slow plant establishment. **Support staking** holds a weak trunk in an upright position. Many trees do not require staking after planting; do not stake a tree unnecessarily.

Until their root systems are well established, trees with large canopies, those with small root-balls, and those planted in areas open to the wind, such as parking lots and parks, are more likely to require **anchor stakes and guy wires** than trees planted in protected areas near buildings or among existing trees. Use two or three anchor stakes for trees with trunk diameters under 2 inches, three stakes for trunks 2 to 3 inches in diameter, and three or four stakes for larger trees (Figure 4.2, *A* and *B*). Stakes should be driven at least 24 inches into the ground. Often wire threaded

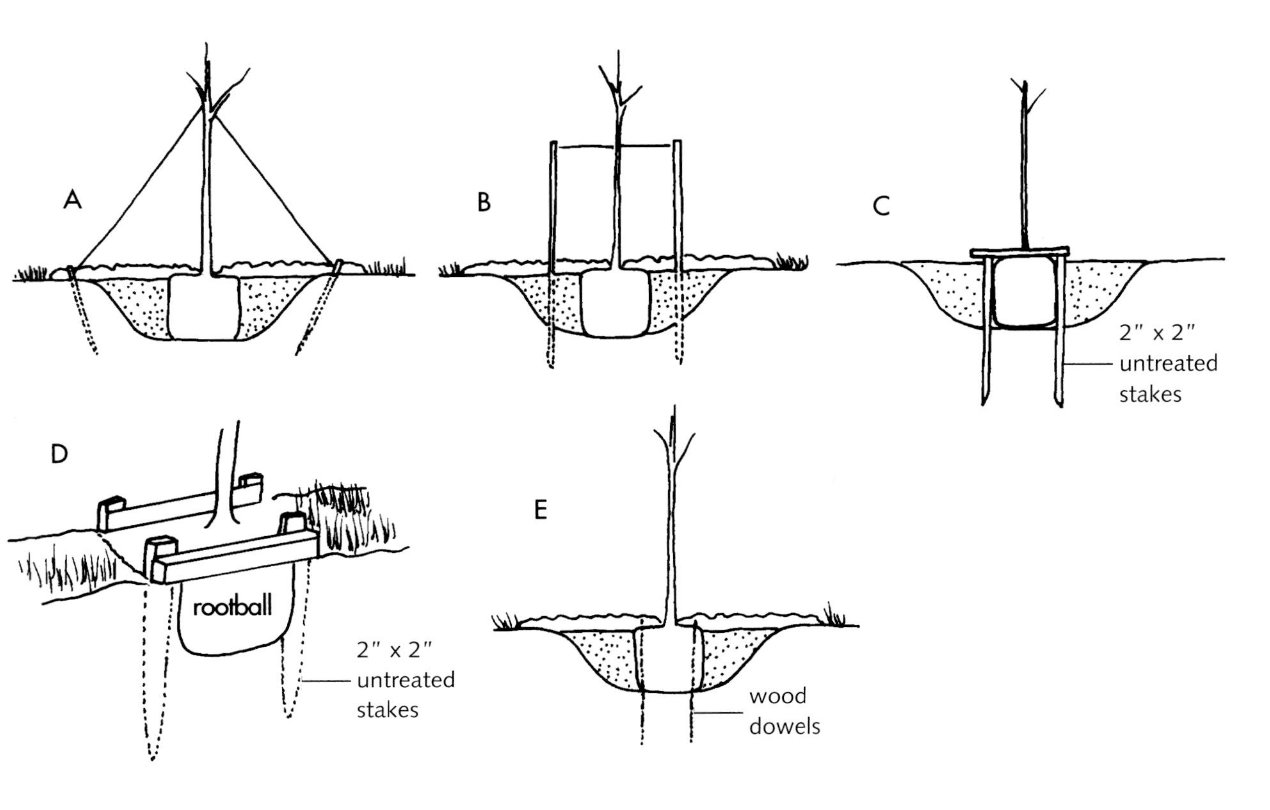

Fig. 4.2. Method of staking: *A* and *B*, anchoring with above-ground stakes and wires; *C*, *D*, and *E*, below-ground anchoring.

through a short piece of garden hose is used to secure the tree to the stake. However, this system can damage the trunk as it moves in the wind and rubs against the hose. You need to use a wide, smooth material such as one of the rubberlike products now available for this purpose. Wrap this material around the trunk above the base of a lower branch. Pull it firmly so there is no slack, and attach to the stake. Guys and stakes should be removed within a year after planting. If anchor stakes are required for more than a year, there may be a problem with the tree.

The anchoring systems shown in Figures 4.2, *C* through *E*, stabilize trees without using aboveground wires or supports. For the techniques shown in *C* and *D*, you will need 2" × 2" stakes (made of untreated lumber) that measure twice the depth of the root-ball. Drive these stakes almost all the way into the ground just *outside* the perimeter of the root-ball *(C)*. Position the stakes so they are nearly opposite each other. Connect them by placing a crosspiece at least 2 inches from the tree trunk and screwed into the sides of the stakes *(D)*; if the crosspiece is attached to the tops of the stakes, it can work loose. Use two stakes and one crosspiece for small trees (that is, those with a root-ball smaller than 30 gallons), and four stakes and two crosspieces for trees that are larger. On container-grown trees, drive ½–¾-inch-

Fig. 4.3. Proper support for a newly installed palm.

diameter dowels that are two times the depth of the root-ball all the way into the ground just *inside* the perimeter of the root-ball.

Poor nursery practices often yield trees with thin, weak trunks that require **support staking** to keep them upright. If you must plant such a tree, the staking must not only provide support but also enable the tree to develop trunk strength. Taking care to avoid major roots, drive the stake approximately 24 inches into the ground immediately next to the trunk being careful not to injure the trunk. The support stake should be secured to the trunk at the lowest position that will hold the trunk erect. To find this point, hold the tree upright and slide your hand from the top of the trunk down to the spot where the top of the tree begins to bend over. Using a wide, smooth material, attach the stake 6 inches above this point. Trim the stake just above the point of attachment so that it does not injure the trunk. Six months after staking and when the foliage is wet, remove the stake to see if the tree can stand erect. If not, repeat the process every two months until sufficient strength is developed. If the tree requires staking for more than one year, it may never develop the strength to support itself. Leaving small branches along the lower trunk will also help the trunk increase in diameter and strength. These branches can be removed once the tree can support itself.

Large transplanted palms usually require anchorage for six to eight months after transplant. Support can be supplied either with guy wires or, more commonly, with wood supports. Wrap three or four boards about 2 feet long in several layers of burlap. Fasten these to the trunk of the palm with metal straps, then nail support posts to the padded boards, being careful not to pierce the trunk with the nails (Figure 4.3). Never nail supports directly into the trunk as such damage is permanent and provides an entryway for pathogens and insect pests as well.

Chapter 5

Plant Maintenance

How plants are cared for not only determines how well they grow but also has an impact on energy and water consumption, and thus the environment. Therefore, apply enough water and fertilizer to keep plants growing and healthy, but not so much as to waste water, encourage excessive growth, or pollute lakes and waterways with fertilizer-contaminated runoff.

Watering

When to Water

Once plants are established, variables such as region of the country, plant species, soil type, time of year, sunlight exposure, and weather conditions determine when plants should be watered and with how much water. Consequently, it is difficult to offer specific watering procedures. Nevertheless, the following guidelines should provide some general information.

Once plants are established and have adapted to the conditions of the site, irrigation is most often needed in late spring (May) and early fall (October), when temperatures are typically high and rainfall amounts low. In many years, little irrigation is needed during the summer rainy period. Irrigate only when plants need water, as indicated by wilting leaves (Figure 5.1). During the summer, if properly selected, established plants located in full sun typically need no water for a couple of weeks after a water application (including rainfall of at least ¾ inch of water). They can go longer without water if planted in the shade or in soils of fine texture, such as marl or clay, as well as during the winter. Established drought tolerant plants may not need to be irrigated at all once they are established.

Plants should be watered early in the morning when wind and temperature levels are low. Irrigating during the late morning, at midday, or during the afternoon usually results in more water loss from evaporation and could violate local irriga-

Fig. 5.1. Some plants will demonstrate their need for water by wilting.

tion ordinances. Because winds are typically stronger at these times of day, overhead irrigation systems are more likely to distribute the water unevenly. Watering at night before dew develops is not advised, as this practice can encourage the development of disease by keeping the foliage wet all night.

Some plants demonstrate their need for water by wilting (Figure 5.1). If they continue to wilt during the evening, water them the following morning if it does not rain. Other plants, however, show no early symptoms of drought stress. If drought conditions continue, however, they may exhibit injury symptoms such as leaf drop, browning of the leaf margins or tips, or both. Plants should be watered just before the appearance of injury symptoms. When you become familiar with your plants, you will be able to determine when they need water just by looking at them. Chances are, all plants in the landscape will not need to be watered on the same day. Only water those that appear to need it. Compared to using a time clock to schedule the irrigation, this is a much more efficient way to irrigate.

When you decide it is time to water, be sure to comply with local and regional water regulations. In many areas, irrigation is allowed only on certain days or during specified hours. Also check your local rain forecasts before irrigating. If a weather front is approaching with rain likely in the next day or two, do not turn on the irrigation. Established plants are unlikely to be damaged by another couple of days of drought. Monitor local rainfall with a simple rain gauge, and install and maintain an automatic rain switch on automatic irrigation systems. A rain switch prevents the irrigation system from operating when it is raining. You will save water by following these guidelines.

How Much Water to Apply

When watering, soak the soil thoroughly. Frequent, light sprinklings on established plants waste water and do little to satisfy the water requirements of a plant growing in hot, dry soil. Plants watered in this way often develop shallow root systems, increasing their susceptibility to damage if watering is interrupted for a few days.

For most sandy soils, ½ to ¾ inch of rainfall or irrigation is sufficient to wet the root zone. Because not all soils and plants are alike, however, some adjustments in the amount of water applied may be necessary.

To determine when a hose-end or in-ground sprinkler system has delivered ¾ inch of water, place cans or cartons at intervals within the spray pattern (as shown in Figure 5.2) and continue watering until the average water level in the cans reaches ¾ inch. Operate the irrigation system for this length of time each time you irrigate.

Watering Methods

Although not commonly used, the most efficient and effective watering method currently in use is microirrigation, which is also known as drip or trickle irrigation. Microirrigation supplies small quantities of water directly to the mulch and soil

Fig. 5.2. Measure water levels in containers placed in a sprinkler's spray pattern to determine the amount of water being applied.

Fig. 5.3. Drip emitters are well suited for narrow strip planting and for new plantings.

through plastic tubing located on or below the ground surface. Low-pressure emitters (nozzles that drip, spray, or sprinkle) are attached to the plastic tubing and slowly release water into the soil around a plant. Wetting only the root zone results in dramatic water savings because less is evaporated. Microirrigation kits are available at many home and garden stores, and individual components of a system can be purchased at irrigation supply stores. More sophisticated systems can be designed and installed by a professional. Irrigation supply stores also carry "retrofit" kits for converting existing irrigation systems to microirrigation.

When microirrigating, you need to know which kind of emitter to install in a given location. With drip emitters placed in sand, water will move laterally only 10 to 12 inches from the emitter. Drip emitters are ideal when such precision is desirable or for narrow strip plantings, such as along hedgerows (Figure 5.3). Because drip emitters are sometimes placed under mulch or buried in the soil, clogging may occur, and this problem is complicated by the difficulty in detecting the location of the clog. Because the action of drip emitters is not readily apparent, it is also difficult to know whether the system is irrigating excessively due to a hole in the tubing or oversight. Regular inspection is required to ascertain that the drip emitters and the overall system are functioning as they should. In fact, all irrigation systems should be inspected for leaks and uniform coverage to assure efficient operation.

On the whole, spray-jets (either microsprayers or microsprinklers) are more desirable than drip emitters for most landscape applications. Because spray-jets can cover areas 3 to 20 feet in diameter, fewer emitters are needed. Not only is their action visible, but also the greater flow rate of water through spray-jets (10 to 20 gallons per hour versus the drip emitter's 0.25 to 2 gallons per hour) makes them less susceptible to clogging. Microsprayers create a fan-shaped distribution of fine water droplets (Figure 5.4). Spray-jets perform well when used for directional spray and confined-area applications, too. Shaping vanes, called "spokes," can be added to create streams of water, or "spoke-jets." A spoke-shaped application pattern works well for a single plant. A deflection cap will confine the application to areas 2

Fig. 5.4. Microsprayers create a fan-shaped distribution of fine water droplets.

Fig. 5.5. Microsprinklers leave more uniform water distribution than microsprayers.

to 5 feet in diameter. Some manufacturers have added spinner devices to create a sprinkler effect (Figure 5.5). These microsprinklers have more uniform water distribution than the fan-shaped spray-jets or spoke-jets and can provide excellent coverage.

Regardless of the emitter style, clogging can be a problem if the water supply is not filtered at the point it enters the irrigation system (Figure 5.6). Filters are easily installed in any irrigation system. It is especially recommended that water from wells be filtered. The safest and easiest way to maintain the emitters in a microirrigation system is to keep a small supply of clean backup emitters on hand. Clogged devices can easily be replaced with clean units and then placed in a small container of the cleaning fluid appropriate for the clogging material.

With systems other than microirrigation, water should be applied only as fast as the soil can absorb it. Using a hose with water pressure at full force can do more damage than good. Fast-flowing water carries away soil and mulch, either exposing plant roots to direct sunlight or covering the root ball with soil. Watering with

Fig. 5.6. Plants can die from drought stress if clogged emitters are not detected.

sprinklers is more efficient. Whether using a sprinkler attached to a hose or an automatic sprinkler system in the ground, the efficiency of the system depends on how well it is managed. A hose-end sprinkler may be placed anywhere in the landscape and allowed to run until it has delivered ¾ inch of water. If the sprinkler is moved too soon, water will not reach the root zone. If the sprinkler runs too long, water will pass below the root zone and be wasted.

Irrigation systems may be operated automatically with a time clock or soil sensor, or they can be manually controlled. Scheduling irrigation with a time clock is easy but wasteful. The time clock turns on the system in rain or sunshine, regardless of whether the plants need water. A sprinkler system with a time clock may be manually controlled by setting the time clock to the "off" position and switching the system on when the plants need water. The automatic position on the time clock is useful when you are away from home for more than a few days. By installing a shutoff device that overrides the system when rain falls, you can make the system operate even more efficiently. Soil moisture sensors often require a lot of maintenance to remain accurate.

Fertilization

Deciding If Fertilization Is Needed

Fertilization of plants usually results in additional growth and production of leaves, stems, branches, and roots. Often this growth results in additional maintenance costs and more yard trimmings to be disposed of, so it is important to determine if growth is the result we want with our plants. Fertilizer is useful for preventing and correcting nutrient deficiencies in acid-loving plants (Figure 5.7) that have been improperly installed into soil with a high pH.

Fertilization is usually desirable when we are trying to establish newly installed plants. We normally want the new plants to get off to a quick start and grow rapidly so they fill the planted area. When this is the case, fertilize about four to six weeks after planting and then two to three times per year for the following three years or so. The first application can be made in the spring, the second in the summer, and the third in the fall.

Established trees and large shrubs may not need additional fertilizer if they are growing in a landscape where turf is fertilized. The plants' root systems extend to take up nutrients (and water) from fertilized areas. However, smaller shrubs and ground covers may benefit from continued fertilization, since they typically have few roots in the fertilized turf.

Soil Testing

Soil testing provides some information about the nutritional status of soil and may aid in the detection of potential nutritional problems. Soil tests can measure soil pH and give an index of the available phosphorus and potassium. If you are prepared to modify your fertilization practices to fit specific fertilization recommendations based on a soil test, the following instructions on conducting soil sampling will be useful. However, if you plan on simply using one of the commonly recommended fertilizers such as 12-4-8 or 15-5-15, there is no logical reason to go to the trouble of testing. Skip to the next section, which discusses how much fertilizer to use.

Test the soil area to be fertilized prior to purchasing fertilizer. Collect the samples and send them to a lab a couple of months before you anticipate needing to fertilize. This allows ample time for the lab to get results back to you.

Obtain a composite soil sample by removing "subsamples" from ten to twelve small holes dug throughout the sample area (such as the front yard of your home).

Fig. 5.7. Iron deficiency in ixora.

Fig. 5.8. Soil testing can determine the pH and nutritional status of soil.

To obtain each subsample, carefully pull back mulch, grass, or ground cover to expose bare soil. With a hand trowel or shovel, dig a small hole, 6 inches deep, and then remove a 1-inch-thick by 6-inch-deep slice of soil from a side of each hole (Figure 5.8). Combine and mix all the subsamples in a clean plastic bucket. You will use about a pint of this mixture as your sample.

When various areas in the landscape have different soil types, receive different fertilization practices, or contain plants that have distinctly different fertilization requirements, obtain separate composite samples from each area. Often a ¼- to 1-acre lot will have two or three areas that require separate sampling. Soil samples need to be sent immediately to a commercial laboratory, or you can check with your local county Cooperative Extension office for testing services.

How Much Fertilizer to Use

Once you have decided to fertilize and know the maintenance level that you can comfortably provide for your landscape plants, use Table 5.1 to determine the amount of fertilizer to apply to individual plants. The number of pounds of various nitrogen-containing fertilizers to apply per 1000 square feet of bed area per year is presented in Table 5.2. Water-soluble (rapidly available fertilizer) should be applied at no more than ½ pound of actual nitrogen per 1000 square feet per application. To calculate the area of a plant bed (Figure 5.9), simply multiply the length of the bed by its width. It is easy to determine how much fertilizer to apply using information given on each bag of fertilizer. Dividing the nitrogen (N) content into 100 gives you the number of pounds of fertilizer to apply per 1000 square feet. You must then figure out how much fertilizer to apply to the plant bed. Because we give fertilizer recommendations on a 1000-square-feet basis, first divide the area of the bed by 1000. Multiply this result by the pounds of fertilizer to apply per 1000 square feet.

Table 5.1. Amounts of nitrogen fertilizer versus the level of maintenance

Level of maintenance	Amount of nitrogen fertilizer
Basic	0–2 lbs N/1000 ft²/year
Moderate	2–4 lbs N/1000 ft²/year
High	4–6 lbs N/1000 ft²/year

Table 5.2. Number of pounds of fertilizer to use containing various percentages of nitrogen

%N in analysis	Rate (lbs N/1000 ft²/yr)						
	0.5	1	2	3	4	5	6
6	8	17	33	50	67	83	100
7	7	14	29	43	57	71	86
8	6	12	25	38	50	63	75
9	6	11	22	33	44	56	67
10	5	10	20	30	40	50	60
11	5	9	18	27	36	45	55
12	4	8	17	25	33	42	50
13	4	8	15	23	31	39	46
14	4	7	14	21	29	36	43
15	3	7	13	20	27	33	40
16	3	6	13	19	25	31	38
17	3	6	12	18	24	29	35
18	3	6	11	17	22	28	33
19	3	5	11	16	21	26	32
20	2	5	10	15	20	25	30
33	1	3	6	9	12	15	18
39	1	3	5	8	10	13	15
46	1	2	4	7	9	11	13

Fig. 5.9. Measure the length and width of a bed to calculate its area.

This gives you the total amount of fertilizer to apply to the bed. If the fertilizer contains more than 50 percent water-soluble nitrogen, divide it in half and apply it in two applications.

What Fertilizer to Use

A complete fertilizer with a ratio of approximately 3:1:2 or 3:1:3 (that is, 12-4-8 or 15-5-15) of nitrogen (N), phosphoric acid (P_2O_5), and potash (K_2O) is often recommended unless the soil test reveals that phosphorus and potassium are adequate. In Florida and other regions, where the phosphorus content of most soils is adequate to sustain plant growth, the phosphorus content of the fertilizer should be 0–2 percent P_2O_5 (e.g., 15-0-15).

Many fertilizers are formulated for use on lawn grasses. Some of these, known as "weed-and-feed" fertilizers, may contain an herbicide that can damage plants that are not grasses. Read labels and carefully follow the directions.

Fertilizers that are "slow release," "controlled release," sulfur coated, or that contain nitrogen as IBDU (isobutylidene diurea) or ureaformaldehyde have extended release periods compared to fertilizers that are readily water soluble (Figure 5.10). Thirty to 50 percent of the nitrogen should be water insoluble or slow-release so that plant roots can absorb the nitrogen over a long period of time.

A fertilizer containing 30 to 50 percent slow-release potassium is often recommended where soil potassium is inadequate. A fertilizer containing magnesium may be needed if soils contain inadequate magnesium or if plants often exhibit magnesium deficiency symptoms. Due to the prevalence of magnesium deficiency on certain landscape plants in many parts of Florida and other regions with sandy soil, magnesium applications of up to 2.5 pounds per 1000 feet per year is recommended.

Fig. 5.10. Controlled-release fertilizers have extended nutrient release periods compared to water-soluble fertilizers.

Water-soluble fertilizers are less expensive than slow-release products. However, the components of a water-soluble fertilizer may leach quickly through the soil and past the roots, which is wasteful and may contaminate groundwater. In sandy, well-drained soils, the soluble fertilizer may move below the root system after only a few inches of rainfall or irrigation. In finer-textured marl, clay, or muck soils, leaching will be slower, but runoff may be greater, which could contribute to pollution of the surface water.

Micronutrient deficiencies can be corrected with foliar sprays if deficiencies are not severe; however, such correction is usually temporary and is not commonly used. Applying a fertilizer with micronutrient supplements to the soil may prevent deficiencies.

Palms have different nutritional requirements than other landscape plants. When palms are important, landscaped areas within 30 feet of large established palms should be fertilized with a 4-1-6-2 Mg (N-P_2O_5-K_2O-Mg) ratio fertilizer (for example, a fertilizer marked "8-2-12-4 Mg"). N, K_2O, and Mg should have equivalent percentages of each nutrient in controlled-release form. Using a fertilizer with a ratio other than that specified may induce or accentuate nutrient deficiencies in palms. Fertilization rates may be based on the rates for nitrogen in Table 5.1, for basic, moderate, and high levels of maintenance. Because palms are highly prone to several potentially fatal micronutrient deficiencies, any fertilizer applied to them should contain 1 to 2 percent iron and manganese, plus trace amounts of zinc, copper, and boron, to prevent these deficiencies.

Where and How to Apply Fertilizer

Because of the naturally high oxygen concentrations near the soil surface, a plant's principal feeding roots are usually within the top 10 to 14 inches of soil. Many of the smaller, fibrous roots of mulched plants are located just beneath the mulch on the soil surface. Consequently, for maximum utilization, fertilizer should be applied to the surface of the soil or mulch. Since most small-diameter (feeder) roots are shallow, there is no need to inject or place fertilizer deep in the soil. However, shallow soil injections in compacted soil or on mounds, berms, and slopes may reduce the amount of fertilizer runoff caused by excessive irrigation or rain.

A large, aesthetically pleasing mulched area should be maintained around plants. This mulched area promotes faster plant establishment by eliminating competition from grass roots for water and nutrients. Ground covers that are not as competitive as grass for water and nutrients can be planted near shrubs and trees.

Pruning

Through the selective removal of shoots and branches, pruning a plant can maintain its health, help develop good branch structure, reduce its size, and enhance fruiting, flowering, or appearance. Pruning should be a part of your gardening routine and not delayed until the landscape is overgrown. An unpruned plant can end up tall and leggy with little foliage close to the ground. In this condition, it cannot be pruned to a desirable size or shape in a single pruning without causing severe damage to the plant. Instead, it must be pruned back gradually over a period of several years.

Proper plant selection can eliminate many pruning requirements. Too often plants are selected for the landscape based on their current size and shape rather than the size and shape they are likely to attain at maturity many years later. The homeowner or landscape manager soon finds it necessary to clip or prune plants frequently to keep them within bounds. It is less time consuming and less costly to select and install a plant that will grow close to the desired size without frequent pruning. Consult this book's Selection Guide for the mature size of the plant species you are considering for your landscape. If a plant needs to be pruned several times each year to control size (with the exception of a formal hedge plant), it is quite likely the wrong species for its location.

Reasons for Pruning

Although we tend to think of pruning as a measure for controlling the form of a plant, plants may be pruned for a number of other reasons. Before pruning, determine which of the following benefits you hope to achieve through your efforts.

Safety

There is no more important reason to prune than to prevent the loss of human life and property. Trees with dead branches and codominant stems (multiple leaders) with included (or embedded) bark (bark pinched or squeezed between two stems indicating a weak union of the stems) are a serious hazard, particularly during a windstorm. These potential hazards can be reduced with proper pruning by a qualified arborist such as one certified by the International Society of Arboriculture.

Health and Improved Vigor

Weekly inspection of your landscape is recommended to detect plants threatened by disease or infestation. Often insect, pest, and disease problems can be "nipped in the bud" by the removal of dead, dying, damaged, or infected plant parts. For example, if several branch tips are infested with aphids or scale, pruning and discarding the affected shoots can be an effective alternative to spraying with insecticides if the infestation is small and localized. Pruning to remove diseased or infested plant parts can also help stop a problem from spreading to neighboring plants.

Plant Size and Form

A common objective of pruning is to maintain or develop a desired size or form. As mentioned earlier, this reason for pruning can be largely eliminated by installing

Fig. 5.11. Properly pruned hedges create privacy but require regular clipping to keep them looking neat.

the proper species. Compact and dwarf plants are now widely available and are a good choice where small or low-growing plants are desired. Once plants grow to the size you want them to be, reduce the number of fertilizer applications and water infrequently to prevent plants from growing more rapidly than desired.

Always work with the natural form of a plant. Frequent light prunings several times each year discourage undesirable sprouting. Several light prunings are preferable to one heavy pruning each year. As a rule, do not attempt to dramatically alter the natural form of a plant; instead, choose a species that has a natural tendency to grow into the form desired. Study the sizes and forms various plants have attained in existing landscapes around town and look at the photographs in this book's Selection Guide.

For special effect, plants can be pruned into geometric shapes or to look like animal figures. This practice, known as topiary, has become popular in recent years. Like hedges (Figure 5.11), topiary plants (Figure 5.12) are high-maintenance attention grabbers and should be used sparingly in most low-maintenance landscapes. Small-leaved shrubs like boxwood, Florida privet, natal plum, dwarf yaupon holly, pyracantha, and others can be trained to achieve specific forms.

An espaliered plant is one that has been trained to grow more or less flat against a wall, fence, or trellis (Figure 5.13). This technique requires frequent pinching and pruning, and not all plants are adaptable to these measures. Pyracantha, sea grape, fatshedra, magnolia, yaupon holly, podocarpus, loquat, and natal plum make excellent espalier plants (Figure 5.14).

Large shrubs (such as cocoplum, photinia, ligustrum, and pittosporum) can be trained into small trees by gradually removing all the foliage and small branches

Fig. 5.12. Plants pruned into geometric shapes are called "topiaries."

from the lower portion of the stem(s). The removal process should take one to three years to complete and should not start before a plant is about 8 feet tall. By allowing the plant to reach this height, the main trunk has time to develop properly. Leaving small branches along the lower trunk during this growing period will create a stronger trunk and sturdier tree. The longer the small branches remain on the trunk, the thicker and stronger the trunk becomes.

When to Prune

Shrubs

Shrubs in hardiness zones 10 and 11 can be pruned year-round. However, those that are pruned in fall or winter could begin actively producing new growth and, therefore, could be damaged by unusually cold weather. Likewise, in cooler regions, some shrubs pruned in late summer and fall could begin growing before winter and cold temperatures hit, which could injure this new growth. In extreme cases, entire plants could be killed.

Some showy flowering shrubs set their flower buds on the previous season's growth and the buds winter over on this older growth (Table 5.3). For example,

Fig. 5.13. Golden dewdrops espaliered on a wooden trellis.

Fig. 5.14. Pyracantha, southern magnolia, and other plants can be trained against a wall as espaliers.

azaleas form flower buds in early summer for the following year's flower display. Therefore, prune spring-flowering plants such as azaleas, spireas, and dogwoods in late spring before the flower buds set for the next season. Additional pruning or pinching between the end of the flower display and early summer will not reduce the number of flower buds set. Pinching back the new shoots on azaleas anytime from several weeks after shoots begin elongating through the early summer will encourage them to branch laterally. Each of these lateral branches is likely to develop a flower bud. For this reason, a pinched plant often produces many more

Table 5.3. Winter- and spring-flowering plants that can be pruned after flowering but before flower buds form for next year's bloom*

azaleas	spiraeas
some hydrangeas	Indian hawthorns
banana shrub	star and saucer magnolia
camellias	

*The only effect from pruning at other times is a reduction in the number of flower buds.

Table 5.4. Plants that can be pruned during the dormant season (flowers are produced on current season's growth)

allamandas	plumbago
abelia	thryallis
hibiscuses	golden dewdrop
oleander	bougainvillea
roses	princess flower
crape myrtles	

flowers the following year than will an unpinched plant. Pruning between July and the beginning of the flower display will remove flower buds and reduce next year's flower display, but it should not affect the health of the plant.

Shrubs that produce showy flowers on the current season's new growth (such as abelia, hibiscus, and rose) can be pruned almost anytime (Table 5.4). However, avoid fall pruning because pruning at this time can stimulate new growth that could be damaged by an early winter freeze. Also, avoid pruning heavily during flowering so as not to reduce the floral display. Save heavy pruning until just before new growth emerges in the spring. Developing shoots can be pinched during the growing season to encourage lateral branching, which will in turn create more flowers on many shrubs. Moderate to severe pruning may encourage production of fewer but larger blossoms or blossom clusters on some species such as crape myrtle.

Most evergreen shrubs (such as podocarpus, holly, boxwood, ligustrum, juniper, and wax myrtle) can be pruned anytime. To encourage rapid shoot development and the greatest overall plant growth, prune just prior to growth in the spring. To retard growth for maximum dwarfing effect, prune just after each growth flush, when leaves have expanded fully. Late summer and fall pruning may stimulate an additional flush of shoot growth on species that flush several times each year. These shoots could be damaged by an early frost.

Cold injury can be minimized if heavy pruning is conducted just prior to spring bud break. Fall and early winter pruning is generally inadvisable, for it can stimulate new growth, particularly during a mild period of the winter. The succulent stems that are produced as a consequence are not cold hardy and can be easily damaged, even by a light frost. Even if pruning does not stimulate growth, low winter temperatures can cause cambium damage. This is particularly true of plants that are marginally hardy and those that cannot stop actively growing soon enough before freezing temperatures arrive. If in doubt about cold susceptibility, it is best to delay heavy pruning until just before growth begins in the spring.

Closure (callusing) of pruning wounds on most plants should be most rapid if pruning is conducted just before or immediately following the spring growth flush. A closed wound is not only more aesthetically pleasing, but it also discourages insects, diseases, and decay organisms from entering the plant.

Trees

Mature trees should not be pruned when they are actively growing in the spring or when they are entering dormancy in the fall. Live branches are best pruned in the dormant season or following a growth flush. But if pruning is needed to improve structure, do it anytime. Removing less than about 10 percent of live foliage can be done at any time with few problems. Removing live foliage on stressed trees increases stress and should be avoided. Dead and diseased limbs can be removed anytime.

Terminal growth of pines can be controlled by removing one-half of the new shoot (candle) in the spring just prior to needle expansion. This encourages new bud formation at the pinch, slows growth on the pinched branch, and creates a more compact plant. Never pinch a pine at other times of the year, since new buds will not form.

When training young trees, begin pruning the second year after planting in order to develop good branch structure. Prune shade trees every 2 to 3 years until a dominant trunk is established. This may take 25 years. Prune at planting only to shorten or remove one side of a double leader.

Pruning Techniques

Shrubs are pruned either by "heading" or by "thinning." Heading is the cutting of the ends of twigs or young branches of shrubs and bedding plants back to a bud or node. This technique should not be used when pruning trees. When heading is done using the thumb and forefinger to remove the tips of soft, newly emerging stems and branches, it is referred to as "pinching" (Figure 5.15). Usually an increased number of shoots and leaves results from heading or pinching, producing denser growth at the outer edge of the canopy of the plant. New growth is typically vigorous and upright, with two to several buds developing into shoots just behind the pruning cut (Figure 5.16). If properly applied to plants, pleasing forms can be created and maintained. Sometimes, however, new foliage may be so thick that it

Fig. 5.15. Removing the tips of branches with thumb and forefinger is called "pinching."

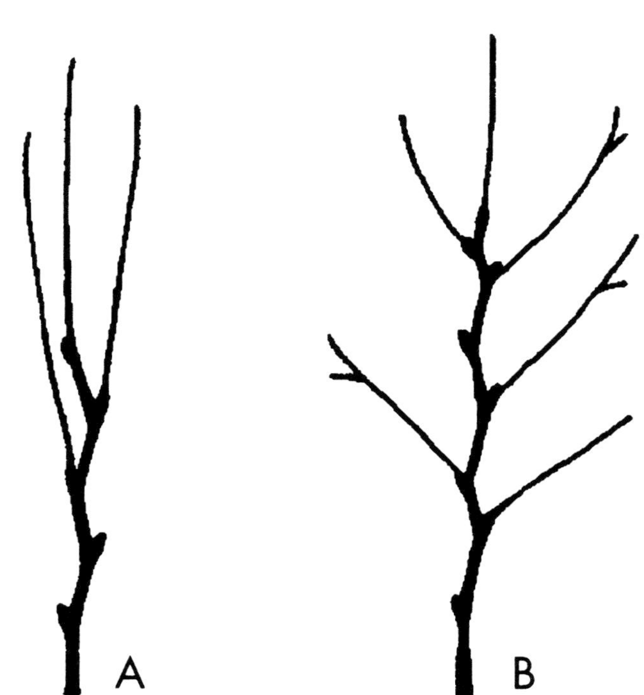

Fig. 5.16. *A,* growth from a shoot that has been headed; *B,* growth from an unpruned shoot.

shades lower and interior foliage, forming a top-heavy plant with few or no leaves on the inside of the plant. To avoid this problem, head back the plant's shoots to several different lengths or reduce their length by cutting back to existing lateral branches (Figure 5.17). When heading, make the cut at a slight slant about ⅛ inch above a healthy bud (Figure 5.18). The bud should be facing the direction preferred for new growth.

Thinning (Figure 5.19) is the removal of branches back to main branches or back to the trunk. A thinned plant usually remains about the same size after pruning.

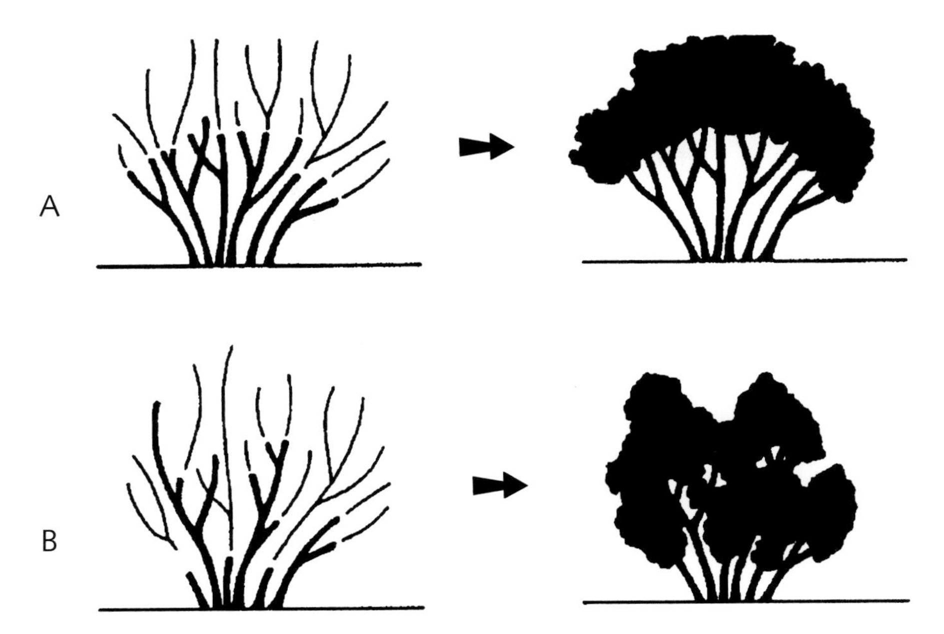

Fig. 5.17. *A,* plant with all shoots headed back to the same height develops new foliage mainly toward the top of the plant; *B,* plant remains fuller when shoots are headed to different heights.

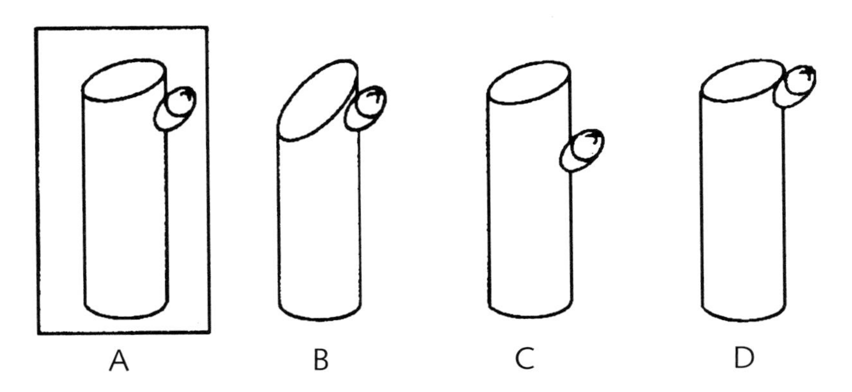

Fig. 5.18. *A,* proper location and angle of pruning cut; *B,* too slanted; *C,* too far from the bud; *D,* too close to the bud.

Reducing the height of a trunk or stem by cutting back to an existing lateral branch is referred to as "reduction." (Some horticulturists refer to this as "drop-crotching"; others call it "heading.") Depending on whether the plant is thinned or reduced, a plant can take on a more open appearance, or new growth can be encouraged inside the crown. If thinning is heavy (as when more than about one-third of foliage is removed), sprouts will form along stems. If the plant is lightly thinned (as when less than 10 percent of foliage is removed), sprouts are not likely to develop. Plants are thinned primarily to reduce plant density while maintaining a natural appearance.

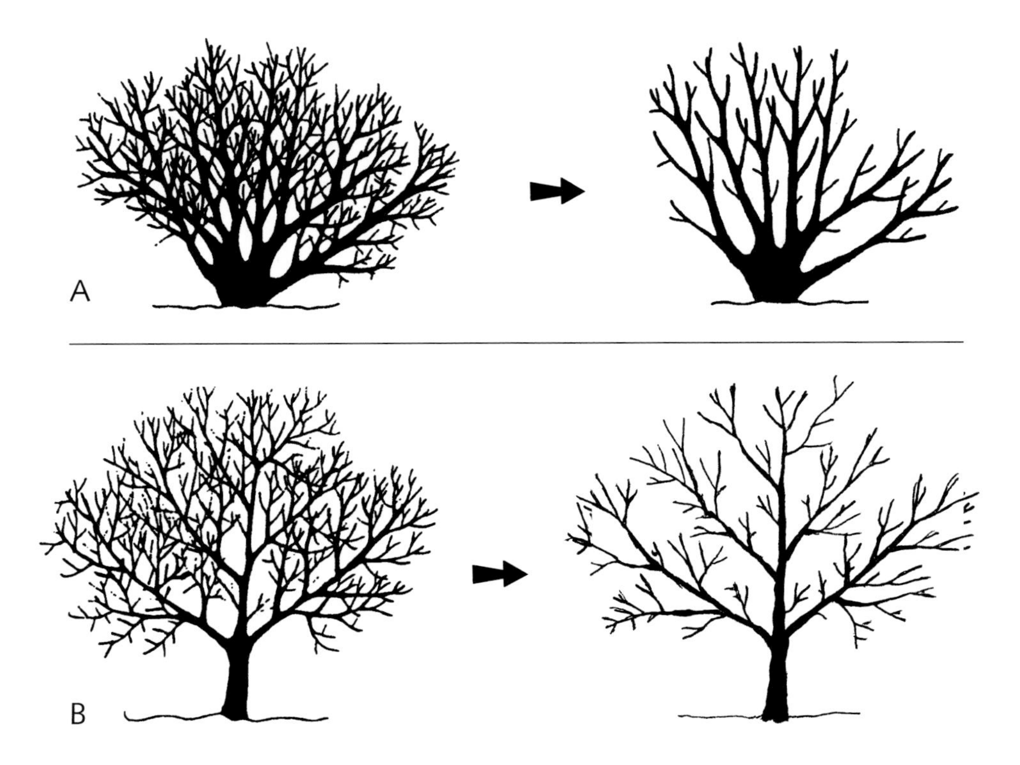

Fig. 5.19. *A*, correctly thinned shrub; *B*, correctly thinned tree.

This technique differs from hedging or heading to the same spot on all branches, which will give a plant a formal, controlled appearance.

Pruning Shrubs

A properly pruned shrub is a work of art and beauty and does not look as if it has been pruned. Pruning cuts should not be visible but located inside the plant where they will be covered by remaining foliage as much as possible. The first step in pruning a shrub is to remove all dead, diseased, or broken branches. Remove branches that cross or touch each other and those that look out of place. If the shrub is still too dense or large, remove some of the oldest branches. Reduce excessively long branches to a lateral branch (Figure 5.20) or bud that is 6 to 12 inches below the desirable plant height (Figure 5.17). Thinning (Figure 5.19) may also be desirable. Do not use hedge shears. Cut each branch separately to different lengths with hand pruners. This type of pruning will maintain a neat informal shrub with a slightly irregular silhouette. (Plants sheared into hard geometric shapes could look out of place in a landscape designed for a soft appearance.) For a discussion of formal pruning, see the following section on hedge pruning.

Fig. 5.20. Cut back excessively long branches to a smaller lateral branch or bud. This has been referred to as a reduction cut.

Rejuvenation of Shrubs

Rejuvenation is a drastic method of pruning old shrubs that have become much too large or have a large amount of nonflowering wood. The best time for rejuvenation is in late winter or early spring, just before growth begins. Large, old shrubs should not be rejuvenated during late summer. Except in hardiness zones 10 and 11, new growth will be stimulated and possibly killed by cold weather in the winter.

Multiple-stem shrubs can be rejuvenated by cutting back all stems at ground level over a period of 12 to 18 months. At the first pruning, remove one-third of the old, mature stems (Figure 5.21*A*). Six months later, take out one-half of the remaining old stems, and head back long shoots growing from the previous pruning cuts (Figure 5.21*B*). At the third pruning, six months later, remove the remaining old wood and head back the long new shoots (Figure 5.21*C*). Some plants can be rejuvenated all at once by cutting the entire plant back to just above ground level. New growth quickly emerges, covering pruning wounds and rapidly producing a smaller, rejuvenated plant. This method of rejuvenation should never be used on junipers because they will not produce new growth when pruned severely.

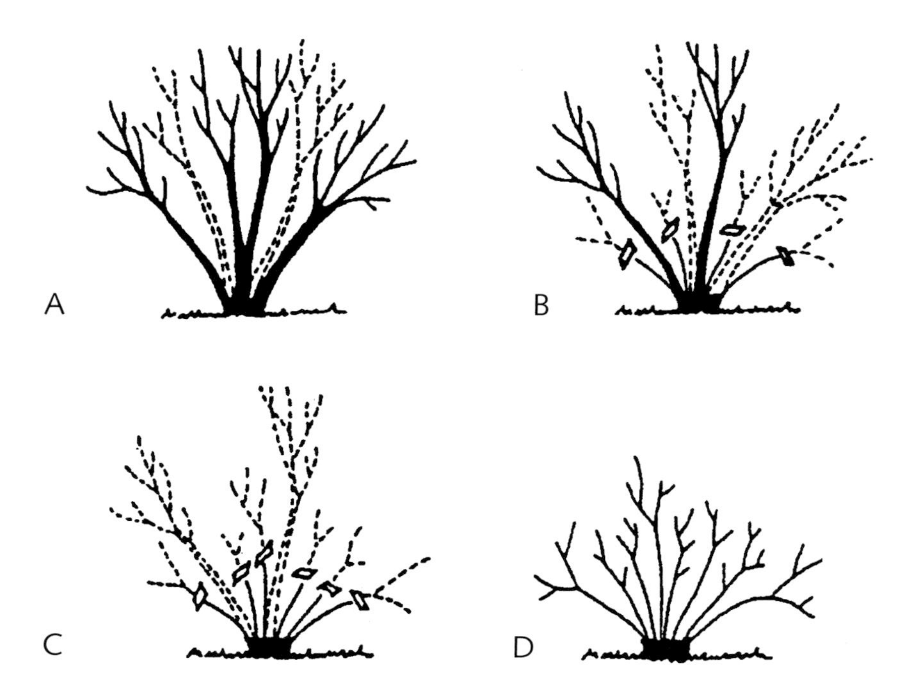

Fig. 5.21. Rejuvenation of multiple stem shrubs: *A*, first pruning; *B*, second pruning; *C*, third pruning; *D*, rejuvenated shrub.

On single-stem shrubs trained to grow in tree form (such as crape myrtle, ligustrum, gardenia), rejuvenation is carried out over a period of 12 to 18 months by severe thinning and heading back to the basic limb framework. One-third to one-half of the old growth is removed in 6-month intervals.

Rejuvenating canelike shrubs, such as nandina and mahonia, is best done on a two- or three-year cycle. The tallest canes are pruned to stubs 3 to 6 inches above the soil line during the first spring, just as growth begins. By the second spring, the previous year's medium-sized canes have grown to become tall canes and should be cut back to 3–inch stubs. By this time, canes from the first year's pruning have already begun to grow and are 1 to 3 feet tall. In the third spring, the canes that were the shortest in the first spring have grown fairly tall and can be cut back. In this way, there is always foliage near the ground and the shrubs can be kept from becoming tall or leggy. After nandina canes are cut, they generally will not flower during the growing season that follows their pruning.

Hedge Pruning

The type of hedge you want will determine the method you choose for hedge pruning. An informal hedge is maintained by heading and reducing only on the

Fig. 5.22. Plants pruned as a solid hedge should be wider at the bottom than at the top.

longest shoots, 6 to 12 inches back inside the outer edge of the hedge. The shorter shoots remain intact and form the outside edge of the now smaller hedge. The outer edge of the canopy appears more open and softer than a clipped formal hedge.

The desired appearance of a formal hedge is a sharply defined geometric shape (Figure 5.11). A square or box shape is most common. There are two important factors to remember when pruning formal hedges: (1) hedges should be clipped while new growth is green and succulent, and (2) plants should be trimmed so the base of the hedge is wider than the top (Figure 5.22). Hedges pruned with a narrow base will lose lower leaves and branches shaded from the top. This condition will worsen with age, resulting in sparse growth at ground level and an unattractive hedge that does not give desired privacy. Flowering hedges grown formally should be sheared only after they have flowered to prevent reduction in the number of blooms. If the blooms are of secondary importance, pruning may be conducted at any time.

Pruning Trees

When improperly performed, pruning can harm the tree's health, stability, and appearance. Several consequences occur when pruning is not performed at all (Figure 5.23). These consequences include development of low limbs and weak, codominant stems, defects such as included bark, and accumulation of dead branches. Formation of codominant stems and defects such as included bark can lead to increased risk of breakage.

When tree pruning is properly executed, a variety of benefits are derived. Benefits include reduced risk of branch and stem breakage, better clearance for vehicles and pedestrians, improved health and appearance, enhanced view, and improved flowering. Several pruning types are used to achieve these benefits. Pruning types include structural, cleaning, thinning, raising, reducing, restoring, and pollarding.

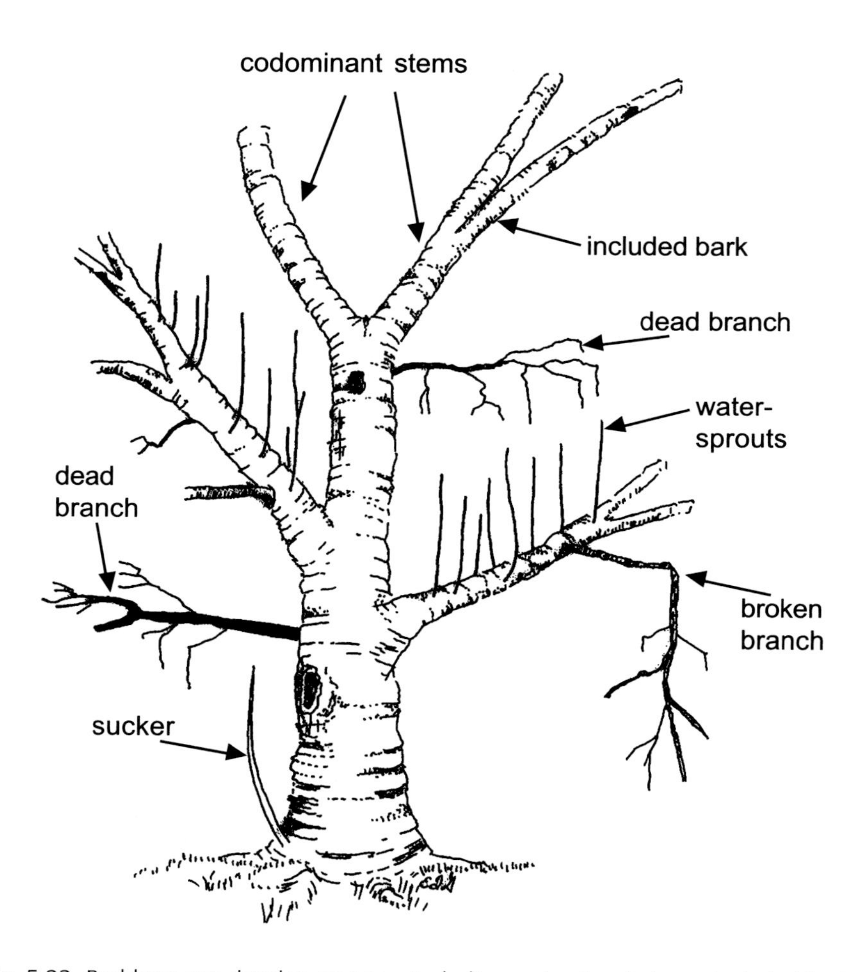

Fig. 5.23. Problems can develop on trees, including codominant stems, included bark, broken and dead branches, suckers and watersprouts, and large, low limbs that require removal.

Table 5.5. Four steps to encourage a leader to dominate the crown on a young or medium-aged tree

1. Choose the one stem that will make the best leader.
2. Identify which stems and branches are competing with this leader.
3. Decide how much to shorten these competing stems.
4. Prevent branches from growing larger than half the trunk diameter by regular pruning.

Pruning for Structure

Establishing a structural pruning program that begins at planting and could carry through the first 25 years or more, depending on the species, can reduce risk of tree failure. This program should be designed to create a structurally sound trunk and branch architecture that will sustain the tree for a long period. Some structural pruning can be conducted on older trees as well.

Four procedures should be considered when structural pruning young to medium-aged, large-maturing trees. The first procedure is to clean the canopy by removing dead, broken, diseased, and dying branches. The second procedure is to choose and develop a dominant leader (Table 5.5). Multiple prunings over time (for example, from 10 to 25 years) usually are required to develop a dominant leader. Competing stems and branches are subordinated (reduced in length) or removed (Figure 5.24). Subordination usually is preferred over removal, especially if the problem stem or stems are larger than half the trunk diameter. Subordination may cause less trunk decay than removal. The offending stem(s) can be removed later, if necessary.

The third procedure is to select and establish the lowest permanent scaffold limb if the tree is old enough. Establish the lowest permanent limb by shortening vigorous branches below it and any lower branches that grow up into the crown (Figure 5.25). This procedure may not be possible on a young tree if all branches are below the best position for the lowest permanent limb. The height of the lowest limb is determined by the location and intended function of the tree. For example, the lowest permanent limb on a street tree might be higher than that on an arboretum specimen.

The fourth procedure is to select and establish scaffold limbs by subordinating or removing competing stems or branches (Figure 5.25). Scaffold selection can take 10 to 20 years or more depending on climate, the type of tree, and its location. Scaffold limbs are located above the lowest permanent limb and provide the base on which to build the permanent crown. Scaffold limbs should be free of serious defects such as included bark and cracks, should be among the largest on the tree, and should be appropriately spaced apart. Vertical spacing should be at least 18 inches for large-maturing trees and about 12 inches for small trees.

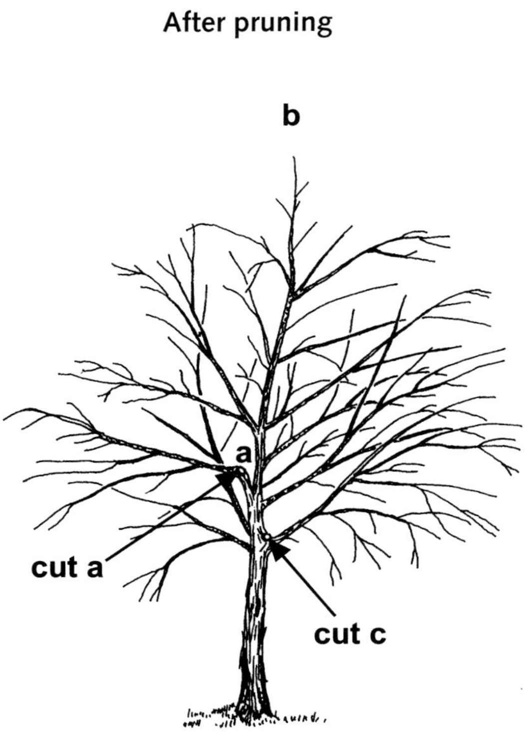

Before pruning **After pruning**

a b c

b

a

cut a

cut c

Problem: Before structural pruning, the young to medium-aged tree had three developing leaders or codominant stems (*a, b,* and *c*). This structure is considered weaker than trees with one dominant stem or trunk. Medium- and large-maturing trees in urban and landscape settings last longest and are easiest to manage if they grow with one dominant trunk. This pruning helps the tree develop one main trunk.

Solution: Reduce the length of (subordinate) leader *a* using a reduction cut to encourage leader *b* to grow faster. Remove leader *c* back to the trunk. After pruning, the tip of leader *b* should be much higher than the tops of all other stems. This technique will help leader *b* become the dominant trunk by slowing growth on competing leaders and allowing more sunlight to reach *b*. In most cases on large-maturing trees, branches in the lower 15 to 20 feet of the tree should be kept smaller than half the trunk diameter using this technique. And they should not be allowed to grow up into the tree to become a permanent part of the canopy. Notice that branches are spaced along the trunk.

Fig. 5.24. Subordinate codominant stems so that one leader dominates medium- and large-maturing shade trees; small-maturing trees can be pruned differently.

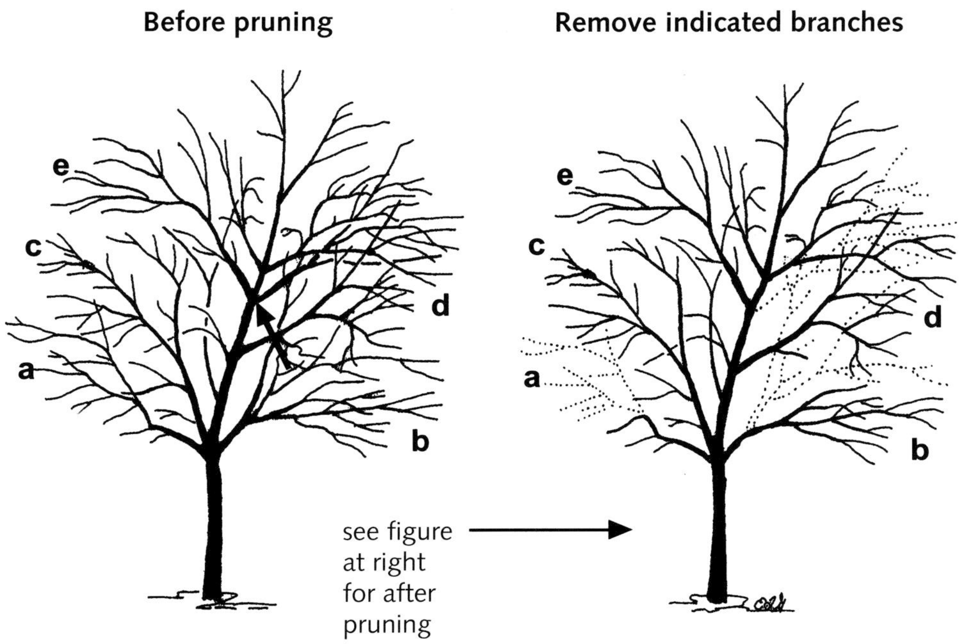

Before pruning | **Remove indicated branches**

see figure at right for after pruning

Problems: 1. Branches *a*, *b*, and *c* are clustered together because they originate from the same point on the trunk. 2. Branches *a* and *b* are too close to the ground. 3. There is a main branch (see arrow) directly opposite where branch *e* is attached to the trunk. Opposite or clustered branches often starve the leader above and grow to become more dominant and larger than the leader. Only one main branch should originate from any one spot on the trunk. Notice the upright-oriented branches growing from lower branches. These branches should be shortened.

Solutions: 1. Cut back on branches *a* and *b* so that branch *c* will become the lowest scaffold branch at this position on the trunk. The upright portion of *b* was removed because it was growing up into the canopy. 2. Remove or cut back (removal is shown) the main branch oppostie *e* so that *e* can become the scaffold branch at this point on the trunk. Notice that branches *c*, *d*, and *e* are now spaced along the trunk. Also notice the two small branches left on the trunk opposite branch *d*. These small branches can remain because they are not likely to grow fast to compete with *d*. This procedure is less appropriate on mature trees because the permanent branch structure is set.

Fig. 5.25. Reduce the growth rate on low branches to prevent them from becoming too large.

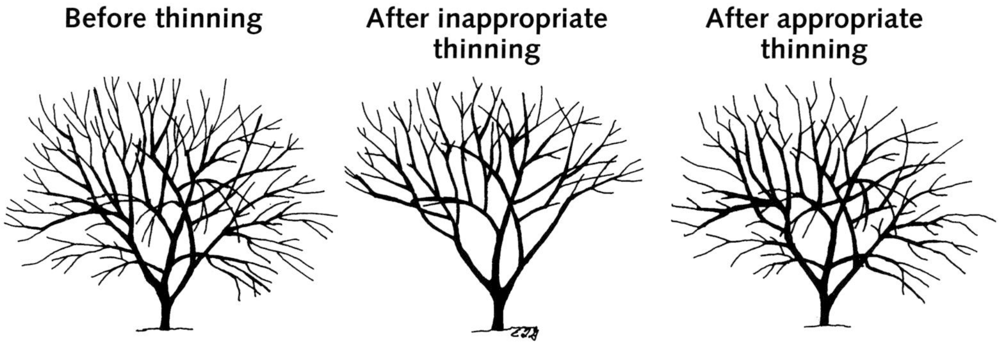

Before thinning | After inappropriate thinning | After appropriate thinning

Inappropriate thinning leaves branches only at the edge of the crown (center). This situation can leave trees more vulnerable to wind damage and other stresses. Appropriate thinning (right) leaves live branches distributed all along limbs by removing live branches primarily from the edge of the crown.

Fig. 5.26. Thinning trees reduces density at the edge of the crown, not on the interior.

Pruning to Clean

Cleaning is the selective removal of dead, diseased, detached, and broken branches. This type of pruning is done to reduce the risk of branches falling from the tree and to reduce the movement of decay, insects, and diseases from dead or dying branches into the rest of the tree. It can be performed on trees of any age but is mostly common on medium-aged and mature trees. Cleaning is the preferred pruning type for mature trees because it does not remove live branches unnecessarily. Cleaning removes branches with cracks that may fail when the interior wood dries.

Pruning to Thin

Thinning is the selective removal of small live branches to reduce crown density (Figure 5.26). Because the majority of small branches are at the outside edge of the crown, thinning is focused in that area. Proper thinning retains crown shape and should provide an even distribution of foliage throughout the crown.

Thinning increases sunlight penetration and air movement through the crown. Increased light and air stimulate and maintain interior foliage, which can encourage taper on scaffold branches. Thinning a limb should be considered if cabling will be performed. Cabling secures limbs on the tree using metal, strapping, or other specially designed devices installed by arborists. Thinning also can involve removing suckers from the base of the tree and some watersprouts on the interior. Watersprouts are new stems that emerge on the lower interior branches, typically in response to a stress such as root damage or overpruning. Excessive removal of watersprouts often produces more watersprouts, so it is not recommended. Vigorous production of watersprouts on interior limbs often is a sign of overthinning.

Excessive branch removal on the lower two-thirds of a branch or stem (lion tailing) can have adverse effects on the tree and therefore is not an acceptable pruning practice (Figure 5.26). Lion tailing transfers weight to the ends of branches and may result in sunburned bark tissue, watersprouts, cracks in branches, reduced branch taper, increased load on branch unions, and weakened branch structure. By changing the weight distribution on the limb, lion tailing often results in excessive branch breakage.

If the entire crown will not be thinned, the areas to be thinned should be specified to the arborist or the person doing the work. The size range and percentage of foliage to be removed also should be specified—usually in the 10 to 15 percent range—but should not exceed 25 percent of the crown, especially on mature trees. Most thinning removes branches ¼ to 1 inch in diameter. If larger branches are removed, large gaps may be created in the crown, or watersprouts can result.

Pruning to Raise

Raising is the selective removal of branches to provide vertical clearance (Figure 5. 27). Crown raising shortens or removes lower branches of a tree to provide clearance for buildings, signs, vehicles, pedestrians, and vistas.

Excessive removal of lower limbs can slow the development of trunk taper, can cause cracks or decay in the trunk, and transfers too much weight to the top of the tree. Mature trees could become stressed if large-diameter lower branches are removed. Shortening some of the low branches, rather than removing them, sometimes can achieve clearance. Live crown ratio should be no less than 66 percent when raising is completed. Live crown ratio is the ratio of the top portion of the tree bearing live foliage to the cleared lower portion without live foliage, including the trunk. Structural pruning should be considered along with raising.

When raising, the desired clearance should be specified. To differentiate between complete branch removal and shortening, specify the size range of the limbs to remove and their location (for example, raise 12 feet above the road by removing downward-growing branches 2 inches in diameter and smaller).

Pruning to Reduce

Reduction is the selective removal of branches and stems to decrease the height and/or the spread of a tree (Figure 5.28). This type of pruning is done to minimize risk of failure, to make the tree smaller in some aspect, for utility line clearance, to clear vegetation from buildings or other structures, or to improve the appearance of the plant. Portions of the crown, such as individual limbs, can be reduced to balance the canopy, provide clearance, or reduce the likelihood of breakage on limbs with defects. Occasionally, the entire crown is reduced. Reducing or thinning should be considered if cabling will be performed. Crown reduction should be accomplished with reduction cuts, not heading cuts.

Not all tree species can be reduced. Therefore, the species and plant health should be considered before starting work. Old, stressed, or mature trees could decline or become more stressed as a result of this treatment. When a limb on a mature tree is cut back to a lateral, no more than one-fourth of its foliage should be removed. More can be removed on a young tree to accomplish particular objectives. More decay can enter the tree following reduction than following other pruning types.

The clearance distance or percentage of the reduction should be specified. Because making many small cuts or just a few larger-diameter cuts can reduce a tree, it

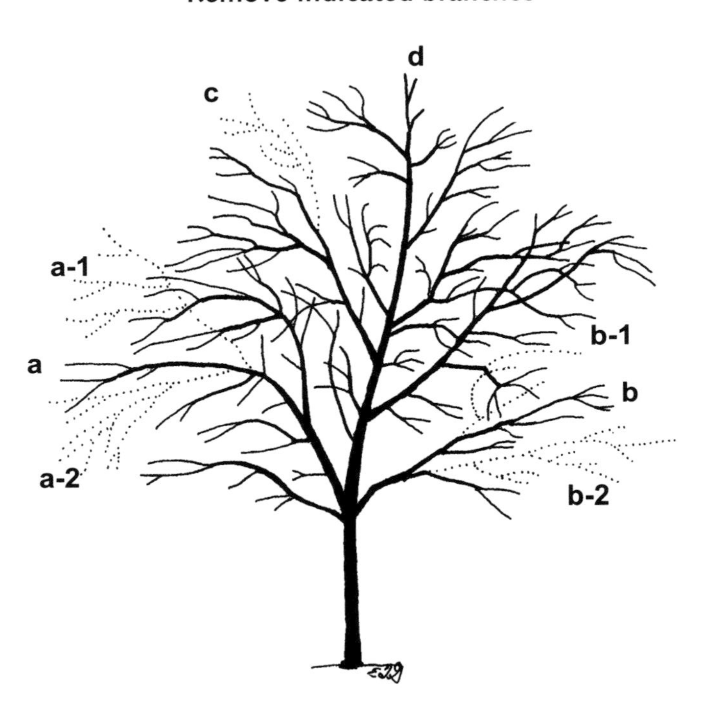

Lower branches *a* and *b* can be removed to raise the crown. However, subordinating branches *a* and *b* by removing upper and lower lateral branches *a-1*, *a-2*, *b-1*, and *b-2* will cause less stress for the tree. Removing *a-2* and *b-2* helps raise the crown. Removing *a-1* and *b-1* ensures that the branches will not grow up to become part of the permanent canopy. This consideration is important because left unpruned, these branches are likely to remain vigorous—forming low, codominant stems. Subordinate branch *c* because it will compete with the leader *d*.

Fig. 5.27. Raising the crown by shortening or removing low branches.

is important also to specify the size range of the cuts. Reduction usually should be done on smaller-diameter branches (those 1 to 4 inches in diameter).

Pruning to Restore

Restoration is the selective removal of branches, sprouts, and stubs from trees that have been topped, severely headed, vandalized, lion tailed, broken in a storm, or otherwise damaged (Figure 5.29). The goal of restoration is to improve a tree structure, form, or appearance.

On trees with many sprouts originating at the tips of branches, one to three sprouts on main branch stubs are selected to become permanent branches and to re-form a more natural-appearing crown. To accomplish this objective, consider shortening some sprouts, removing others, and leaving some untouched. Some vigorous sprouts that will remain as branches may need to be shortened to control growth and ensure adequate attachment for the size of the sprout. Lion-tailed trees

After canopy reduction

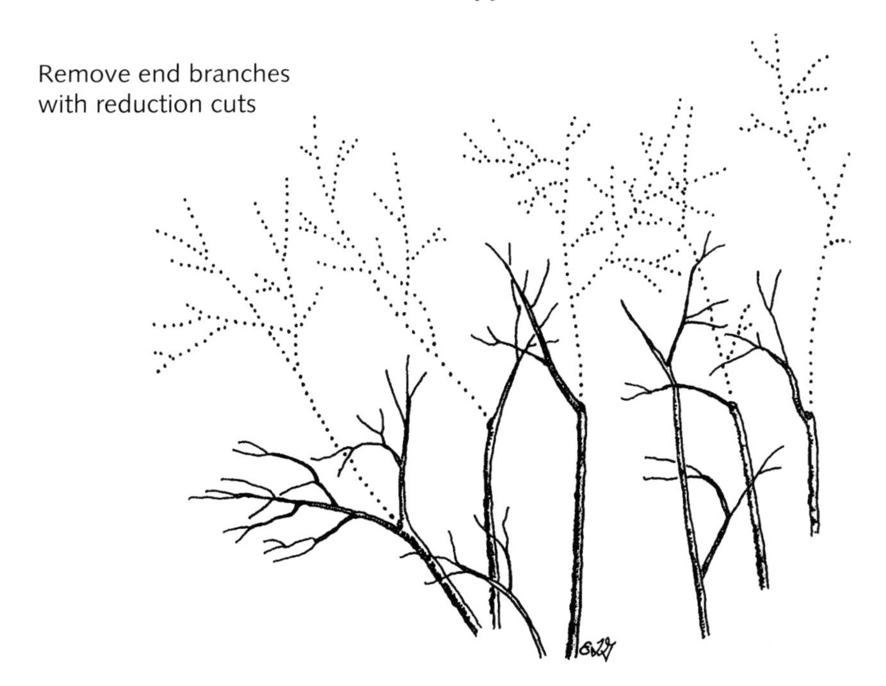

Reduction shortens stems and branches back to live lateral branches. (Removed stem and branch sections are shown as dotted lines.) Notice that live, unpruned branches were left on the edge of the new, smaller canopy and that no heading cuts were used. Properly done, this technique provides a more pleasing, unpruned natural look to the tree or shrub compared to topping or shearing. Compared to topping, less decay is likely to enter the tree following reduction.

Fig. 5.28. Reduction makes a plant, or a portion of a plant, smaller in size.

Before restoration

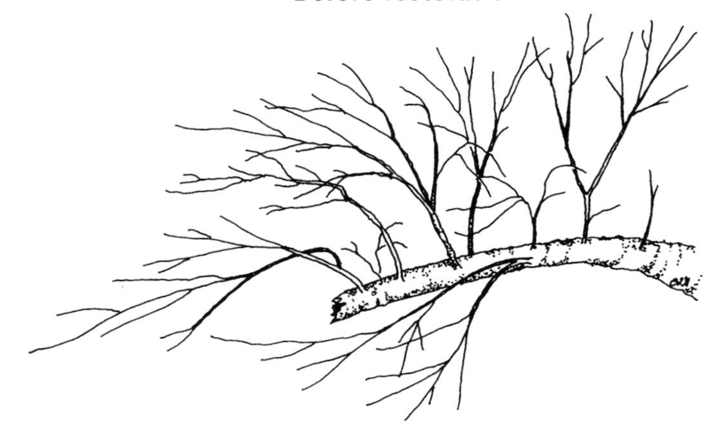

Problem: Many sprouts form from the cut ends of topped or storm-damaged trees. Some sprouts also develop behind the cuts. All are poorly attached to the tree—at least for several years—and can break easily. Notice the eight sprouts that developed from the damaged branch. There are too many sprouts too close together.

Remove some sprouts and shorten others

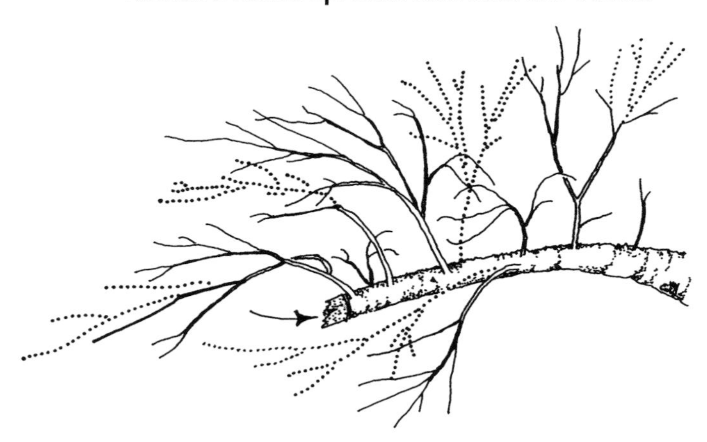

Solution: Begin by removing dead stubs (see arrow), removing some sprouts completely, and shortening others using reduction cuts (indicated by dotted lines). This procedure helps rebuild structure by spacing unpruned sprouts apart so that they can develop into branches. The shortened branches help protect the sprouts that remain.

Fig. 5.29. Restoration attempts to improve structure by removing or reducing sprouts.

Table 5.6. Some species in these genera are known to withstand pollarding

ash *(Fraxinus)*	Japanese quince *(Chaenomeles)*
beech *(Fagus)*	linden (Tilia)
catalpa *(Catalpa)*	maple *(Acer)*
crape myrtle *(Lagerstroemia)*	oak *(Quercus)*
elm *(Ulmus)*	pear *(Pyrus)*
hawthorn *(Crataegus)*	planetree *(Platanus)*
horsechestnut *(Aesculus)*	sweet gum *(Liquidambar)*

can be restored by allowing sprouts to develop along the interior portion of limbs for one to three years, depending on size, age, and condition of the tree. Then remove and shorten some of the sprouts along the entire length of the limbs, so they are evenly distributed and spaced apart. Restoration usually requires several prunings over a number of years.

The location in the tree (top or interior) and the percentage of sprouts to be removed or reduced should be determined before restoration is begun. Typically, one-third of the sprouts are removed and one-third of the sprouts are reduced at each pruning until adequate branches have developed.

Pollarding

Pollarding is a training system that involves severe heading the first year followed by annual sprout removal to maintain trees at a predetermined size or to maintain a "formal" appearance. Pollarding is not the same as "topping." Pollarding historically was used to generate shoots for fuel, shelter, and various products because of the abundance of adventitious sprouts that a tree produces in this process. The pollarding process should be started on deciduous trees when they are young by making heading cuts through stems and branches no more than about three years old. Severe heading (topping) through older tissue may kill or start a decline syndrome on some tree species. Table 5.6 lists several trees that can withstand pollarding.

Heading cuts are made at strategic locations so that the sprouts from all cuts have access to sunlight. After the initial cuts are made, no additional heading cuts should be necessary. After a few pruning cycles, pollard heads (also called "knuckles" or "knobs") develop, and the tree produces sprouts from these knuckles. Sprouts that grow from knuckles should be removed during the dormant season, taking care not to cut into or below the knobs. The knobs are the key differentiating factor between pollarding and topping. If knobs are damaged or removed in subsequent pruning, the cut branches could decay.

Fig. 5.30. Removing a branch over 1 inch in diameter: First *(A)* and second *(B)* cuts prevent bark from tearing; third cut *(C)* is detailed in figures 5.31 and 5.32.

Removing Large Tree Branches

Large branches too heavy to be held by hand (that is, 1 inch or more in diameter) require three separate cuts to prevent the bark from stripping (Figure 5.30). The first cut is made on the underside of the branch, about 15 inches away from the trunk and as far up through the branch as possible before the branch weight binds the saw. The second cut, which takes the limb off, is made downward from the top of the branch, about 18 inches from the main trunk, to cause the limb to split between the two cuts without tearing the trunk bark under the limb. The remaining stub can then be supported easily with one hand while it is cut from the tree. This final cut should begin on the outside of the branch bark ridge and end just outside of the branch collar swelling on the lower side of the branch (Figure 5.31). (The bark ridge is usually rough, always darker than the surrounding bark, and fairly obvious on most species.) Note that the cut is usually made angling down and outward from the tree. If the cut must be made straight down (parallel to the trunk), do not make it flush with the tree trunk. A flush cut will cause serious injury. Although flush cutting was once standard practice, research has conclusively shown that this method can cause extensive trunk decay because wood that is actually part of the trunk gets cut. When the bottom of the branch collar is hard to see, prune as shown in Figure 5.32. In this way, only branch tissue is cut, and there is no damage to the trunk.

Painting wounds with tree wound dressing has become a controversial practice. The standard recommendation was to paint wounds with a quality tree wound dressing to protect the cut surface from wood rotting organisms and from cracking upon drying. However, research has shown that wound dressings do not prevent decay. When exposed to the sun, the protective coating often cracks, allowing moisture to enter and accumulate in pockets between the wood and the wound covering. This situation may be more inviting to wood-rotting organisms than one with no wound cover. In situations where aesthetics or perception are important, however, the practice may be justified.

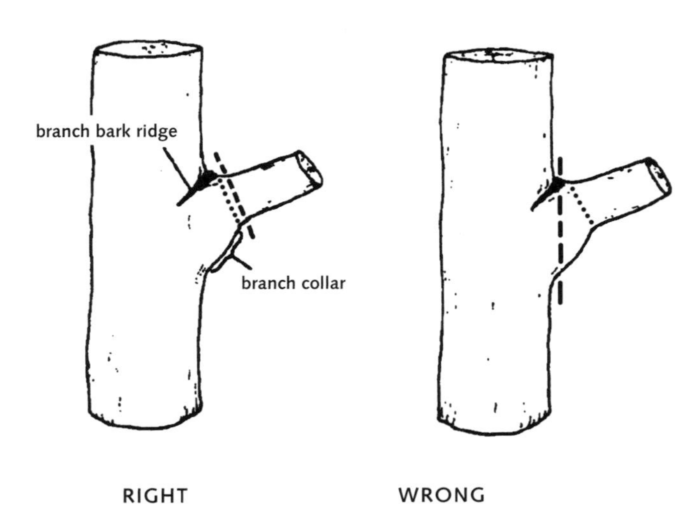

Fig. 5.31. *Left,* correct, and *right,* incorrect final pruning cuts for branches of any size.

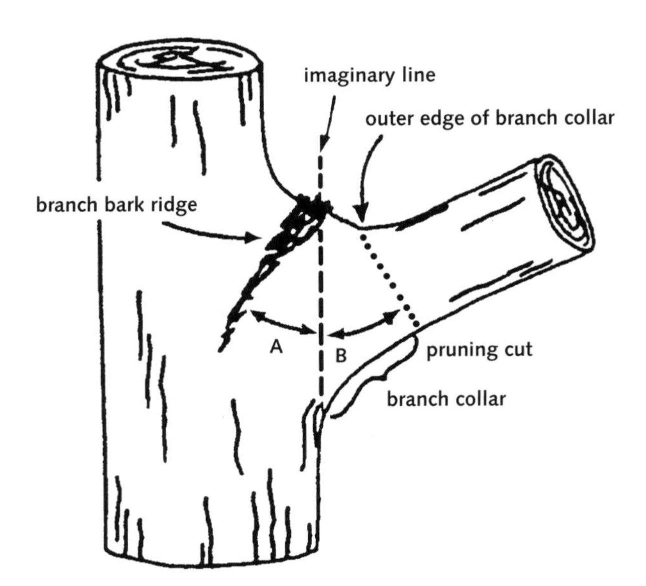

Fig. 5.32. The angle *(A)* created by the branch bark ridge and an imaginary line flush with the tree trunk is the approximate angle *(B)* at which to make the pruning cut; this calculation is useful when the bottom of the branch collar cannot be seen.

Pruning Palms

Care must be taken when pruning palms not to cut or otherwise injure the terminal bud, or the whole tree will die. Old dead leaves on palms such as the Washington palm should be removed, for they often harbor insects and rodents and may become a fire hazard. Remove palm leaves by cutting them from the underside to avoid tearing the fibers of the palm's stem. Palms such as the royal palm shed their leaves, which are heavy and could pose a hazard to those under them. Thus it is best

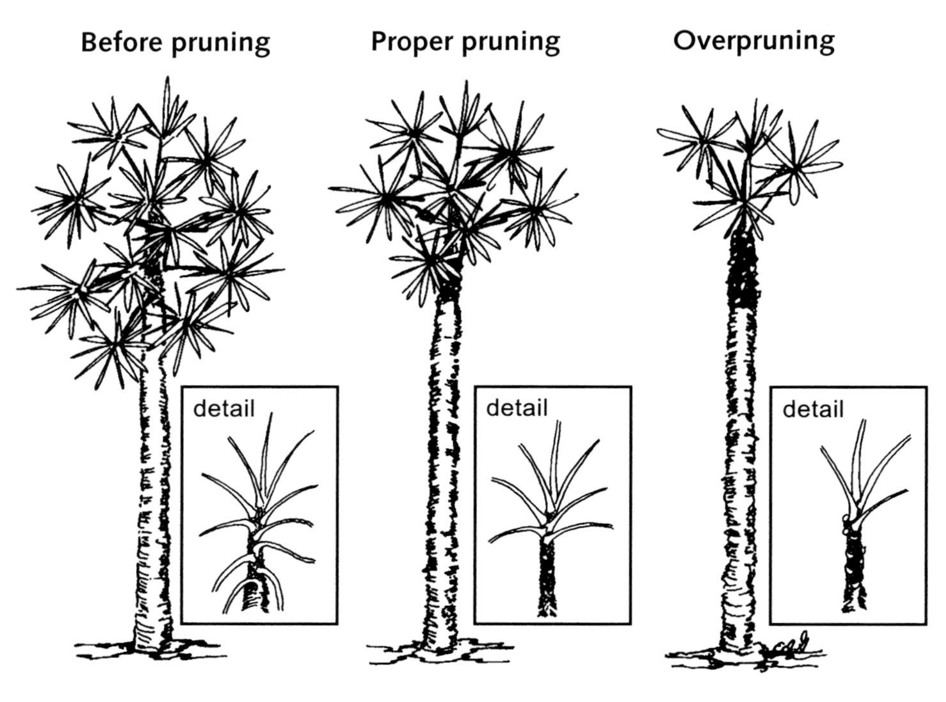

Consider treating nutrient deficiencies along with pruning. Pruning nutrient-deficient palms could cause symptoms to appear in remaining foliage. Remove lower fronds that are chlorotic or dead. There is no biological reason to remove live green fronds on palms. Removing live green fronds is not known to reduce future pruning requirements.

Remove lower fronds that are dead or more than about half chlorotic. It is best for the palm if green fronds remain intact. (If you decide to remove green fronds, the ANSI A300 pruning standard advises never to remove those growing at an angle of more than 45 degrees from the horizontal. Some arborists remove no green fronds above a horizontal line drawn across the base of the crown.)

Overpruned palms look terrible, have slow growth, and can attract pests. In the detail above, you can see that many upright fronds were removed. Green fronds are almost always removed during this overpruning.

Fig. 5.33. Palm pruning primarily removes dead or chlorotic fronds.

to remove them before they drop. The large fruit of coconut palms can be dangerous in areas where pedestrians and automobiles pass beneath. Prevent formation of fruits by removing the flower stalks. On small-fruited palms such as Christmas and cabbage palms, these safety precautions are of course not necessary. Nevertheless, the fallen fruits from these and many other palms can become slippery on paved surfaces; consider removing the flower stalks if this is a concern.

Live, healthy leaves should not be removed. Removal of these leaves reduces the food-making ability of the palm and can result in a narrowing of the trunk just below the crown. However, if they must be removed, avoid removing those that initiate at an angle of 45 degrees or greater above horizontal (Figure 5.33). Leaves removed should be severed close to the petiole base without damaging living trunk tissue. Climbing spikes should not be used to climb palms for pruning. It is preferable to hire a professional arborist, who will have ropes, ladders, or a cherry picker.

Chapter 6

Plant Selection Guide

This section is a guide to help you select the right plant for your landscape, as well as a reference for maintenance of the plants once they are established. The plants are arranged in alphabetical order by botanical name and are divided into the categories "trees," "shrubs," "vines and ground covers," and "palms." Plants that grow equally well as large shrubs or small trees were each placed into one category or the other depending on the most common landscape use. Plants in the "trees," "shrubs, " and "vines and ground covers" categories are subdivided by their degree of tolerance to salt as "highly," "moderately," and "slightly" salt tolerant. Palms are subdivided into two categories, "highly" and "moderately" salt tolerant. Refer to the map of hardiness zones (Figure 2.1) to determine whether a plant is suitable for your region.

Some plants listed in this selection guide are reported to be invasive in some regions and could seed themselves and reproduce in nearby landscapes, woodlands, or natural plant communities on conservation lands. Invasive plants can form self-sustaining and expanding populations within plant communities with which they were not previously associated. They can displace native plants and associated wildlife, including endangered plants, and they can alter natural processes such as fire and water flow. When landscaping, do not use plants that have the potential to be invasive in natural areas near where you live. Local land managers, park biologists, and county governments can provide information on invasive plants that are the greatest problem in your area. Plants with invasive potential are noted in the "uses" category of the plant lists.

Salt-Tolerant Trees

Highly Salt-Tolerant Trees

Botanical name: *Avicennia germinans*
Common name: Black Mangrove
Hardiness range: 9A to 11
Mature size: 20–30 feet tall by 15–20 feet wide
Light requirement: full sun
Leaf persistence: evergreen
Flower: white; inconspicuous in spring and summer
Soil moisture: tolerates wet and submerged soil
Soil pH tolerance: neutral to slightly alkaline
Uses: erosion control
Attributes: pest tolerant; wetlands plant
Native: tropical America, western Africa, along the coast from Cedar Key, Florida, south through the Keys, then north to Daytona
Notes: grows in the tidal area of the shore; helps to stabilize the coast and will help prevent shoreline changes during storms; leaves are olive green; salt is exported through glands at bases of leaf blades

Botanical name: *Bucida buceras*
Common name: Black Olive
Hardiness range: 10B to 11
Mature size: 30–60 feet tall by 40–60 feet wide
Light requirement: partial shade to full sun
Leaf persistence: evergreen
Flower: yellow; inconspicuous in spring and summer
Soil moisture: tolerates drought
Soil pH tolerance: acid to alkaline
Uses: street tree; standard; specimen; shade tree
Attributes: pest tolerant; urban tough
Native: West Indies, Mexico to Panama
Notes: often planted in parking lot islands; fruit and leaves can stain cars; commonly topped or "hat-racked" (improper pruning) to prevent the branches from growing over the cars

Botanical name: *Bulnesia arborea*
Common name: Bulnesia
Hardiness range: 10A to 11
Mature size: 20–40 feet tall by 15–35 feet wide
Light requirement: full sun
Leaf persistence: evergreen
Flower: yellow; very showy in spring and summer
Soil moisture: tolerates drought
Soil pH tolerance: acid to alkaline
Uses: border; street tree; specimen; shade tree
Attributes: pest tolerant
Native: Colombia and Venezuela
Notes: excellent low-growing tree for small yards and patios; can be grown as a multistemmed clump or can be trained into a single trunk

Botanical name: *Bursera simaruba*
Common name: Gumbo Limbo
Hardiness range: 10A to 11
Mature size: 25–50 feet tall by 35–50 feet wide
Light requirement: partial shade to full sun
Leaf persistence: semievergreen
Flower: green; inconspicuous in spring
Soil moisture: tolerates drought
Soil pH tolerance: acid to alkaline
Uses: street tree; standard; specimen; shade tree
Attributes: pest tolerant
Native: Florida throughout the Keys, Puerto Rico, and the Virgin Islands
Notes: adapts to shallow, alkaline, rocky, or poor soil, or even deep white sands, but will also grow quickly on more fertile soil; deciduous toward the end of the dry season (spring in Florida); prune to one leader

Botanical name: *Calophyllum inophyllum*
Common name: Beauty Leaf, Indian Laurel, Laurelwood
Hardiness range: 10B to 11
Mature size: 25–50 feet tall by 35–50 feet wide
Light requirement: partial shade to full sun
Leaf persistence: evergreen
Flower: white; fragrant and showy in summer
Soil moisture: tolerates drought well
Soil pH tolerance: acid to slightly alkaline
Uses: invasive
Attributes: pest tolerant; attractive and fragrant flowers
Native: coastal, southern India to Malay Peninsula
Notes: has been used for coastal locations; becomes twisted and contorted when exposed to constant wind; naturalized in undisturbed native habitats in parts of Florida

Botanical name: *Canella winterana*
Common name: Wild Cinnamon, Winter Cinnamon
Hardiness range: 10B to 11
Mature size: 15–25 feet tall to 8–12 feet wide
Light requirement: partial shade to full sun
Leaf persistence: evergreen
Flower: purple and white; showy in summer and fall
Soil moisture: tolerates drought
Soil pH tolerance: acid to alkaline
Uses: border; screen; espalier; specimen
Attributes: pest tolerant; attractive bright green foliage
Native: Miami to Key West along the coast to Cape Sable, Florida
Notes: bright red berries follow the showy, purple and white flowers; good native plant for locating near patios and decks in exposed locations

Botanical name: *Casuarina* spp.
Common name: Australian Pine
Hardiness range: 9A to 11
Mature size: 50–75 feet tall by 35–50 feet wide
Light requirement: partial shade to full sun
Leaf persistence: evergreen
Flower: yellow; inconspicuous in spring
Soil moisture: tolerates drought and occasional wetness
Soil pH tolerance: acid to alkaline
Uses: **invasive;** prohibited to plant in Florida by the Florida Department of Environmental Protection
Attributes: tolerates sea salt well
Native: Australia and the Pacific Islands
Notes: vigorous sprouts often originate from the roots of older trees killed to the ground by freezing temperatures; outlawed in Florida due to its invasive nature, rapid growth, and non-native status

Botanical name: *Clusia major* (syn. *Clusia rosea*)
Common name: Pitch Apple, Balsam Apple, Florida Clusia
Hardiness range: 10B to 11
Mature size: 15–25 feet tall and wide
Light requirement: full shade to full sun
Leaf persistence: evergreen
Flower: pink and white; showy in summer
Soil moisture: tolerates drought and occasional wetness
Soil pH tolerance: acid to alkaline
Uses: border; screen; espalier; street tree; standard; specimen
Attributes: pest tolerant; attractive flowers and fruit; urban tough
Native: West Indies and in Florida, possibly the Keys
Notes: pruning required to remove prop roots and aerial roots as they form from the trunk base and lower branches; some prop roots should be allowed to remain to ensure that long horizontal branches remain well attached to the tree

Botanical name: *Coccoloba diversifolia*
Common name: Pigeon Plum
Hardiness range: 10B to 11
Mature size: 20–30 feet tall and wide
Light requirement: partial shade to full sun
Leaf persistence: evergreen
Flower: white; showy in summer
Soil moisture: tolerates drought
Soil pH tolerance: acid to alkaline
Uses: street tree; standard; specimen; parking lot
Attributes: pest tolerant; attracts birds
Native: Florida, Mexico, Puerto Rico, and the Virgin Islands
Notes: fallen fruit may create a litter problem on patios, sidewalks, and streets; tolerates urban conditions and has performed well as a street tree

Botanical name: *Coccoloba uvifera*
Common name: Sea Grape, Platter Leaf
Hardiness range: 10A to 11
Mature size: 25–35 feet tall by 25–40 feet wide
Light requirement: partial shade to full sun
Leaf persistence: evergreen
Flower: white; inconspicuous in winter
Soil moisture: tolerates drought
Soil pH tolerance: acid to alkaline
Uses: street tree; standard; specimen; parking lot
Attributes: pest tolerant; urban tough
Native: Florida, Mexico, Puerto Rico, and the Virgin Islands
Notes: perfect for seaside landscapes; can be pruned to become a loose hedge, screen, or windbreak with several prunings each year; can be trained to become a strong tree with regular pruning

Botanical name: *Conocarpus erectus*
Common name: Buttonwood, Buttonwood Mangrove
Hardiness range: 10B to 11
Mature size: 25–40 feet tall by 30–40 feet wide
Light requirement: full sun
Leaf persistence: evergreen
Flower: purple and white; inconspicuous year-round
Soil moisture: tolerates drought and flooding
Soil pH tolerance: acid to alkaline
Uses: screen; street tree; standard; specimen; shade tree; parking lot
Attributes: pest tolerant; wetlands plant; urban tough
Native: Florida
Notes: withstands the rigors of urban conditions very well and makes a durable street or parking lot tree

Botanical name: *Conocarpus erectus* var. *sericeus*
Common name: Silver Buttonwood
Hardiness range: 10B to 11
Mature size: 15–25 feet tall and wide
Light requirement: full sun
Leaf persistence: evergreen
Flower: purple and white; inconspicuous year-round
Soil moisture: tolerates drought and flooding
Soil pH tolerance: acid to alkaline
Uses: seashore planting; street and parking lot; patio tree; small shade tree
Attributes: attractive silver-blue foliage; urban tough
Native: Florida
Notes: tolerates brackish areas and alkaline soils; tough and long lasting in the landscape

Botanical name: *Cordia sebestena*
Common name: Geiger Tree
Hardiness range: 10B to 11
Mature size: 15–25 feet tall and wide
Light requirement: partial shade to full sun
Leaf persistence: evergreen
Flower: orange; very showy in spring and summer
Soil moisture: tolerates drought
Soil pH tolerance: acid to alkaline
Uses: street tree; standard; specimen; parking lot
Attributes: pest tolerant; attracts butterflies
Native: Caribbean Islands, probably naturalized in Florida
Notes: quite tolerant of salt and brackish water; ideal for use in coastal landscapes as a freestanding specimen, patio, or framing tree

Botanical name: *Cupaniopsis anacardiopsis*
Common name: Carrotwood
Hardiness range: 10A to 11
Mature size: 25–50 feet tall by 25–35 feet wide
Light requirement: full sun
Leaf persistence: evergreen
Flower: green; inconspicuous in summer
Soil moisture: tolerates drought and occasional wetness
Soil pH tolerance: acid to alkaline
Uses: **invasive;** noxious weed listed by Fla. Dept. of Agriculture and Consumer Services and/or USDA
Attributes: pest tolerant; wetlands plant
Native: Australia
Notes: durable, urban-tolerant tree, able to grow in confined planting pits in sidewalks; fruit is soft, abundant, and messy; invasive and banned in many communities in Florida

Botanical name: *Gleditsia triacanthos*
Common name: Honeylocust
Hardiness range: 4A to 8A
Mature size: 40–75 feet tall by 35–60 feet wide
Light requirement: partial shade to full sun
Leaf persistence: deciduous
Flower: yellow; fragrant and inconspicuous in spring
Soil moisture: tolerates drought and occasional wetness
Soil pH tolerance: acid to alkaline
Uses: specimen; street tree; shade tree; parking lot
Attributes: fragrant flowers
Native: eastern North America
Notes: has no particular soil preferences and is useful in dry or alkaline areas; tolerates compacted, poorly aerated soil and flooding for a period of time once it is well established

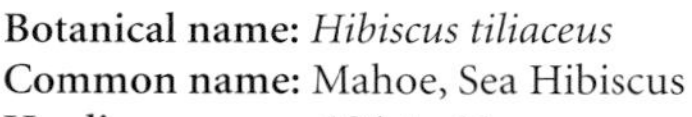

Botanical name: *Hibiscus tiliaceus*
Common name: Mahoe, Sea Hibiscus
Hardiness range: 10A to 11
Mature size: 25–50 feet tall by 35–50 feet wide
Light requirement: full sun
Leaf persistence: evergreen
Flower: red and yellow in one day; showy year-round
Soil moisture: tolerates drought and occasional wetness
Soil pH tolerance: acid to alkaline
Uses: invasive
Attributes: attractive flowers
Native: Old and New World tropics
Notes: tends to naturalize into nearby landscapes; engulfs everything nearby with its rank growth habit; plant something else

Botanical name: *Ilex vomitoria*
Common name: Yaupon Holly
Hardiness range: 7A to 10A
Mature size: 15–18 feet tall by 10–15 feet wide
Light requirement: full shade to full sun
Leaf persistence: evergreen
Flower: white; inconspicuous in spring
Soil moisture: tolerates drought and flooding
Soil pH tolerance: acid to slightly alkaline
Uses: woodland garden; seashore planting; border; screen; espalier; street tree; standard; specimen
Attributes: wetlands plant; attracts birds; hedge
Native: eastern North America to central Florida
Notes: crown will thin in shade; sprouts readily from the roots, forming clumps of upright shoots beneath the canopy

Botanical name: *Juniperus silicicola*
Common name: Southern Redcedar, Juniper
Hardiness range: 7B to 10A
Mature size: 25–50 feet tall by 15–35 feet wide
Light requirement: partial shade to full sun
Leaf persistence: evergreen
Flower: inconspicuous
Soil moisture: tolerates drought
Soil pH tolerance: acid to alkaline
Uses: screen; specimen; street tree; Christmas tree
Attributes: attracts birds
Native: southeastern United States
Notes: growth may be poor in landscapes that are overirrigated; water until well-established and then forget about the tree except to prune for shape and structure

Botanical name: *Juniperus virginiana*
Common name: Eastern Redcedar
Hardiness range: 3B to 9A
Mature size: 25–50 feet tall by 10–35 feet wide
Light requirement: partial shade to full sun
Leaf persistence: evergreen
Flower: green and yellow; inconspicuous in summer
Soil moisture: tolerates drought
Soil pH tolerance: acid to alkaline
Uses: seashore planting; screen; street tree; standard; specimen
Attributes: attracts birds and butterflies; Christmas tree
Native: eastern North America
Notes: will not do well on soils kept continually moist; once established, it performs admirably with no care

Botanical name: *Laguncularia racemosa*
Common name: White Buttonwood, White Mangrove
Hardiness range: 10B to 11
Mature size: 25–50 feet tall by 25–35 feet wide
Light requirement: full sun
Leaf persistence: evergreen
Flower: green and white; fragrant and inconspicuous in spring
Soil moisture: tolerates flooding
Soil pH tolerance: acid to alkaline
Uses: seashore planting
Attributes: stabilizes shoreline; tolerates some pruning
Native: southern part of Florida into the Keys and throughout the Caribbean Basin
Notes: roots bind the soil along the shore; most common in upland tidal area a few feet above sea level; excretes salt from glands at the bases of leaves

Botanical name: *Leptospermum laevigatum*
Common name: Australian Tea Tree
Hardiness range: 9A to 11
Mature size: 15–30 feet tall by 20–35 feet wide
Light requirement: partial shade to full sun
Leaf persistence: evergreen
Flower: pink, red, and white; showy in spring
Soil moisture: tolerates drought
Soil pH tolerance: acid to slightly alkaline
Uses: containers; seashore planting; cascades; pollarding; specimen
Attributes: low-branched habit
Native: southeastern Australia and Tasmania
Notes: tolerates pruning and clipping; tolerates poor soil, but shows chlorosis on soils with a high pH

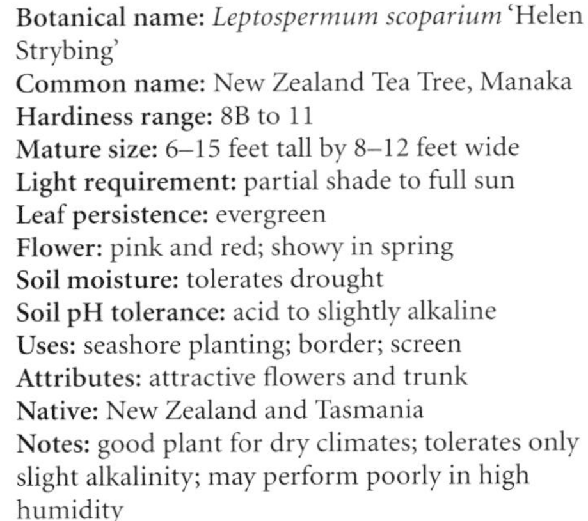

Botanical name: *Leptospermum scoparium* 'Helen Strybing'
Common name: New Zealand Tea Tree, Manaka
Hardiness range: 8B to 11
Mature size: 6–15 feet tall by 8–12 feet wide
Light requirement: partial shade to full sun
Leaf persistence: evergreen
Flower: pink and red; showy in spring
Soil moisture: tolerates drought
Soil pH tolerance: acid to slightly alkaline
Uses: seashore planting; border; screen
Attributes: attractive flowers and trunk
Native: New Zealand and Tasmania
Notes: good plant for dry climates; tolerates only slight alkalinity; may perform poorly in high humidity

Botanical name: *Lysiloma latisiliqua* (syn. *Lysiloma bahamensis*)
Common name: Wild Tamarind, Cuban Tamarind
Hardiness range: 10B to 11
Mature size: 25–50 feet tall by 30–50 feet wide
Light requirement: partial shade to full sun
Leaf persistence: evergreen
Flower: white; fragrant and inconspicuous in spring and summer
Soil moisture: tolerates drought
Soil pH tolerance: acid to alkaline
Uses: street tree; standard; specimen; parking lot; shade tree
Attributes: pest tolerant; attracts butterflies; urban tough
Native: Florida
Notes: should be grown in full sun or partial shade on rich, well-drained soil; needs structural pruning for strong form

Botanical name: *Manilkara zapota*
Common name: Sapodilla
Hardiness range: 10B to 11
Mature size: 25–50 feet tall by 35–50 feet wide
Light requirement: full sun
Leaf persistence: evergreen
Flower: white; inconspicuous year-round
Soil moisture: tolerates drought
Soil pH tolerance: acid to alkaline
Uses: **invasive** in the Florida Keys
Attributes: pest tolerant; tasty fruit
Native: Mexico, Central America
Notes: grows well in urban sites with poor soil; poor drainage can slow growth and cause decline

Botanical name: *Mastichodendron foetidissimum*
Common name: Mastic
Hardiness range: 10A to 11
Mature size: 35–60 feet tall by 35–50 feet wide
Light requirement: full sun
Leaf persistence: evergreen
Flower: white and yellow; inconspicuous spring through fall
Soil moisture: tolerates drought
Soil pH tolerance: acid to alkaline
Uses: specimen; shade tree
Attributes: pest tolerant; edible fruit
Native: Florida
Notes: large-growing tree casting deep shade; edible fruit creates a mess when it falls to the ground

Botanical name: *Myrcianthes fragrans*
Common name: Simpson's Stopper, Twinberry
Hardiness range: 9B to 11
Mature size: 15–25 feet tall and wide
Light requirement: full shade to full sun
Leaf persistence: evergreen
Flower: white; fragrant and showy year-round
Soil moisture: tolerates drought and occasional wetness
Soil pH tolerance: acid to alkaline
Uses: screen; hedge; specimen
Attributes: pest tolerant; attracts butterflies
Native: Florida
Notes: an attractive, hardy tropical; tiny, deep green leaves contain aromatic oils with the fragrance of nutmeg; flowers develop into attractive red berries that are edible by birds

Botanical name: *Myrica cerifera*
Common name: Southern Wax Myrtle, Southern Bayberry
Hardiness range: 7B to 11
Mature size: 15–25 feet tall and wide
Light requirement: partial shade to full sun
Leaf persistence: evergreen
Flower: green; inconspicuous in spring
Soil moisture: tolerates some drought and flooding
Soil pH tolerance: acid to slightly alkaline
Uses: border; screen; specimen; erosion control
Attributes: wetlands plant; attracts birds and butterflies
Native: southeastern United States to southern Florida
Notes: has a tendency to sprout from the roots and is sensitive to disease; only female trees produce fruit; plants typically live for about 15 years, if pruning is kept to a bare minimum

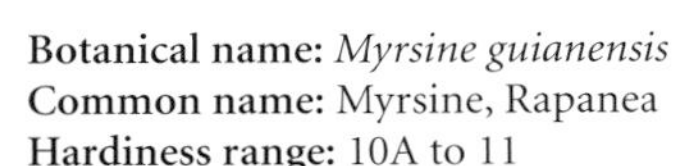

Botanical name: *Myrsine guianensis*
Common name: Myrsine, Rapanea
Hardiness range: 10A to 11
Mature size: 15–25 feet tall by 10–15 feet wide
Light requirement: full shade to partial sun
Leaf persistence: evergreen
Flower: green, white, and yellow; inconspicuous year-round
Soil moisture: tolerates drought and occasional wetness
Soil pH tolerance: acid to slightly alkaline
Uses: border; screen; street tree; standard; specimen; parking lot
Attributes: pest tolerant; attracts butterflies; attractive foliage and fruit
Native: Florida
Notes: flowers are followed by decorative, shiny, black berries; plants of both sexes must be planted for fruiting to occur; good background plant in a shrub border; also useful as an understory plant and lends itself well to dune conditions

Botanical name: *Noronhia emarginata*
Common name: Madagascar Olive
Hardiness range: 10B to 11
Mature size: 15–25 feet tall and wide
Light requirement: partial shade to full sun
Leaf persistence: evergreen
Flower: yellow; fragrant and inconspicuous year-round
Soil moisture: tolerates drought
Soil pH tolerance: acid to alkaline
Uses: screen; espalier; street tree; standard; specimen; parking lot
Attributes: pest tolerant
Native: Madagascar
Notes: tolerance to salt and wind makes it well suited for screen or windbreak; can form an ideal specimen or framing tree for landscapes with limited room

Botanical name: *Ochrosia elliptica*
Common name: Ochrosia
Hardiness range: 10B to 11
Mature size: 15–25 feet tall and wide
Light requirement: partial shade to full sun
Leaf persistence: evergreen
Flower: yellow; fragrant and showy summer through winter
Soil moisture: tolerates some drought
Soil pH tolerance: acid to slightly alkaline
Uses: seashore planting; border; screen; specimen
Attributes: pest tolerant; attractive fruit
Native: New Caledonia to Australia
Notes: grows well close to the ocean in full sun or partial shade on a wide range of moist soils, including sandy and alkaline; bright red fruit is considered poisonous

Botanical name: *Osmanthus americanus*
Common name: Devilwood, Wild Olive
Hardiness range: 5B to 9B
Mature size: 15–25 feet tall by 10–15 feet wide
Light requirement: partial shade to full sun
Leaf persistence: evergreen
Flower: white; fragrant and showy in spring
Soil moisture: tolerates flooding
Soil pH tolerance: acid to slightly alkaline
Uses: woodland garden; border; screen; specimen
Attributes: attracts birds; wetlands plant
Native: southeastern United States to south-central Florida
Notes: naturally found along stream banks or swamp margins; trees usually trained to multiple stems, but nurseries can grow them as single trunk for use along streets

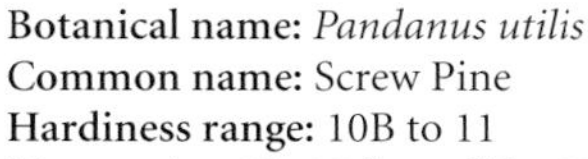

Botanical name: *Pandanus utilis*
Common name: Screw Pine
Hardiness range: 10B to 11
Mature size: 15–25 feet tall by 10–15 feet wide
Light requirement: partial shade to full sun
Leaf persistence: evergreen
Flower: white; fragrant and inconspicuous in winter
Soil moisture: tolerates some drought and flooding
Soil pH tolerance: acid to slightly alkaline
Uses: specimen
Attributes: pest tolerant; attractive foliage
Native: Madagascar
Notes: produces an abundance of large fruit when grown in full sun; regularly drops foliage and fruit, potentially becoming messy beneath the canopy

Botanical name: *Parkinsonia aculeata* (syn. *Cercidium aculeate*)
Common name: Jerusalem Thorn
Hardiness range: 8B to 11
Mature size: 15–25 feet tall by 15–40 feet wide
Light requirement: full sun
Leaf persistence: evergreen
Flower: yellow; fragrant and very showy in spring and summer
Soil moisture: tolerates drought
Soil pH tolerance: acid to alkaline
Uses: rock garden; standard; specimen
Attributes: pest tolerant; winter interest; attractive flowers; lanky open habit; thorns
Native: tropical America
Notes: tolerates heat, drought, alkaline soil, and salt, but cannot tolerate wet, soggy soil; does best without frequent irrigation once established; poor drainage may account for short life on many sites

Botanical name: *Persea borbonia*
Common name: Red Bay
Hardiness range: 7B to 11
Mature size: 25–40 feet tall by 35–50 feet wide
Light requirement: partial shade to full sun
Leaf persistence: evergreen
Flower: green and white; inconspicuous in spring
Soil moisture: tolerates drought and occasional wetness
Soil pH tolerance: acid to alkaline
Uses: street tree; specimen; park
Attributes: pest tolerant; attracts birds and butterflies
Native: southeastern United States to the Florida Keys
Notes: suitable to many landscape applications including coastal beachfront property; tolerates urban conditions well and grows well along streets; harmless gall deforms leaves

Botanical name: *Pinus thunbergii* (syn. *Pinus thunbergiana*)
Common name: Japanese Black Pine
Hardiness range: 6A to 9A
Mature size: 15–40 feet tall by 15–25 feet wide
Light requirement: full sun
Leaf persistence: evergreen
Flower: yellow; inconspicuous in spring
Soil moisture: tolerates drought
Soil pH tolerance: acid to slightly alkaline
Uses: screen; specimen
Attributes: attractive fruit
Native: Japan
Notes: thrives in dry, sandy soil and is extremely salt tolerant, being used successfully along beachfront property in the full sun; has been under attack by pests lately in some eastern regions of the United States; tolerates ozone

Botanical name: *Piscidia piscipula*
Common name: Fish Poison Tree, Jamaican Dogwood, West Indian Dogwood
Hardiness range: 10 to 11
Mature size: 35–45 feet tall by 25–45 feet wide
Light requirement: partial shade to full sun
Leaf persistence: evergreen
Flower: lavender and white; showy in spring
Soil moisture: tolerates drought
Soil pH tolerance: acid to alkaline
Uses: specimen
Attributes: pest tolerant; attracts butterflies
Native: southern Florida, West Indies
Notes: outstanding wood for woodworking; very resistant to decay; all parts of the plant are poisonous

Botanical name: *Pithecellobium mexicanum*
Common name: Pithecellobium, Palo Chinu, Mexican Pithecellobium
Hardiness range: 10A to 11
Mature size: 25–35 feet tall by 20–25 feet wide
Light requirement: full sun
Leaf persistence: evergreen
Flower: white and yellow; showy and fragrant in spring
Soil moisture: tolerates drought
Soil pH tolerance: acid to alkaline
Uses: barrier
Attributes: attractive and fragrant flowers; pest tolerant
Native: arroyos and desert slopes in Sonora and Baja California, Mexico
Notes: often found in sandy pinelands, hammocks, and dunes; will continue to thrive when subjected to high levels of salt spray

Botanical name: *Plumeria* spp.
Common name: Frangipani, Plumeria
Hardiness range: 10B to 11
Mature size: 15–25 feet tall and wide
Light requirement: partial shade to full sun
Leaf persistence: deciduous
Flower: pink, red, yellow, white, and rose; fragrant and very showy spring through fall
Soil moisture: tolerates drought
Soil pH tolerance: acid to alkaline
Uses: espalier; street tree; standard; specimen
Attributes: pest tolerant; fragrant and showy flowers
Native: tropical America
Notes: wonderful small garden tree for tropical and subtropical landscapes; very susceptible to freezing temperatures; works well as a specimen, as a patio tree, or as part of a shrub border

Botanical name: *Podocarpus nagi* (syn. *Nageia nagi*)
Common name: Broadleaf Podocarpus, Nagi Podocarpus
Hardiness range: 9A to 11
Mature size: 25–40 feet tall by 15–25 feet wide
Light requirement: full shade to full sun
Leaf persistence: evergreen
Flower: yellow; inconspicuous in spring
Soil moisture: tolerates drought
Soil pH tolerance: acid to slightly alkaline
Uses: border; screen; street tree; specimen
Attributes: adaptable to urban conditions
Native: central and southwestern Japan, Ryukyu Islands
Notes: will show nutrient deficiencies on alkaline soils; the most common symptom is a wide yellow band or stripe across the leaves, commonly attributed to magnesium deficiency

Botanical name: *Prunus serrulata*
Common name: Oriental Cherry, Japanese Flowering Cherry
Hardiness range: 5B to 8A
Mature size: 15–25 feet tall by 15–30 feet wide
Light requirement: full sun
Leaf persistence: deciduous
Flower: pink; very showy and fragrant in spring
Soil moisture: tolerates some drought and occasional wetness
Soil pH tolerance: acid to alkaline
Uses: specimen; street tree; parking lot
Attributes: attractive fall color
Native: eastern Asia
Notes: this species rarely seen in cultivation because the market is dominated by cultivars; rarely produces fruit; useful life of the species is limited to about 15 years; 'Kwanzan' is a popular cultivar

Botanical name: *Quercus alba*
Common name: White Oak
Hardiness range: 3B to 9A
Mature size: 40–75 feet tall by 50–80 feet wide
Light requirement: partial shade to full sun
Leaf persistence: deciduous
Flower: brown; inconspicuous in spring
Soil moisture: tolerates some drought and occasional wetness
Soil pH tolerance: acid to slightly alkaline
Uses: street tree; standard; specimen
Attributes: pest tolerant
Native: eastern North America
Notes: grows best in moist soil that does not dry out for long periods

Botanical name: *Quercus geminata*
Common name: Sand Live Oak
Hardiness range: 8A to 10A
Mature size: 25–50 feet tall by 50–80 feet wide
Light requirement: partial shade to full sun
Leaf persistence: evergreen and semievergreen
Flower: brown; inconspicuous in spring
Soil moisture: tolerates drought and occasional wetness
Soil pH tolerance: acid to slightly alkaline
Uses: seashore planting; street tree; standard; specimen
Attributes: very good wind resistance
Native: North America
Notes: will thrive in almost any location and has very good wind and salt resistance; a tough, enduring tree that will respond with vigorous growth to plentiful moisture on well-drained soil

Botanical name: *Quercus macrocarpa*
Common name: Burr Oak, Mossy Cup Oak
Hardiness range: 3A to 8A
Mature size: 50–75 feet tall by 50–80 feet wide
Light requirement: full sun
Leaf persistence: deciduous
Flower: brown; inconspicuous in spring
Soil moisture: tolerates drought and flooding
Soil pH tolerance: acid to slightly alkaline
Uses: specimen
Attributes: pest tolerant
Native: eastern United States
Notes: well adapted to alkaline soils, poor drainage, and high clay content; most drought tolerant of the temperate oaks

Botanical name: *Quercus phellos*
Common name: Willow Oak
Hardiness range: 5A to 9A
Mature size: 50–75 feet tall by 35–50 feet wide
Light requirement: full sun
Leaf persistence: deciduous
Flower: brown; inconspicuous in spring
Soil moisture: tolerates drought and occasional wetness
Soil pH tolerance: acid to slightly alkaline
Uses: street tree; standard; specimen; parking lot
Attributes: pest tolerant; urban tough
Native: eastern United States
Notes: grows in acid, wet sites of floodplains yet is drought-tolerant; well adapted to urban conditions

Botanical name: *Quercus virginiana*
Common name: Southern Live Oak, Live Oak
Hardiness range: 7B to 10B
Mature size: 50–75 feet tall by 60–100 feet wide
Light requirement: partial shade to full sun
Leaf persistence: evergreen and semievergreen
Flower: brown; inconspicuous in spring
Soil moisture: tolerates drought and occasional wetness
Soil pH tolerance: acid to alkaline
Uses: espalier; street tree (overused); standard; specimen; parking lot
Attributes: attracts butterflies; urban tough
Native: coastal southeastern United States
Notes: grows best in moist, acid soil, in sand, loam, or clay, but is amazingly adapted to drought; also tolerates alkaline soil well; performs well along streets and in parking lot islands but grows to be quite large

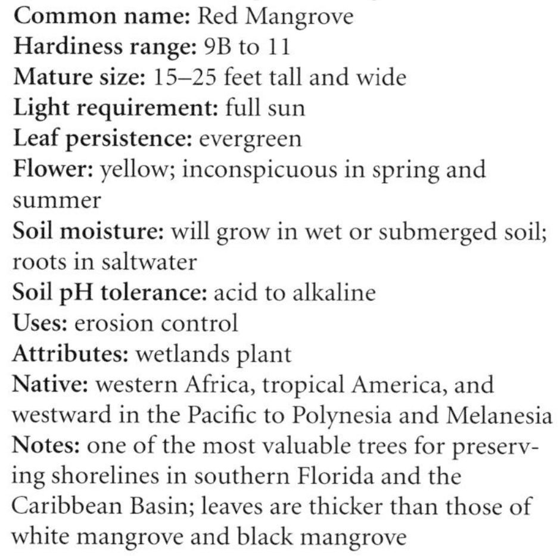

Botanical name: *Rhizophora mangle*
Common name: Red Mangrove
Hardiness range: 9B to 11
Mature size: 15–25 feet tall and wide
Light requirement: full sun
Leaf persistence: evergreen
Flower: yellow; inconspicuous in spring and summer
Soil moisture: will grow in wet or submerged soil; roots in saltwater
Soil pH tolerance: acid to alkaline
Uses: erosion control
Attributes: wetlands plant
Native: western Africa, tropical America, and westward in the Pacific to Polynesia and Melanesia
Notes: one of the most valuable trees for preserving shorelines in southern Florida and the Caribbean Basin; leaves are thicker than those of white mangrove and black mangrove

Botanical name: *Sapindus saponaria*
Common name: Soapberry, Florida Soapberry, Wingleaf Soapberry
Hardiness range: 9A to 11
Mature size: 25–50 feet tall by 25–35 feet wide
Light requirement: full sun
Leaf persistence: evergreen
Flower: white; inconspicuous in spring
Soil moisture: tolerates drought
Soil pH tolerance: acid to slightly alkaline
Uses: specimen; street tree
Attributes: pest tolerant
Native: tropical America, Florida
Notes: tolerance to alkaline soil makes it a good choice for planting in southern Florida; foliage is reported to be poisonous when ingested

Botanical name: *Simarouba glauca*
Common name: Paradise Tree
Hardiness range: 10B to 11
Mature size: 25–50 feet tall by 25–35 feet wide
Light requirement: partial shade to full sun
Leaf persistence: evergreen
Flower: yellow; showy in spring
Soil moisture: tolerates some drought
Soil pH tolerance: acid to slightly alkaline
Uses: street tree; standard; specimen
Attributes: attracts butterflies; outstanding flowers and foliage
Native: southern Florida, West Indies, and Mexico to Costa Rica
Notes: outstanding yellow flowers and compound foliage that glistens in the sun; grows quickly on rich soils high in organic matter

Botanical name: *Terminalia catappa*
Common name: Tropical Almond, India Almond
Hardiness range: 10B to 11
Mature size: 25–50 feet tall by 25–35 feet wide
Light requirement: full sun
Leaf persistence: deciduous
Flower: green; inconspicuous in spring
Soil moisture: tolerates drought
Soil pH tolerance: acid to alkaline
Uses: invasive
Attributes: pest tolerant
Native: Malay Peninsula
Notes: quite tolerant of wind, salt, and drought; has the potential to naturalize; form varies from vase to pyramid

Botanical name: *Thespesia populnea*
Common name: Portia Tree, Seaside Mahoe
Hardiness range: 10B to 11
Mature size: 25–50 feet tall by 25–35 feet wide
Light requirement: full sun
Leaf persistence: evergreen
Flower: yellow; showy year-round
Soil moisture: tolerates drought and occasional wetness
Soil pH tolerance: acid to alkaline
Uses: invasive
Attributes: attractive flowers
Native: pantropical, especially on shores
Notes: invasive and is not recommended for planting

Botanical name: *Zanthoxylum fagara*
Common name: Wild Lime
Hardiness range: 9B to 11
Mature size: 15–25 feet tall and wide
Light requirement: partial shade to full sun
Leaf persistence: evergreen
Flower: yellow; inconspicuous and appearing periodically throughout the year
Soil moisture: tolerates drought
Soil pH tolerance: acid to alkaline
Uses: border; massing; containers; understory tree
Attributes: attracts butterflies
Native: southwestern Texas and Florida, south to South America and West Indies
Notes: plant grown in the full sun is full, nearly symmetrical and makes a nice multitrunk small patio tree

Moderately Salt-Tolerant Trees

Botanical name: *Acacia auriculiformis*
Common name: Earleaf Acacia, Black Wattle
Hardiness range: 10A to 11
Mature size: 60–90 feet tall and wide
Light requirement: full sun
Leaf persistence: evergreen
Flower: yellow; showy in spring
Soil moisture: tolerates drought and occasional wetness
Soil pH tolerance: acid to alkaline
Uses: invasive
Attributes: fast growing; abundance of bright yellow flowers; pest resistant
Native: Australia
Notes: has brittle wood and weak branch unions; badly damaged during thunderstorms; invasive weed in some areas; pollen causes allergies in many people

Botanical name: *Acacia farnesiana*
Common name: Sweet Acacia, Huisache
Hardiness range: 9A to 11
Mature size: 15–25 feet tall and wide
Light requirement: full sun
Leaf persistence: evergreen and semievergreen
Flower: yellow; fragrant and showy year-round
Soil moisture: tolerates drought and occasional wetness
Soil pH tolerance: acid to alkaline
Uses: bonsai; containers; buffer strip; reclamation; specimen; highway
Attributes: pest tolerant; attracts birds
Native: tropical America; naturalized in parts of South Florida
Notes: shrub or small tree with feathery, finely divided leaflets; low branching; routinely grown with multiple trunks; thorns are present on trunk or branches; open canopy

Botanical name: *Acer buergerianum*
Common name: Trident Maple
Hardiness range: 5A to 9A
Mature size: 25–50 feet tall by 25–40 feet wide
Light requirement: partial shade to full sun
Leaf persistence: deciduous
Flower: yellow; somewhat showy in spring
Soil moisture: tolerates some drought
Soil pH tolerance: acid to alkaline
Uses: street tree; specimen; shade tree; parking lot; bonsai
Attributes: pest tolerant; urban tough
Native: China
Notes: performs well in urban areas where soils are often poor and compacted; easily transplanted due to its fibrous, branching root system

Botanical name: *Acer negundo*
Common name: Boxelder, Ashleafed Maple
Hardiness range: 3A to 8A
Mature size: 25–50 feet tall by 35–50 feet wide
Light requirement: partial shade to full sun
Leaf persistence: deciduous
Flower: yellow; inconspicuous in spring
Soil moisture: tolerates drought and flooding
Soil pH tolerance: acid to alkaline
Uses: woodland garden; pollarding; erosion control
Attributes: good fall color
Native: North America
Notes: occasional good fall color in the south; highly drought tolerant; usually not recommended as a street tree due to its weak structure

Botanical name: *Ailanthus altissima*
Common name: Tree of Heaven
Hardiness range: 5A to 8A
Mature size: 50–75 feet tall by 35–50 feet wide
Light requirement: partial shade to full sun
Leaf persistence: deciduous
Flower: green; showy in spring
Soil moisture: tolerates drought and occasional wetness
Soil pH tolerance: acid to alkaline
Uses: invasive
Attributes: pest tolerant; attractive flowers
Native: China
Notes: survives almost anywhere, under urban or suburban conditions; spreads rapidly by seed and suckers and is considered a weed tree; tends to have weak wood and to split at the crotches

Botanical name: *Aleurites moluccana*
Common name: Candlenut, Candleberry Tree, Kukui
Hardiness range: 9B to 11
Mature size: 35–60 feet tall by 35–50 feet wide
Light requirement: partial shade to full sun
Leaf persistence: semievergreen
Flower: white; showy in spring
Soil moisture: tolerates drought and occasional wetness
Soil pH tolerance: acid to slightly alkaline
Uses: specimen
Attributes: coarse texture
Native: Southeast Asia and Hawaii
Notes: could be used more in both low-maintenance and manicured landscapes; its coarse texture makes it a real standout in the landscape; appears whitish due to hairs on leaves; Hawaii state tree

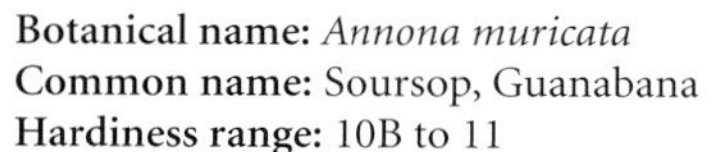

Botanical name: *Annona muricata*
Common name: Soursop, Guanabana
Hardiness range: 10B to 11
Mature size: 15–25 feet tall and wide
Light requirement: full sun
Leaf persistence: evergreen
Flower: yellow; fragrant and inconspicuous year-round
Soil moisture: tolerates some drought
Soil pH tolerance: acid to alkaline
Uses: screen; specimen
Attributes: pest tolerant
Native: tropical America
Notes: can enhance any landscape with its delightful spring flush of foliage; can be the centerpiece of a landscape, if properly located

Botanical name: *Araucaria bidwillii*
Common name: False Monkey Puzzle, Monkey Puzzle Tree
Hardiness range: 9A to 11
Mature size: 40–70 feet tall by 20–30 feet wide
Light requirement: full sun
Leaf persistence: evergreen
Flower: inconspicuous
Soil moisture: tolerates drought
Soil pH tolerance: acid to alkaline
Uses: containers; specimen; screen
Attributes: pest tolerant
Native: northeastern Australia
Notes: should be grown with one central leader, so prune out multiple trunks or leaders; best for large-scale landscapes like parks and municipal buildings; fruit is very large, weighing several pounds

Botanical name: *Araucaria heterophylla* (syn. *Araucaria excelsa*)
Common name: Norfolk Island Pine
Hardiness range: 10A to 11
Mature size: 70–100 feet tall by 35–50 feet wide
Light requirement: full sun
Leaf persistence: evergreen
Flower: inconspicuous
Soil moisture: tolerates drought
Soil pH tolerance: acid to alkaline
Uses: containers; specimen
Attributes: pest tolerant; Christmas tree
Native: Norfolk Island
Notes: the upright habit makes this a poor shade tree; large surface roots can heave pavement and patios; pollen can cause significant allergies for some people

Botanical name: *Betula nigra*
Common name: River Birch, Black Birch, Water Birch
Hardiness range: 3B to 9A
Mature size: 25–50 feet tall by 25–35 feet wide
Light requirement: partial shade to full sun
Leaf persistence: deciduous
Flower: brown; inconspicuous in spring and winter
Soil moisture: tolerates some drought and flooding
Soil pH tolerance: acid to slightly alkaline
Uses: woodland garden; specimen
Attributes: attractive bark; pest tolerant; attracts birds and butterflies
Native: eastern United States to northern Florida
Notes: needs moist conditions to thrive and tolerates low soil oxygen, flooding, and clay soil; tends to be short-lived (30 to 40 years) in many urban settings in the south; chlorosis occurs in alkaline soil

Botanical name: *Bischofia javanica*
Common name: Bischofia, Toog Tree
Hardiness range: 10A to 11
Mature size: 25–50 feet tall by 25–35 feet wide
Light requirement: partial shade to full sun
Leaf persistence: evergreen
Flower: green; inconspicuous in spring
Soil moisture: tolerates some drought and flooding
Soil pH tolerance: acid to alkaline
Uses: invasive
Attributes: grows well in confined urban soil spaces
Native: tropical Asia
Notes: grows easily and quickly in full sun on various soil types; the fruit is messy and stains sidewalks; aggressive roots can lift pavement

Botanical name: *Bixa orellana*
Common name: Lipstick Tree, Annatto
Hardiness range: 10B to 11
Mature size: 15–20 feet tall by 8–12 feet wide
Light requirement: partial shade to full sun
Leaf persistence: evergreen
Flower: pink; showy in spring
Soil moisture: tolerates some drought
Soil pH tolerance: acid to slightly alkaline
Uses: specimen
Attributes: winter interest
Native: tropical America
Notes: the colorful display of flowers and fruit suits it for many tropical landscapes

Botanical name: *Bombax ceiba*
Common name: Red Silk Cotton Tree
Hardiness range: 10A to 11
Mature size: 50–75 feet tall by 35–50 feet wide
Light requirement: full sun
Leaf persistence: deciduous
Flower: red; showy in winter
Soil moisture: tolerates some drought
Soil pH tolerance: acid to slightly alkaline
Uses: specimen
Attributes: pest tolerant
Native: tropical Asia
Notes: huge tree for parks and golf courses; trunk is thorny when young and smooths with age; large buttress roots can form

Botanical name: *Callistemon viminalis*
Common name: Weeping Bottlebrush
Hardiness range: 9B to 11
Mature size: 15–25 feet tall and wide
Light requirement: full sun
Leaf persistence: evergreen
Flower: red; very showy in spring and summer
Soil moisture: tolerates drought
Soil pH tolerance: acid to slightly alkaline
Uses: screen; street tree; standard; specimen
Attributes: attracts birds and butterflies
Native: Australia
Notes: roots often rot in wet soils; best growth and flowering is obtained with ample moisture and fertilization; can spread to nearby disturbed areas and become naturalized; susceptible to a witches'-broom disease

Botanical name: *Carya glabra*
Common name: Pignut Hickory
Hardiness range: 4B to 9A
Mature size: 50–75 feet tall by 25–35 feet wide
Light requirement: partial shade to full sun
Leaf persistence: deciduous
Flower: yellow; inconspicuous in spring
Soil moisture: tolerates drought and occasional wetness
Soil pH tolerance: acid to slightly alkaline
Uses: shade tree; woodland garden
Attributes: pest tolerant; attracts butterflies; good fall color
Native: North America to south-central Florida
Notes: will show minor-element deficiencies on alkaline soils; grows well in sand or clay; resists breakage in ice storms; host for butterfly larvae; fruit source of food for wildlife

Botanical name: *Castanea pumila*
Common name: Allegheny Chinquapin
Hardiness range: 6A to 9B
Mature size: 10–25 feet tall by 20–30 feet wide
Light requirement: full sun
Leaf persistence: deciduous
Flower: white or yellow; fragrant and very showy in summer
Soil moisture: tolerates drought
Soil pH tolerance: acid to slightly alkaline
Uses: woodland garden; specimen
Attributes: attractive and fragrant flowers
Native: eastern North America to north-central Florida
Notes: any advantages of using this tree may be overshadowed by potential disease problems (although it is moderately resistant to chestnut blight)

Botanical name: *Catalpa* spp.
Common name: Catalpa
Hardiness range: 5A to 9A
Mature size: 25–50 feet tall by 35–50 feet wide
Light requirement: partial shade to full sun
Leaf persistence: deciduous
Flower: white; very showy spring to summer
Soil moisture: tolerates drought and occasional wetness
Soil pH tolerance: acid to alkaline
Uses: specimen
Attributes: asymmetrical with a coarse texture and a moderately dense canopy
Native: North America
Notes: tough tree suited for large-scale landscapes; can escape cultivation and invade surrounding woodlands

Botanical name: *Ceiba pentandra*
Common name: Kapok Tree
Hardiness range: 10B to 11
Mature size: 45–55 feet tall by 40–50 feet wide
Light requirement: full sun
Leaf persistence: deciduous
Flower: pink, white, and yellow; showy in winter
Soil moisture: tolerates drought
Soil pH tolerance: acid to slightly alkaline
Uses: specimen
Attributes: pest tolerant; attractive root buttresses, flowers, and bark
Notes: develops enormous trunk and foot buttresses lifting sidewalks and cracking foundations; plant away from buildings, giving plenty of space for root expansion such as in a park

Botanical name: *Celtis laevigata*
Common name: Sugar Hackberry, Sugarberry
Hardiness range: 5A to 10A
Mature size: 50–75 feet tall by 50–85 feet wide
Light requirement: partial shade to full sun
Leaf persistence: deciduous
Flower: green; inconspicuous in spring
Soil moisture: tolerates drought and flooding; will grow in very wet or submerged soil
Soil pH tolerance: acid to alkaline
Uses: woodland garden; street tree; erosion control
Attributes: pest tolerant; wetlands plant; attracts butterflies
Native: eastern North America through Florida
Notes: grows best in moist, fertile soils in full sun, but tolerates worse conditions; sensitive to highly alkaline soils

Botanical name: *Chrysophyllum oliviforme*
Common name: Satin Leaf, Damson Plum
Hardiness range: 10B to 11
Mature size: 25–40 feet tall by 15–25 feet wide
Light requirement: partial shade to full sun
Leaf persistence: evergreen
Flower: white; inconspicuous year-round
Soil moisture: tolerates drought and occasional wetness
Soil pH tolerance: acid to alkaline
Uses: street tree; standard; specimen; shade tree; parking lot
Attributes: pest tolerant; attractive foliage; urban tough
Native: southern Florida to Cuba, Puerto Rico, and Jamaica
Notes: tolerates urban conditions and has performed well as a street tree; foliage is very attractive

Botanical name: *Citrus* spp.
Common name: Citrus
Hardiness range: 9A to 11
Mature size: 15–25 feet tall and wide
Light requirement: full sun
Leaf persistence: evergreen
Flower: white; very fragrant and showy in spring and winter
Soil moisture: tolerates some drought
Soil pH tolerance: acid to slightly alkaline
Uses: espalier; specimen; fruit tree
Attributes: attracts butterflies; edible fruit; urban tough
Native: southern and Southeast Asia and Malay Peninsula
Notes: withstands heat well; regular fertilization and pest control is needed to keep trees looking good and producing quality fruit; can invade parks and woodlands

Botanical name: *Cupressocyparis leylandii*
Common name: Leyland Cypress
Hardiness range: 6A to 10A
Mature size: 25–50 feet tall by 15–25 feet wide
Light requirement: full sun
Leaf persistence: evergreen
Flower: no flowers
Soil moisture: tolerates some drought
Soil pH tolerance: acid to alkaline
Uses: seashore planting; border; screen; specimen
Attributes: Christmas tree; symmetrical with fine texture and dense canopy
Notes: tolerates severe pruning; short lived in most of the United States due to a fungus canker disease; suggest using a different plant

Botanical name: *Cupressus sempervirens*
Common name: Italian Cypress
Hardiness range: 7B to 11
Mature size: 25–50 feet tall by 6–10 feet wide
Light requirement: full sun
Leaf persistence: evergreen
Flower: inconspicuous
Soil moisture: tolerates drought; will grow in very dry soil
Soil pH tolerance: acid to alkaline
Uses: border; screen; specimen
Attributes: symmetrical with a fine texture and a dense crown
Native: southern Europe and western Asia
Notes: should not be pruned; very susceptible to mites; allow for good air circulation to help prevent disease problems

Botanical name: *Dalbergia sissoo*
Common name: Indian Rosewood
Hardiness range: 10A to 11
Mature size: 50–75 feet tall by 35–50 feet wide
Light requirement: partial shade to full sun
Leaf persistence: semievergreen
Flower: white; fragrant and inconspicuous in spring
Soil moisture: tolerates some drought and occasional wetness
Soil pH tolerance: acid to slightly alkaline
Uses: invasive
Attributes: pest tolerant
Native: India
Notes: sprouts develop from the roots, sometimes far from the canopy, and can become a maintenance problem; branches are brittle and tend to break in storms; chlorosis occurs on alkaline soils

Botanical name: *Delonix regia*
Common name: Royal Poinciana, Peacock Flower
Hardiness range: 10B to 11
Mature size: 25–50 feet tall by 50–70 feet wide
Light requirement: full sun
Leaf persistence: semievergreen
Flower: orange and red; very showy spring into summer
Soil moisture: tolerates drought
Soil pH tolerance: acid to alkaline
Uses: street tree; specimen; shade tree
Attributes: one of the most beautiful flowering trees on the planet; attracts hummingbirds; urban tough
Native: Madagascar
Notes: provides fullest flowering and best growth when planted in full sun; fruit pods are large and litter the ground; roots are large and invasive

Botanical name: *Diospyros digyna*
Common name: Black Sapote
Hardiness range: 10B to 11
Mature size: 25–50 feet tall by 15–25 feet wide
Light requirement: full sun
Leaf persistence: evergreen
Flower: green and yellow; fragrant and inconspicuous in spring
Soil moisture: tolerates some drought
Soil pH tolerance: acid to alkaline
Uses: specimen
Attributes: pest tolerant
Native: Mexico and Central America
Notes: can enhance any landscape with its delightful spring flush of foliage and flowers; can be the centerpiece of a landscape if properly located

Botanical name: *Elaeagnus angustifolia*
Common name: Russian Olive, Oleaster
Hardiness range: 2A to 7A
Mature size: 15–30 feet tall by 20–30 feet wide
Light requirement: full sun
Leaf persistence: deciduous
Flower: white; fragrant and inconspicuous in spring
Soil moisture: tolerates drought and occasional wetness
Soil pH tolerance: acid to alkaline
Uses: invasive
Attributes: attractive silver-gray foliage
Native: Europe and western Asia
Notes: fixes its own nitrogen, thus it can improve the soil it grows in; probably is better suited for dry climates than the moist climate typical of the southeastern United States

Botanical name: *Eriobotrya japonica*
Common name: Loquat, Japanese Loquat
Hardiness range: 8A to 11
Mature size: 15–25 feet tall by 25–35 feet wide
Light requirement: partial shade to full sun
Leaf persistence: evergreen
Flower: white; fragrant and showy in fall and winter
Soil moisture: tolerates some drought
Soil pH tolerance: acid to alkaline
Uses: containers; screen; espalier; street tree; standard; specimen
Attributes: edible fruit; urban tough
Native: China, central and southern Japan
Notes: provides the best fruit and form when grown in full sun; grows best and maintains the characteristic dark green foliage in soils with a high pH; fruit can be messy on the ground; seeds germinate under and near the tree

Botanical name: *Eucalyptus cinerea*
Common name: Silver Eucalyptus, Silver Gum, Silver Dollar Gum
Hardiness range: 8B to 11
Mature size: 25–50 feet tall by 25–35 feet wide
Light requirement: partial shade to full sun
Leaf persistence: evergreen
Flower: white; inconspicuous in spring and winter
Soil moisture: tolerates drought
Soil pH tolerance: acid to slightly alkaline
Uses: specimen
Attributes: aromatic foliage; striking silver-blue foliage
Native: New South Wales and Victoria
Notes: grows best on the West Coast of the United States and Arizona; especially useful along coasts; pollen can cause allergies

Botanical name: *Eucalyptus robusta*
Common name: Swamp Mahogany, Eucalyptus, Gum
Hardiness range: 8A to 11
Mature size: 35–50 feet tall by 35–40 feet wide
Light requirements: partial shade to full sun
Leaf persistence: evergreen
Flower: white; inconspicuous in spring and summer
Soil moisture: tolerates drought and occasional wetness
Soil pH tolerance: acid to slightly alkaline
Uses: street tree; specimen
Attributes: aromatic foliage
Native: Queensland
Notes: overirrigated trees can develop chlorosis; recovers from periodic flooding better than many other trees

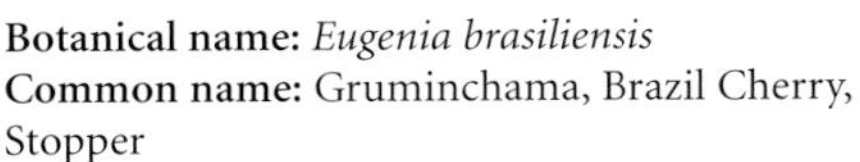

Botanical name: *Eugenia brasiliensis*
Common name: Gruminchama, Brazil Cherry, Stopper
Hardiness range: 10A to 11
Mature size: 15–25 feet tall by 10–15 feet wide
Light requirement: partial shade to full sun
Leaf persistence: evergreen
Flower: white; inconspicuous in summer
Soil moisture: tolerates some drought and occasional wetness
Soil pH tolerance: acid to alkaline
Uses: screen; street tree; standard; specimen
Attributes: pest tolerant; edible fruit
Native: southern Brazil
Notes: native to sandy coastal areas; fruits are showy, edible, juicy cherrylike berries that can make a mess on a sidewalk

Botanical name: *Eugenia* spp.
Common name: Stopper
Hardiness range: 10B to 11
Mature size: 15–25 feet tall and wide
Light requirement: partial shade to full sun
Leaf persistence: evergreen
Flower: white; inconspicuous in spring and summer
Soil moisture: tolerates drought and occasional wetness
Soil pH tolerance: acid to alkaline
Uses: border; screen
Attributes: pest tolerant; attractive bark; urban tough
Native: Florida
Notes: multiple trunk trees are often specified for specimen planting so the beautiful bark can be displayed; larger growing types are used as street trees; *E. uniflora* is considered invasive; *E. confusa, E. foetida,* and *E. rhombea* are good native species

Botanical name: *Ficus aurea*
Common name: Golden Fig, Strangler Fig
Hardiness range: 10B to 11
Mature size: 40–50 feet tall by 50–60 feet wide
Light requirement: full shade to full sun
Leaf persistence: evergreen
Flower: inconspicuous
Soil moisture: tolerates drought and flooding
Soil pH tolerance: acid to alkaline
Uses: specimen; large shade tree
Attributes: pest tolerant; wetlands plant; attracts butterflies
Native: Florida
Notes: much too big for most landscapes but can make a nice addition to a large park

Botanical name: *Ficus benghalensis*
Common name: Banyan Tree
Hardiness range: 10B to 11
Mature size: 50–75 feet tall by 50–70 feet wide
Light requirement: partial shade to full sun
Leaf persistence: evergreen
Flower: white; inconspicuous
Soil moisture: tolerates drought and occasional wetness
Soil pH tolerance: acid to alkaline
Uses: specimen
Attributes: pest tolerant
Native: India, Pakistan
Notes: aerial roots descend from branches and root into the ground under the canopy; these aerial roots help support the branches; too large for residential landscapes

Botanical name: *Ficus benjamina*
Common name: Weeping Fig
Hardiness range: 10B to 11
Mature size: 50–75 feet tall by 50–70 feet wide
Light requirement: full shade to full sun
Leaf persistence: evergreen
Flower: inconspicuous
Soil moisture: tolerates drought and occasional wetness
Soil pH tolerance: acid to alkaline
Uses: containers; hedge; indoor plant
Attributes: pest tolerant; attracts birds
Native: India, Southeast Asia, Malay Archipelago, northern tropical Australia
Notes: can be successfully used as a clipped hedge or screen, or can be trained into an espalier or topiary

Botanical name: *Ficus carica*
Common name: Common Fig
Hardiness range: 7B to 11
Mature size: 10–15 feet tall and wide
Light requirement: partial shade to full sun
Leaf persistence: semievergreen
Flower: inconspicuous
Soil moisture: tolerates some drought
Soil pH tolerance: acid to slightly alkaline
Uses: containers; specimen; fruit tree
Attributes: delicious fruit
Native: Mediterranean region
Notes: large foliage makes a great textural statement in the landscape; invasive in California; can look a bit messy in winter

Botanical name: *Ficus citrifolia*
Common name: Shortleaf Fig, Wild Banyan Tree
Hardiness range: 10B to 11
Mature size: 25–50 feet tall by 35–50 feet wide
Light requirement: full shade to partial shade or partial sun
Leaf persistence: evergreen
Flower: inconspicuous
Soil moisture: tolerates drought and occasional wetness
Soil pH tolerance: acid to alkaline
Uses: specimen; shade tree
Attributes: pest tolerant, attracts butterflies
Native: Palm Beach to Key West
Notes: considered semideciduous; there are up to three flowering and fruiting seasons per year; fruits are maroon when ripe, sweet to the taste, and attractive to birds; large size makes it ill suited for home landscapes

Botanical name: *Ficus elastica*
Common name: India Rubber Tree, India Rubber Fig, Rubber Tree
Hardiness range: 10B to 11
Mature size: 25–50 feet tall by 25–35 feet wide
Light requirement: partial shade to full sun
Leaf persistence: evergreen
Flower: inconspicuous
Soil moisture: tolerates drought and occasional wetness
Soil pH tolerance: acid to alkaline
Uses: containers; screen; espalier; specimen; indoor plant; shade tree
Attributes: pest tolerant; attractive large foliage
Native: Nepal, to Assam, India, to Myanmar (Burma)
Notes: takes over a landscape, shading out everything below and making a mess with dropping foliage; makes a nice houseplant if it is not overwatered

Botanical name: *Ficus lyrata* (syn. *Ficus pandurata*)
Common name: Fiddleleaf Fig
Hardiness range: 10B to 11
Mature size: 25–50 feet tall by 35–50 feet wide
Light requirement: full shade to partial shade or partial sun
Leaf persistence: evergreen
Flower: inconspicuous
Soil moisture: tolerates drought and occasional wetness
Soil pH tolerance: acid to alkaline
Uses: containers; street tree; specimen; shade tree; indoor plant
Attributes: pest tolerant; attractive large foliage
Native: tropical Africa
Notes: some aerial roots are produced but not as many as on some other *Ficus*

Botanical name: *Ficus microcarpa* (syns. *Ficus nitida; Ficus retusa*)
Common name: Cuban Laurel, Fig Laurel, Indian Laurel
Hardiness range: 10B to 11
Mature size: 50–75 feet tall by 50–100 feet wide
Light requirement: partial shade to full sun
Leaf persistence: evergreen
Flower: inconspicuous
Soil moisture: tolerates drought and occasional wetness
Soil pH tolerance: acid to alkaline
Uses: invasive
Attributes: pest tolerant; hedges well
Native: Malay Peninsula to Borneo
Notes: grows fast and has a dense canopy; tolerates trimming well and can be sheared into a hedge; used as a street tree or ditch bank tree in some communities; may clog canals when they blow over in a hurricane

Botanical name: *Ficus religiosa*
Common name: Bo Tree, Sacred Fig
Hardiness range: 10B to 11
Mature size: 50–75 feet tall by 50–60 feet wide
Light requirement: partial shade to full sun
Leaf persistence: evergreen
Flower: inconspicuous
Soil moisture: tolerates drought
Soil pH tolerance: acid to alkaline
Uses: containers; specimen
Attributes: pest tolerant
Native: India to Southeast Asia
Notes: prune to maintain a dominant leader; fruit is fleshy, round, inconspicuous, and a litter problem

Botanical name: *Ficus rubiginosa*
Common name: Rusty Fig, Little-Leaf Fig
Hardiness range: 10B to 11
Mature size: 40–60 feet tall and wide
Light requirement: partial shade to full sun
Leaf persistence: evergreen
Flower: inconspicuous
Soil moisture: tolerates some drought
Soil pH tolerance: acid to alkaline
Uses: containers; specimen; indoor plant
Attributes: pest tolerant
Native: New South Wales
Notes: growth habit makes it better suited for residential landscapes than most other ficus trees, but it eventually grows quite large

Botanical name: *Ficus sycomorus* (syn. *Ficus gnaphalocarpa*)
Common name: Sycamore Fig
Hardiness range: 10B to 11
Mature size: 50–70 feet tall by 50–80 feet wide
Light requirement: partial shade to full sun
Leaf persistence: evergreen
Flower: inconspicuous
Soil moisture: tolerates drought and occasional wetness
Soil pH tolerance: acid to alkaline
Uses: containers; specimen
Attributes: pest tolerant; very large plant
Native: Africa, Arabian Peninsula
Notes: huge tree that grows quickly in sun or partial shade; trunk forms an enormous buttress

Botanical name: *Fraxinus pennsylvanica*
Common name: Green Ash, Red Ash, Water Ash
Hardiness range: 3A to 9A
Mature size: 50–75 feet tall by 35–50 feet wide
Light requirement: full sun
Leaf persistence: deciduous
Flower: green; inconspicuous in spring
Soil moisture: tolerates drought and flooding
Soil pH tolerance: acid to alkaline
Uses: street tree; pollarding; shade tree
Attributes: attracts butterflies; good fall color; urban tough
Native: eastern North America to Florida panhandle
Notes: adapts quite well to city landscapes

Botanical name: *Geijera parviflora*
Common name: Australian Willow
Hardiness range: 9A to 11
Mature size: 25–50 feet tall by 15–25 feet wide
Light requirement: full sun
Leaf persistence: evergreen
Flower: white; showy in spring and fall
Soil moisture: tolerates some drought; will grow in dry soil
Soil pH tolerance: acid to alkaline
Uses: screen; street tree; specimen; shade tree
Attributes: pest tolerant; urban tough
Native: eastern Australia and New Caledonia
Notes: casts light shade, so it is ideal for lawn specimen; drooping branches

Botanical name: *Ginkgo biloba*
Common name: Ginkgo, Maidenhair Tree
Hardiness range: 4A to 8A
Mature size: 50–75 feet tall by 40–50 feet wide
Light requirement: partial shade to full sun
Leaf persistence: deciduous
Flower: green; inconspicuous in spring
Soil moisture: tolerates drought and occasional wetness
Soil pH tolerance: acid to alkaline
Uses: street tree; standard; specimen
Attributes: pest tolerant; urban tough
Native: southeastern China
Notes: geological evidence suggests that the ginkgo has been growing on earth for the past 150 million years; wonderfully suited for city conditions; female trees produce abundant quantities of seeds, which have an unpleasant odor

Botanical name: *Grevillea robusta*
Common name: Silk Oak
Hardiness range: 9B to 11
Mature size: 70–120 feet tall by 25–35 feet wide
Light requirement: partial shade to full sun
Leaf persistence: evergreen
Flower: orange and yellow; showy in spring
Soil moisture: tolerates drought and occasional wetness
Soil pH tolerance: acid to slightly alkaline
Uses: containers; specimen; street tree
Attributes: attractive orange flowers
Native: Queensland and New South Wales
Notes: often develops mushroom root rot in poorly drained, wet soils; branches are brittle and tend to break in storms; roots are invasive into gardens; a messy tree, dropping foliage regularly

Botanical name: *Guaiacum officinale*
Common name: Lignum Vitae
Hardiness range: 10B to 11
Mature size: 10–30 feet tall by 10–15 feet wide
Light requirement: partial shade to full sun
Leaf persistence: evergreen
Flower: blue; showy year-round
Soil moisture: tolerates drought
Soil pH tolerance: acid to alkaline
Uses: street tree; standard; specimen; street tree
Attributes: pest tolerant; urban tough
Native: West Indies, Panama, to northern South America
Notes: makes one of the nicest small ornamental trees for tropical landscapes and can be used as a street tree; especially useful for small, restricted soil spaces

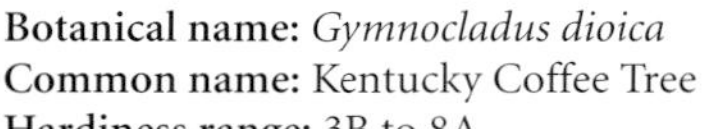

Botanical name: *Gymnocladus dioica*
Common name: Kentucky Coffee Tree
Hardiness range: 3B to 8A
Mature size: 50–75 feet tall by 45–50 feet wide
Light requirement: full sun
Leaf persistence: deciduous
Flower: white; fragrant and inconspicuous in spring
Soil moisture: tolerates drought
Soil pH tolerance: acid to alkaline
Uses: specimen
Attributes: pest tolerant
Native: eastern North America
Notes: amazingly tolerant of drought and poor soil once established; used as a street tree in some communities; seedpods from female trees could become projectiles from mowing equipment

Botanical name: *Ilex* × *attenuata* cultivars
Common name: Holly, Topal Holly
Hardiness range: 6A to 9B
Mature size: 15–40 feet tall by 6–12 feet wide
Light requirement: partial shade to full sun
Leaf persistence: evergreen
Flower: white; inconspicuous in spring; attracts bees
Soil moisture: tolerates drought and occasional wetness
Soil pH tolerance: acid to alkaline
Uses: border; screen; espalier; specimen; parking lot; street tree
Attributes: fruit attractive and attracts wildlife
Native: hybrid origin
Notes: growth is poor and foliage chlorotic on alkaline soils; training into a single-trunk tree will increase durability; native cultivars include 'East Palatka' and 'Savannah'; disease sensitive in some regions

Botanical name: *Ilex cassine*
Common name: Dahoon Holly
Hardiness range: 7A to 11
Mature size: 25–40 feet tall by 10–30 feet wide
Light requirement: partial shade to full sun
Leaf persistence: evergreen
Flower: white; inconspicuous in spring; attracts bees
Soil moisture: tolerates some drought and flooding
Soil pH tolerance: acid to slightly alkaline
Uses: specimen; small shade tree; street tree; parking lot
Attributes: pest tolerant; wetlands plant; attracts birds
Native: southeastern United States to southern Florida
Notes: does best on moist soils since the wet, boggy soils of swamps is its native environment; not recommended in the southern part of its range in a dry, exposed site unless irrigation is provided

Botanical name: *Ilex cornuta* 'Burfordii'
Common name: Burford Holly, Chinese Holly, Horned Holly
Hardiness range: 7A to 9A
Mature size: 10–20 feet tall and wide
Light requirement: partial shade to full sun
Leaf persistence: evergreen
Flower: white; inconspicuous in spring
Soil moisture: tolerates drought and occasional wetness
Soil pH tolerance: acid to alkaline
Uses: border; screen; hedge; patio tree; parking lot
Attributes: pest tolerant; fragrant flowers; attract bees; urban tough
Native: eastern China
Notes: flowering and subsequent fruiting is reduced in shady locations; though typically planted as a shrub, can eventually grow to nearly 20 feet tall

Botanical name: *Ilex myrtifolia*
Common name: Myrtle Holly, Myrtle Dahoon
Hardiness range: 7A to 11
Mature size: 25–50 feet tall by 10–15 feet wide
Light requirement: partial shade to full sun
Leaf persistence: evergreen
Flower: white; inconspicuous in spring
Soil moisture: tolerates some drought and flooding
Soil pH tolerance: acid to alkaline
Uses: woodland garden; border
Attributes: pest tolerant; tolerates wet soil
Native: southeastern United States to northern Florida
Notes: does best on moist to wet soils; adapts well to the confined spaces of urban landscapes

Botanical name: *Ilex opaca*
Common name: American Holly
Hardiness range: 5B to 9A
Mature size: 25–50 feet tall by 15–25 feet wide
Light requirement: full shade to full sun
Leaf persistence: evergreen
Flower: green and white; fragrant and inconspicuous in spring
Soil moisture: tolerates drought and occasional wetness
Soil pH tolerance: acid to slightly alkaline
Uses: woodland garden; screen; espalier; street tree; specimen; parking lot
Attributes: attracts birds and butterflies
Native: eastern North America
Notes: berry production is highest in full sun; female trees produce fruit only if pollinated by a male plant; foliage thins during drought; tolerates ozone

Botanical name: *Koelreuteria bipinnata*
Common name: Chinese Flame Tree, Goldenrain Tree
Hardiness range: 6A to 8B
Mature size: 35–45 feet tall and wide
Light requirement: full sun
Leaf persistence: deciduous
Flower: yellow; fragrant and very showy in summer
Soil moisture: tolerates drought and flooding
Soil pH tolerance: acid to alkaline
Uses: street tree; specimen; shade tree
Attributes: pest tolerant; attractive flowers and fruit
Native: southwestern China
Notes: may break up as it reaches about 30 years old if not properly pruned; becomes leggy and thin in partial shade; appears identical to *Koelreuteria elegans* except *K. elegans* is less cold hardy

Botanical name: *Koelreuteria elegans*
Common name: Goldenrain Tree, Flamegold
Hardiness range: 9A to 11
Mature size: 25–35 feet tall by 35–45 feet wide
Light requirement: full sun
Leaf persistence: deciduous
Flower: yellow; very showy in summer and fall
Soil moisture: tolerates drought and flooding
Soil pH tolerance: acid to alkaline
Uses: invasive
Attributes: pest tolerant; showy pink fruit
Native: Taiwan, Fiji
Notes: does well in many parts of central and southern Florida where soils can be alkaline; has escaped cultivation and invades ditch banks, gardens, and woodlands

Botanical name: *Koelreuteria paniculata*
Common name: Goldenrain Tree, Varnish Tree
Hardiness range: 5B to 8A
Mature size: 25–40 feet tall by 30–40 feet wide
Light requirement: full sun
Leaf persistence: deciduous
Flower: yellow; very showy in summer
Soil moisture: tolerates drought and flooding
Soil pH tolerance: acid to alkaline
Uses: specimen; street tree; parking lot
Attributes: pest tolerant
Native: China, Korea
Notes: transplant success in the fall is reportedly limited; performs well as a street tree; hard to find a more adaptive yellow-flowering tree for urban planting

Botanical name: *Lagerstroemia fauriei*
Common name: Japanese Crape Myrtle
Hardiness range: 6B to 10A
Mature size: 25–50 feet tall by 25–35 feet wide
Light requirement: full sun
Flower: white; showy in summer
Soil moisture: tolerates some drought
Soil pH tolerance: acid to slightly alkaline
Uses: specimen; standard; border; street tree; parking lot
Attributes: attractive flowers and wonderful showy bark and trunk structure
Native: Japan and Ryukyu Islands
Notes: grows well in limited soil spaces in urban areas; flowers very nicely without pruning

Botanical name: *Lagerstroemia speciosa*
Common name: Queen's Crape Myrtle
Hardiness range: 10B to 11
Mature size: 25–50 feet tall by 35–45 feet wide
Light requirement: full sun
Leaf persistence: semievergreen
Flower: lavender and pink; very showy in spring and summer
Soil moisture: tolerates some drought
Soil pH tolerance: acid to slightly alkaline
Uses: street tree; standard; specimen; parking lot
Attributes: attractive flowers
Native: India to China, south to New Guinea and Australia
Notes: appreciates regular fertilization or leaves become chlorotic; tolerates alkaline soil with regular fertilizer applications

Botanical name: *Ligustrum lucidum*
Common name: Tree Ligustrum, Chinese Privet, Glossy Privet
Hardiness range: 8A to 11
Mature size: 25–40 feet tall by 25–35 feet wide
Light requirement: partial shade to full sun
Leaf persistence: evergreen
Flower: white; showy in summer
Soil moisture: tolerates some drought
Soil pH tolerance: acid to alkaline
Uses: invasive
Attributes: pest tolerant; attracts birds
Native: China, Korea
Notes: grows quickly while young but slows with age; seems to thrive on neglect; invades adjacent woodlands

Botanical name: *Liquidambar styraciflua*
Common name: Sweet Gum, American Sweet Gum
Hardiness range: 5B to 9B
Mature size: 50–75 feet tall by 35–50 feet wide
Light requirement: partial shade to full sun
Leaf persistence: deciduous
Flower: green and yellow; inconspicuous in spring
Soil moisture: tolerates some drought and occasional wetness
Soil pH tolerance: acid to slightly alkaline
Uses: street tree; specimen; shade tree
Attributes: pest tolerant
Native: southeastern United States to central Florida
Notes: tolerates wet soils, but chlorosis is often seen in alkaline soils; grows well in deep soil but poorly in shallow, droughty soil

Botanical name: *Maclura pomifera*
Common name: Osage Orange, Bois D'Arc
Hardiness range: 4A to 9A
Mature size: 25–50 feet tall by 25–35 feet wide
Light requirement: full sun
Leaf persistence: deciduous
Flower: white; inconspicuous in spring
Soil moisture: tolerates drought and flooding
Soil pH tolerance: acid to alkaline
Uses: barrier; fruitless cultivars can be used in parking lots
Attributes: pest tolerant; urban tough
Native: Texas, Oklahoma, and Arkansas
Notes: roots and bark are a source of yellow dye; wood used for bows; fruitless cultivars are available; all parts may be poisonous

Botanical name: *Magnolia grandiflora*
Common name: Southern Magnolia, Bull Bay
Hardiness range: 6B to 10A
Mature size: 60–80 feet tall by 35–50 feet wide
Light requirement: partial shade to full sun
Leaf persistence: evergreen
Flower: white; fragrant and showy in spring and summer
Soil moisture: tolerates some drought and occasional wetness
Soil pH tolerance: acid to slightly alkaline
Uses: screen; espalier; street tree; specimen
Attributes: pest tolerant; attracts birds
Native: southeastern United States
Notes: thrives in moist soil, full sun, and hot conditions once established; performs best in fertile soil or with a regular fertilization program when young; many cultivars to choose from; flooding kills young trees

Botanical name: *Malpighia glabra*
Common name: Barbados Cherry
Hardiness range: 9B to 11
Mature size: 10–15 feet tall and wide
Light requirement: partial shade to full sun
Leaf persistence: evergreen
Flower: pink; showy in summer
Soil moisture: tolerates drought
Soil pH tolerance: acid to slightly alkaline
Uses: border; screen; specimen
Attributes: edible fruit
Native: Texas, south to northern South America, West Indies
Notes: well-suited as a foundation plant for larger buildings or used in the rear of a shrubbery border; often planted on residential property for the edible fruit

Botanical name: *Mammea americana*
Common name: Mammee Apple, South American Apricot, Mammee
Hardiness range: 10A to 11
Mature size: 30–40 feet tall by 25–30 feet wide
Light requirement: partial shade to full sun
Leaf persistence: evergreen
Flower: white; fragrant and showy in fall
Soil moisture: tolerates drought
Soil pH tolerance: acid to alkaline
Uses: specimen
Attributes: aromatic fruit
Native: Caribbean and South America
Notes: resembles an evergreen magnolia tree; seeds are said to be extremely poisonous

Botanical name: *Mangifera indica*
Common name: Mango
Hardiness range: 10B to 11
Mature size: 25–50 feet tall by 25–35 feet wide
Light requirement: full sun
Leaf persistence: evergreen
Flower: white; showy in spring and winter
Soil moisture: tolerates some drought
Soil pH tolerance: acid to alkaline
Uses: espalier; pollarding; specimen; fruit
Attributes: edible fruit
Native: northern India, Myanmar (Burma), Malay Peninsula
Notes: grows best in full sun on rich, well-drained soils and should have regular irrigation in dry weather; some people are allergic to the fruit, which causes rashes and itching around the mouth

Botanical name: *Nolina recurvata* (syn. *Beucarnea recurvata*)
Common name: Ponytail Palm, Bottle Palm, Elephant's Foot
Hardiness range: 10A to 11
Mature size: 10–15 feet tall and wide
Light requirement: partial shade to full sun
Leaf persistence: evergreen
Flower: white and yellow; very showy in spring and summer
Soil moisture: tolerates drought
Soil pH tolerance: acid to slightly alkaline
Uses: containers; specimen
Attributes: attractive flowers
Native: Mexico
Notes: not a true palm; has a tendency to develop root rot in poorly drained soil

Botanical name: *Nyssa sylvatica*
Common name: Black Tupelo, Black Gum, Sour Gum
Hardiness range: 4B to 9A
Mature size: 30–75 feet tall by 25–35 feet wide
Light requirement: partial shade to full sun
Leaf persistence: deciduous
Flower: white; inconspicuous in spring
Soil moisture: tolerates drought and flooding
Soil pH tolerance: acid to alkaline
Uses: specimen
Attributes: pest tolerant; wetlands plant; attracts birds and butterflies
Native: eastern United States, from Maine to Lake Okeechobee, Florida
Notes: excellent fall color; very tolerant of urban conditions and grows well along streets; defoliates early in the southern portion of its range, remaining bare for 6 months

Botanical name: *Oxydendrum arboreum*
Common name: Sourwood, Sorrel Tree
Hardiness range: 5A to 8A
Mature size: 25–50 feet tall by 20–30 feet wide
Light requirement: partial shade to full sun
Leaf persistence: deciduous
Flower: white; showy in summer and fall
Soil moisture: tolerates some drought
Soil pH tolerance: acid to slightly alkaline
Uses: specimen
Attributes: pest tolerant; attracts butterflies
Native: eastern North America to Florida panhandle
Notes: grows slowly and adapts to about any light conditions; irrigation is needed during hot, dry weather to keep leaves on the tree in southern portions of its range

Botanical name: *Paulownia tomentosa*
Common name: Princess Tree, Empress Tree, Royal Paulownia
Hardiness range: 6A to 9A
Mature size: 30–50 feet tall and wide
Light requirement: partial shade to full sun
Leaf persistence: deciduous
Flower: lavender; very showy in spring
Soil moisture: tolerates some drought and occasional wetness
Soil pH tolerance: acid to slightly alkaline
Uses: specimen
Attributes: pest tolerant; very attractive flowers
Native: China
Notes: often considered a weed tree; naturalizes in the edges of woodlands; fruit capsules hang on the tree and can be objectionable to some; trunk buttress could form large surface roots

Botanical name: *Peltophorum pterocarpum*
Common name: Yellow Poinciana
Hardiness range: 9B to 11
Mature size: 25–50 feet tall by 25–35 feet wide
Light requirement: full sun
Leaf persistence: semievergreen
Flower: yellow; fragrant and very showy in summer
Soil moisture: tolerates drought and occasional wetness
Soil pH tolerance: acid to alkaline
Uses: has invaded roadsides
Attributes: pest tolerant; attractive flowers
Native: Ceylon, Malay Archipelago, to northern Australia, especially on seashores
Notes: fast-growing tree performing best in full sun on any well-drained soil; temperatures slightly below freezing cause the leaves to drop but these are quickly replaced when spring arrives; some people consider this a junk tree

Botanical name: *Persea americana*
Common name: Avocado
Hardiness range: 9B to 11
Mature size: 25–50 feet tall by 25–35 feet wide
Light requirement: partial shade to full sun
Leaf persistence: evergreen
Flower: green; inconspicuous in spring and winter
Soil moisture: tolerates some drought
Soil pH tolerance: acid to alkaline
Uses: containers; specimen
Attributes: attracts butterflies; edible fruit
Native: tropical and Central America
Notes: naturally has a dominant leader growing up through the center of the canopy unless the tree is topped; fruits are large, and they drop to the ground, causing a mess unless picked up; other parts of the plant are suspected to be poisonous

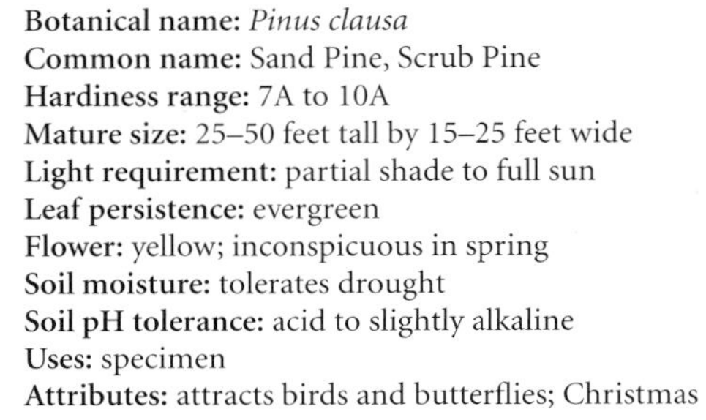

Botanical name: *Pinus clausa*
Common name: Sand Pine, Scrub Pine
Hardiness range: 7A to 10A
Mature size: 25–50 feet tall by 15–25 feet wide
Light requirement: partial shade to full sun
Leaf persistence: evergreen
Flower: yellow; inconspicuous in spring
Soil moisture: tolerates drought
Soil pH tolerance: acid to slightly alkaline
Uses: specimen
Attributes: attracts birds and butterflies; Christmas tree
Native: Alabama to central Florida
Notes: tolerance to dry, sandy soils should make this tree adaptable to conditions created near asphalt and other hot areas in urban landscapes; often leans, forming an asymmetrical canopy

Botanical name: *Pinus echinata*
Common name: Shortleaf Pine
Hardiness range: 6A to 8B
Mature size: 30–50 feet tall by 25–35 feet wide
Light requirement: full sun
Leaf persistence: evergreen
Flower: yellow; inconspicuous in spring
Soil moisture: tolerates some drought
Soil pH tolerance: acid
Uses: specimen
Attributes: attracts birds
Native: southeastern United States to Florida panhandle
Notes: grows well on acid, well-drained soils in full sun; horizontal branches break easily

Botanical name: *Pinus elliottii*
Common name: Slash Pine
Hardiness range: 7B to 11
Mature size: 40–70 feet tall by 35–40 feet wide
Light requirement: partial shade to full sun
Leaf persistence: evergreen
Flower: yellow; inconspicuous in spring
Soil moisture: tolerates some drought and occasional wetness
Soil pH tolerance: acid to slightly alkaline
Uses: specimen
Attributes: attracts birds and butterflies
Native: southeastern United States
Notes: grows well on a variety of acid soils, from wet to moist, in full sun or partial shade; does poorly in basic soil (high pH) or where irrigation water has a high pH; keep turf 10–15 feet from the trunk; plant var. *densa* south of Orlando

Botanical name: *Pinus taeda*
Common name: Lobolly Pine
Hardiness range: 6B to 9A
Mature size: 50–60 feet tall by 25–35 feet wide
Light requirement: full sun
Leaf persistence: evergreen
Flower: yellow; inconspicuous in spring
Soil moisture: tolerates some drought and occasional wetness
Soil pH tolerance: acid to slightly alkaline
Uses: specimen
Attributes: pest tolerant; attracts birds
Native: southeastern United States to central Florida
Notes: commonly planted for timber and pulpwood; creates a light shade; very susceptible to southern pine beetle

Botanical name: *Pithecellobium flexicaule*
Common name: Ebony Blackbead, Texas Ebony
Hardiness range: 8B to 11
Mature size: 25–40 feet tall by 15–25 feet wide
Light requirement: full sun
Leaf persistence: evergreen
Flower: white and yellow; fragrant and showy in spring and summer
Soil moisture: tolerates drought
Soil pH tolerance: acid to alkaline
Uses: specimen; parking lot
Attributes: pest tolerant; attracts butterflies
Native: Texas to northeastern Mexico
Notes: tolerates wind and compacted soil; will thrive in full sun with little water once established

Botanical name: *Platanus × acerifolia*
Common name: London Planetree
Hardiness range: 5A to 8A
Mature size: 40–70 feet tall by 50–60 feet wide
Light requirement: full sun
Leaf persistence: deciduous
Flower: red; inconspicuous in spring
Soil moisture: tolerates drought and flooding
Soil pH tolerance: acid to alkaline
Uses: street tree; pollarding
Attributes: attractive bark and fruit
Native: hybrid origin
Notes: urban-tolerant tree, withstanding typical city conditions; most years infested with lace bugs, which causes premature defoliation; best suited for planting along waterways and parks

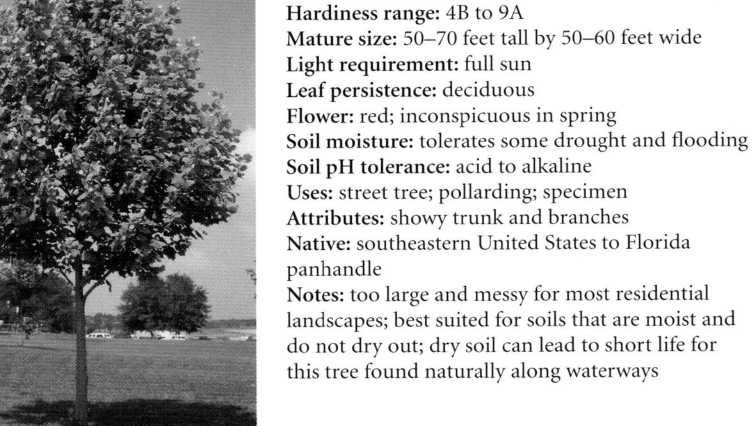

Botanical name: *Platanus occidentalis*
Common name: American Sycamore, American Planetree
Hardiness range: 4B to 9A
Mature size: 50–70 feet tall by 50–60 feet wide
Light requirement: full sun
Leaf persistence: deciduous
Flower: red; inconspicuous in spring
Soil moisture: tolerates some drought and flooding
Soil pH tolerance: acid to alkaline
Uses: street tree; pollarding; specimen
Attributes: showy trunk and branches
Native: southeastern United States to Florida panhandle
Notes: too large and messy for most residential landscapes; best suited for soils that are moist and do not dry out; dry soil can lead to short life for this tree found naturally along waterways

Botanical name: *Platanus orientalis*
Common name: Oriental Sycamore, Oriental Planetree
Hardiness range: 7A to 9A
Mature size: 70–90 feet tall by 70–80 feet wide
Light requirement: partial shade to full sun
Leaf persistence: deciduous
Flower: inconspicuous in spring
Soil moisture: tolerates some drought and occasional wetness
Soil pH tolerance: acid to alkaline
Uses: street tree; pollarding; specimen
Attributes: showy trunk and branches
Native: southeastern Europe and western Asia
Notes: grows on acid or alkaline soil; should be grown primarily for its resistance to anthracnose disease, which can be devastating to American Sycamore

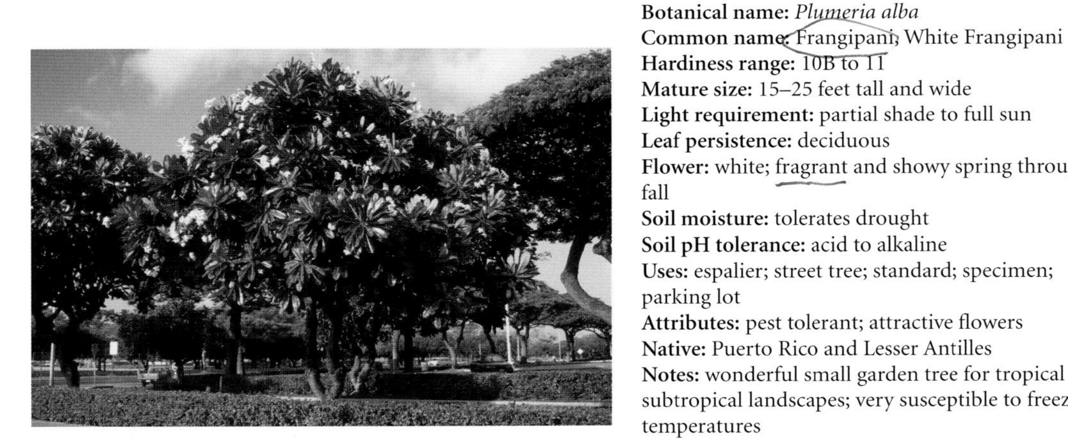

Botanical name: *Plumeria alba*
Common name: Frangipani, White Frangipani
Hardiness range: 10B to 11
Mature size: 15–25 feet tall and wide
Light requirement: partial shade to full sun
Leaf persistence: deciduous
Flower: white; fragrant and showy spring through fall
Soil moisture: tolerates drought
Soil pH tolerance: acid to alkaline
Uses: espalier; street tree; standard; specimen; parking lot
Attributes: pest tolerant; attractive flowers
Native: Puerto Rico and Lesser Antilles
Notes: wonderful small garden tree for tropical and subtropical landscapes; very susceptible to freezing temperatures

Botanical name: *Pongamia pinnata*
Common name: Karum Tree, Poonga Oil Tree, Pongam
Hardiness range: 10B to 11
Mature size: 25–45 feet tall by 30–40 feet wide
Light requirement: full sun
Leaf persistence: evergreen
Flower: lavender, pink, and white; fragrant and showy in spring
Soil moisture: tolerates drought
Soil pH tolerance: acid to slightly alkaline
Uses: street tree; specimen
Attributes: pest tolerant; fast growing
Native: tropical Asia and Australia
Notes: grows rapidly and presents showy fragrant flowers; tends to form included bark in the crotch of large-diameter branches; fruit can be messy; requires regular pruning for good structure

Botanical name: *Populus alba*
Common name: White Poplar
Hardiness range: 3A to 9A
Mature size: 50–75 feet tall by 35–50 feet wide
Light requirement: full sun
Leaf persistence: deciduous
Flower: yellow; inconspicuous in spring
Soil moisture: tolerates drought
Soil pH tolerance: acid to alkaline
Uses: specimen; erosion control
Attributes: attractive bark; asymmetrical with a coarse texture
Native: Europe, Asia
Notes: planted for its rapid growth and large size; has invasive roots; drops leaves in midsummer when the weather is dry

Botanical name: *Populus deltoides*
Common name: Eastern Cottonwood, Necklace Poplar
Hardiness range: 3A to 9A
Mature size: 70–90 feet tall by 45–60 feet wide
Light requirement: full sun
Leaf persistence: deciduous
Flower: red and yellow; inconspicuous in spring
Soil moisture: tolerates some drought and flooding
Soil pH tolerance: acid to alkaline
Uses: erosion control
Attributes: wetlands plant
Native: eastern North America
Notes: prefers moist conditions near water; huge tree is fast growing and weak wooded; pollen is produced copiously and can lead to allergies in many individuals

Botanical name: *Prunus angustifolia*
Common name: Chickasaw Plum
Hardiness range: 5B to 9B
Mature size: 15–25 feet tall and wide
Light requirement: partial shade to full sun
Leaf persistence: deciduous
Flower: pink and white; fragrant and very showy in mid- to late winter
Soil moisture: tolerates drought
Soil pH tolerance: acid to slightly alkaline
Uses: espalier; specimen
Attributes: attracts butterflies; attractive flowers
Native: southeastern United States to central Florida
Notes: very easily grown and has no special horticultural requirements; tolerates drought and sandy or clay soil but does poorly in alkaline pH; grows quickly but has a relatively short life

Botanical name: *Prunus × blireiana*
Common name: Blireiana Plum; Purple-leafed Plum
Hardiness range: 3B to 7A
Mature size: 15–25 feet tall and wide
Light requirement: full sun
Leaf persistence: deciduous
Flower: pink and white; showy in late winter and spring
Soil moisture: tolerates some drought
Soil pH tolerance: acid to slightly alkaline
Uses: specimen
Attributes: attractive fall color
Native: hybrid origin
Notes: crown becomes one-sided unless it receives light from all around the plant; does not tolerate poorly drained soil

Botanical name: *Prunus caroliniana*
Common name: Carolina Laurel Cherry
Hardiness range: 7B to 10A
Mature size: 25–30 feet tall by 15–25 feet wide
Light requirement: full shade to full sun
Leaf persistence: evergreen
Flower: white; fragrant and showy in spring
Soil moisture: tolerates drought
Soil pH tolerance: acid to slightly alkaline
Uses: woodland garden; screen; street tree; standard; hedge
Attributes: pest tolerant; attracts birds
Native: southeastern United States to central Florida
Notes: for best growth, provide good drainage and acid soils; foliage is considered poisonous; fast growth

Botanical name: *Prunus cerasifera*
Common name: Cherry Plum, Pissard Plum, Purple-Leafed Plum
Hardiness range: 5B to 8A
Mature size: 15–25 feet tall and wide
Light requirement: full sun
Leaf persistence: deciduous
Flower: pink and white; very showy in late winter and spring
Soil moisture: tolerates some drought
Soil pH tolerance: acid to slightly alkaline
Uses: specimen
Attributes: attractive flowers
Native: central Asia to the Balkans
Notes: for best growth, provide good drainage and acid soils; often begins to decline within 10 years of planting in the southeastern United States

Botanical name: *Prunus laurocerasus*
Common name: Common Cherry Laurel, English Laurel
Hardiness range: 6A to 8B
Mature size: 12–20 feet tall and wide
Light requirement: full shade to full sun
Leaf persistence: evergreen
Flower: white; fragrant and showy in spring
Soil moisture: tolerates drought
Soil pH tolerance: acid to slightly alkaline
Uses: border; screen; specimen
Attributes: attractive foliage
Native: southeastern Europe, southwestern Asia
Notes: a fast-growing shrub that can be trained to a small tree; tolerates wet soil for only a short period of time; often pruned as a tall hedge or screen

Botanical name: *Prunus salicifolia*
Common name: Mexican Bird Cherry
Hardiness range: 3B to 10A
Mature size: 30–40 feet tall by 20–25 feet wide
Light requirement: partial shade to full sun
Leaf persistence: evergreen
Flower: white; showy in spring
Soil moisture: tolerates drought
Soil pH tolerance: acid to alkaline
Uses: specimen
Attributes: attractive fall color and fruit
Native: Mexico to Peru
Notes: responds best to rich, moist soil and a heavy mulch to keep the root zone cool in the south

Botanical name: *Prunus serotina*
Common name: Wild Black Cherry
Hardiness range: 3B to 9B
Mature size: 50–75 feet tall by 35–50 feet wide
Light requirement: partial shade to full sun
Leaf persistence: deciduous
Flower: white; fragrant and showy in spring
Soil moisture: tolerates drought and occasional wetness
Soil pH tolerance: acid to alkaline
Uses: specimen
Attributes: attracts birds and butterflies
Native: eastern North America except lower Mississippi Valley, into Mexico and Florida
Notes: usually seen in the woods or growing along a fencerow as birds devour the fruit; plant away from walks or driveways because fruit can make a mess; foliage is poisonous to cattle and humans

Botanical name: *Pseudobombax ellipticum*
Common name: Shaving Brush Tree, Pachira
Hardiness range: 10B to 11
Mature size: 20–25 feet tall and wide
Light requirement: partial shade to full sun
Leaf persistence: deciduous
Flower: pink, red, and white; showy in winter and spring
Soil moisture: tolerates some drought
Soil pH tolerance: acid to slightly alkaline
Uses: specimen
Attributes: attractive flowers; pest tolerant
Native: Mexico to Guatemala
Notes: flowers are spectacular, resembling a shaving brush; allow plenty of space for root expansion for this large-trunk tree

Botanical name: *Psidium guajava*
Common name: Guava
Hardiness range: 10A to 11
Mature size: 15–25 feet tall by 10–15 feet wide
Light requirement: full sun
Leaf persistence: evergreen
Flower: white; showy in spring
Soil moisture: tolerates drought and occasional wetness
Soil pH tolerance: acid to alkaline
Uses: invasive
Attributes: pest tolerant; edible fruit
Native: tropical America
Notes: this is the guava that is grown commercially; has escaped cultivation and has infested ditch banks and other wild areas in southern Florida

Botanical name: *Psidium littorale*
Common name: Cattley Guava, Strawberry Guava
Hardiness range: 10A to 11
Mature size: 15–25 feet tall by 10–15 feet wide
Light requirement: partial shade to full sun
Leaf persistence: evergreen
Flower: white; showy in spring
Soil moisture: tolerates drought and occasional wetness
Soil pH tolerance: acid to alkaline
Uses: invasive
Attributes: pest tolerant; showy bark; edible fruit
Native: Brazil
Notes: has escaped cultivation and become a weed in Hawaii and southern Florida; this weedy habit makes it a potential liability to the natural landscapes in these states; fruit is edible and makes nice jellies and jams

Botanical name: *Pyrus calleryana* cultivars
Common name: Callery Pear
Hardiness range: 5A to 9A
Mature size: 25–40 feet tall by 25–35 feet wide
Light requirement: full sun
Leaf persistence: deciduous
Flower: white; very showy in spring
Soil moisture: tolerates drought and occasional wetness
Soil pH tolerance: acid to alkaline
Uses: screen; espalier; street tree; parking lot
Attributes: attractive flowers and fall color; urban tough
Native: China
Notes: very adaptable tree; fallen fruits are a nuisance to some; prune when the tree is young to space lateral branches along a central trunk; 'Bradford' is the most common cultivar, but others have better structure and last longer

Botanical name: *Quercus acutissima*
Common name: Sawtooth Oak
Hardiness range: 5B to 9A
Mature size: 40–50 feet tall by 50–70 feet wide
Light requirement: full sun
Leaf persistence: deciduous
Flower: brown and yellow; showy in spring
Soil moisture: tolerates drought and occasional wetness
Soil pH tolerance: acid to slightly alkaline
Uses: street tree; specimen; parking lot
Attributes: attractive fall color
Native: Korea, Japan, China
Notes: micronutrient-deficiency chlorosis occurs on high pH soils; one of the fastest growing oaks in North America; rounded canopy makes it useful as a shade, street, or parking lot tree

Botanical name: *Quercus bicolor*
Common name: Swamp White Oak
Hardiness range: 4A to 8A
Mature size: 50–75 feet tall by 50–75 feet wide
Light requirement: partial shade to full sun
Leaf persistence: deciduous
Flower: brown; inconspicuous in spring
Soil moisture: tolerates drought and flooding
Soil pH tolerance: acid to slightly alkaline
Uses: street tree; specimen
Attributes: pest tolerant; attracts birds and butterflies
Native: northeastern and upper midwestern United States
Notes: native to wet places; sturdy with branches well attached to trunk; chlorosis can occur on alkaline soils

Botanical name: *Quercus coccinea*
Common name: Scarlet Oak
Hardiness range: 4A to 8A
Mature size: 50–75 feet tall by 40–50 feet wide
Light requirement: full sun
Leaf persistence: deciduous
Flower: brown; inconspicuous in spring
Soil moisture: tolerates some drought
Soil pH tolerance: acid to slightly alkaline
Uses: street tree
Attributes: attracts birds
Native: Appalachian region from Maine to Alabama
Notes: appears to adapt to compacted clay soil; leaf chlorosis often develops on alkaline soils

Botanical name: *Quercus falcata*
Common name: Southern Red Oak, Spanish Oak
Hardiness range: 7A to 9A
Mature size: 40–70 feet tall by 50–60 feet wide
Light requirement: full sun
Leaf persistence: deciduous
Flower: brown; inconspicuous in spring
Soil moisture: tolerates drought
Soil pH tolerance: acid to slightly alkaline
Uses: street tree; specimen; parking lot
Attributes: attracts butterflies
Native: eastern United States
Notes: commonly found growing in the wild in poor soils on slopes and hilltops; also found in sandy flat woods near the coast

Botanical name: *Quercus imbricaria*
Common name: Shingle Oak, Northern Laurel Oak
Hardiness range: 4A to 8A
Mature size: 50–75 feet tall by 35–45 feet wide
Light requirement: full sun
Leaf persistence: deciduous
Flower: brown; inconspicuous in spring
Soil moisture: tolerates drought and flooding
Soil pH tolerance: acid to slightly alkaline
Uses: street tree; specimen
Attributes: attracts birds; urban tough
Native: Pennsylvania to Nebraska; Arkansas to Georgia
Notes: native habitat along streams; tolerates wet soil once well established; usually grows with a central leader

Botanical name: *Quercus laevis*
Common name: American Turkey Oak
Hardiness range: 7B to 9A
Mature size: 25–50 feet tall by 25–35 feet wide
Light requirement: full sun
Leaf persistence: deciduous
Flower: brown; inconspicuous in spring
Soil moisture: tolerates drought
Soil pH tolerance: acid to slightly alkaline
Uses: street tree; specimen
Attributes: attracts butterflies
Native: southeastern United States to south-central Florida
Notes: very tolerant to drought; mostly seen in native dry, sandy soils; can live 80 to 160 years; often becomes hollow with age

Botanical name: *Quercus laurifolia*
Common name: Laurel Oak
Hardiness range: 6B to 10A
Mature size: 50–75 feet tall by 45–60 feet wide
Light requirement: partial shade to full sun
Leaf persistence: deciduous
Flower: brown; inconspicuous in spring
Soil moisture: tolerates some drought and occasional wetness
Soil pH tolerance: acid to slightly alkaline
Uses: street tree; parking lot; parks
Attributes: attracts butterflies
Native: southeastern United States to southern Florida
Notes: quite tolerant of a wide range of soils, from moist and rich to dry and sandy; *Q. hemisphaerica* is native to drier sites; trunk decays readily when large branches are removed

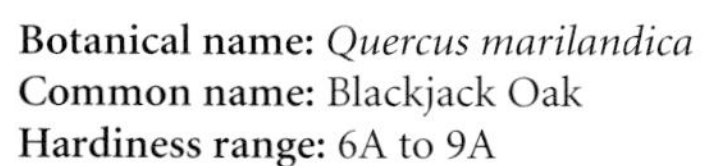

Botanical name: *Quercus marilandica*
Common name: Blackjack Oak
Hardiness range: 6A to 9A
Mature size: 20–50 feet tall by 30–40 feet wide
Light requirement: full sun
Leaf persistence: deciduous
Flower: brown; inconspicuous in spring
Soil moisture: tolerates drought
Soil pH tolerance: acid to slightly alkaline
Uses: specimen
Attributes: attracts birds
Native: eastern United States to Florida panhandle
Notes: very drought tolerant; common in dry deciduous forests in the eastern United States; not grown by many landscape nurseries; roots damaged by construction equipment decay quickly

Botanical name: *Quercus muehlenbergii*
Common name: Yellow Chestnut Oak, Chinkapin Oak
Hardiness range: 4B to 8B
Mature size: 50–75 feet tall and wide
Light requirement: full sun
Leaf persistence: deciduous
Flower: brown; inconspicuous in spring
Soil moisture: tolerates drought and occasional wetness
Soil pH tolerance: acid to alkaline
Uses: street tree; specimen; parking lot
Attributes: pest tolerant; attractive fall color; urban tough
Native: central and eastern United States to central Texas and Florida panhandle
Notes: adapted to alkaline soils; superb tree for city streets

Botanical name: *Quercus myrsinifolia*
Common name: Chinese Evergreen Oak, Japanese Live Oak
Hardiness range: 7A to 9B
Mature size: 25–35 feet tall and wide
Light requirement: partial shade to full sun
Leaf persistence: evergreen
Flower: brown; inconspicuous in spring
Soil moisture: tolerates some drought
Soil pH tolerance: acid to slightly alkaline
Uses: screen; street tree
Attributes: pest tolerant
Native: eastern Asia
Notes: tough tree for residential and street use; not usually available in nurseries

Botanical name: *Quercus myrtifolia*
Common name: Myrtle Oak
Hardiness range: 8A to 9B
Mature size: 6–20 feet tall by 10–25 feet wide
Light requirement: partial shade to full sun
Leaf persistence: evergreen
Flower: brown; inconspicuous in spring
Soil moisture: tolerates drought
Soil pH tolerance: acid to slightly alkaline
Uses: woodland garden; screen; massing; erosion control
Attributes: pest tolerant
Native: southeastern United States
Notes: could be used for coastal reclamation and in any dry situation; great large shrub or small tree for stabilizing banks; not usually available in landscape nurseries

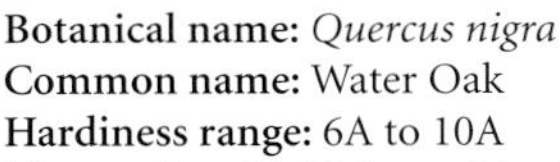

Botanical name: *Quercus nigra*
Common name: Water Oak
Hardiness range: 6A to 10A
Mature size: 50–75 feet tall by 50–80 feet wide
Light requirement: partial shade to full sun
Leaf persistence: semievergreen
Flower: brown; inconspicuous in spring
Soil moisture: tolerates drought and occasional wetness
Soil pH tolerance: acid to slightly alkaline
Uses: ditch banks; retention ponds; wet soils
Attributes: wetlands plant
Native: southeastern United States
Notes: adapted to wet, swampy areas; a good choice for planting in urban areas that have poorly drained soil; decay spreads quickly in the trunk and branches and shortens the tree's life if the trunk is injured or large branches removed

Botanical name: *Quercus shumardii*
Common name: Shumard Oak
Hardiness range: 5B to 9A
Mature size: 60–75 feet tall by 35–60 feet wide
Light requirement: full sun
Leaf persistence: deciduous
Flower: brown; inconspicuous in spring
Soil moisture: tolerates drought and occasional wetness
Soil pH tolerance: acid to slightly alkaline
Uses: street tree; specimen
Attributes: pest tolerant; attractive fall color
Native: eastern United States from Indiana to central Texas to northern Florida
Notes: prefers moist, rich bottomland soil, where it grows rapidly; it will tolerate somewhat drier locations; well adapted to clay soils, even those that are poorly drained

Botanical name: *Quercus stellata*
Common name: Post Oak
Hardiness range: 5B to 9A
Mature size: 40–50 feet tall by 35–50 feet wide
Light requirement: full sun
Leaf persistence: deciduous
Flower: brown; inconspicuous in spring
Soil moisture: tolerates drought
Soil pH tolerance: acid to slightly alkaline
Uses: specimen; shade tree; street tree; parking lot
Attributes: attracts birds
Native: eastern United States from Massachusetts to central Texas to central Florida
Notes: most often found on dry, nutrient-poor, sandy soils; extremely drought tolerant; very sensitive to soil compaction, drainage changes, and soil disturbances; usually not available in nurseries

Botanical name: *Robinia pseudoacacia*
Common name: Black Locust, Yellow Locust
Hardiness range: 4A to 9A
Mature size: 50–75 feet tall by 30–45 feet wide
Light requirement: partial shade to full sun
Leaf persistence: deciduous
Flower: white; fragrant and very showy in spring
Soil moisture: tolerates drought
Soil pH tolerance: acid to alkaline
Uses: erosion control
Attributes: attracts butterflies
Native: eastern and central United States
Notes: able to tolerate drought, salt, and poor soil; should be used for the toughest sites, such as roadsides, landfills, and strip mines; reseeds itself

Botanical name: *Salix babylonica*
Common name: Weeping Willow, Babylon Weeping Willow
Hardiness range: 6A to 9A
Mature size: 40–50 feet tall by 40–60 feet wide
Light requirement: partial shade to full sun
Leaf persistence: deciduous
Flower: yellow; inconspicuous in spring
Soil moisture: tolerates some drought and flooding
Soil pH tolerance: acid to alkaline
Uses: pollarding; specimen; erosion control
Attributes: wetlands plant
Native: Asia
Notes: old-time favorite plant for large landscapes; roots are notoriously invasive, growing into gardens and lawns, making mowing difficult

Botanical name: *Schaefferia frutescens*
Common name: Florida Boxwood
Hardiness range: 10B to 11
Mature size: 15–25 feet tall by 10–15 feet wide
Light requirement: partial shade to full sun
Leaf persistence: evergreen
Flower: green; inconspicuous in spring
Soil moisture: tolerates drought
Soil pH tolerance: acid to alkaline
Uses: border; screen; standard; specimen; hedge
Attributes: attractive red fruit
Native: Key Biscayne to Key West
Notes: usually found close to the tidewater area on sandy soil; it is seen mostly as a small to medium-sized shrub; fruit turn from green to yellow then bright red; small leaves borne close together make this plant suitable for hedges

Botanical name: *Sophora japonica*
Common name: Japanese Pagoda Tree, Scholar Tree
Hardiness range: 4A to 7B
Mature size: 50–75 feet tall by 40–60 feet wide
Light requirement: full sun
Leaf persistence: deciduous
Flower: white and yellow; showy in summer
Soil moisture: tolerates drought and occasional wetness
Soil pH tolerance: acid to alkaline
Uses: street tree; specimen; parking lot
Attributes: pest tolerant; urban tough
Native: China, Korea
Notes: can tolerate typical urban conditions; makes a nice medium-sized patio tree (but can eventually grow to a huge size); well-suited for parking lot planting

Botanical name: *Sophora secundiflora*
Common name: Texas Mountain Laurel, Mescal Bean
Hardiness range: 7B to 10A
Mature size: 15–25 feet tall by 10–15 feet wide
Light requirement: partial shade to full sun
Leaf persistence: evergreen
Flower: purple; inconspicuous in spring
Soil moisture: tolerates drought
Soil pH tolerance: neutral to alkaline
Uses: border; espalier; street tree; parking lot; massing; specimen
Attributes: pest tolerant; showy and fragrant flowers
Native: North America
Notes: will tolerate exposed, hot, windy conditions and alkaline or wet soil; nicely suited for planting in a rock garden or as an accent in any small place

Botanical name: *Styrax japonicum*
Common name: Japanese Snowball
Hardiness range: 5B to 8A
Mature size: 15–25 feet tall and wide
Light requirement: partial shade to full sun
Leaf persistence: deciduous
Flower: white; showy in spring and summer
Soil moisture: tolerates some drought
Soil pH tolerance: acid to slightly alkaline
Uses: specimen; parking lot
Attributes: pest tolerant; showy flowers
Native: Japan, China
Notes: excellent small patio tree where the flowers and bark can be viewed up close; locate tree in an area protected from winter winds; most are grown with multiple trunks but can be trained to one trunk

Botanical name: *Swietenia mahagoni*
Common name: Mahogany, West Indies Mahogany
Hardiness range: 10B to 11
Mature size: 40–60 feet tall by 35–60 feet wide
Light requirement: partial shade to full sun
Leaf persistence: evergreen and semievergreen
Flower: green; inconspicuous in spring
Soil moisture: tolerates drought and occasional wetness
Soil pH tolerance: acid to alkaline
Uses: street tree; specimen; parking lot border
Attributes: pest tolerant
Native: Florida
Notes: grows in the Florida Everglades and throughout the Caribbean in moist soils; large fruit can dent cars

Botanical name: *Tabebuia chrysotricha*
Common name: Golden Trumpet Tree
Hardiness range: 9A to 11
Mature size: 25–40 feet tall by 25–35 feet wide
Light requirement: full sun
Leaf persistence: semievergreen
Flower: yellow; very showy in spring
Soil moisture: tolerates some drought
Soil pH tolerance: acid to slightly alkaline
Uses: containers; specimen; parking lot
Attributes: pest tolerant; very attractive flowers
Native: Colombia, Brazil
Notes: one of the most beautiful flowering trees in the world; grows and flowers best in full sun; may survive the winters in hardiness zone 8B for many years

Botanical name: *Tabebuia heterophylla*
Common name: Pink Trumpet Tree
Hardiness range: 10A to 11
Mature size: 15–35 feet tall by 15–25 feet wide
Light requirement: full sun
Leaf persistence: semievergreen
Flower: pink and white; very showy in spring and summer
Soil moisture: tolerates drought and occasional wetness
Soil pH tolerance: acid to alkaline
Uses: street tree; specimen; parking lot
Attributes: pest tolerant; very attractive flowers; urban tough
Native: West Indies to Puerto Rico
Notes: can be used as a residential shade tree near the patio or deck; well suited for planting in parking lot islands and other small spaces

Botanical name: *Tabebuia impetiginosa* (syns. *Tabebuia heptaphylla; Tabebuia palmeri*)
Common name: Purple Trumpet Tree
Hardiness range: 9B to 11
Mature size: 15–50 feet tall by 30–50 feet wide
Light requirement: full sun
Leaf persistence: deciduous
Flower: purple; very showy in spring
Soil moisture: tolerates drought
Soil pH tolerance: acid to slightly alkaline
Uses: street tree; specimen; parking lot
Attributes: pest tolerant; attractive flowers
Native: Brazil
Notes: foliage drops from tree just before it flowers; tolerates urban conditions well, surviving in parking lots and medians

Botanical name: *Tabebuia umbellata*
Common name: Trumpet Tree
Hardiness range: 9B to 11
Mature size: 15–25 feet tall by 10–15 feet wide
Light requirement: full sun
Leaf persistence: deciduous
Flower: purple; very showy in spring
Soil moisture: tolerates drought
Soil pH tolerance: acid to slightly alkaline
Uses: specimen
Attributes: pest tolerant; very attractive flowers
Native: Brazil
Notes: responds especially well to rich soil; once established it is highly drought tolerant; has a beautiful layered canopy that fills with flowers in the spring

Botanical name: *Tamarindus indica*
Common name: Tamarind
Hardiness range: 10A to 11
Mature size: 50–75 feet tall by 40–60 feet wide
Light requirement: full sun
Leaf persistence: evergreen
Flower: red and yellow; inconspicuous in spring
Soil moisture: tolerates drought and occasional wetness
Soil pH tolerance: acid to alkaline
Uses: street tree; specimen
Attributes: pest tolerant
Native: possibly India
Notes: tolerates alkaline soil well; large tree for big spaces

Botanical name: *Tetrazygia bicolor*
Common name: Florida Tetrazygia, West Indian Lilac
Hardiness range: 10B to 11
Mature size: 15–25 feet tall by 6–10 feet wide
Light requirement: partial shade to full sun
Leaf persistence: evergreen
Flower: white and pinkish; showy in spring and summer
Soil moisture: tolerates drought
Soil pH tolerance: acid to alkaline
Uses: border; foundation planting; specimen
Attributes: pest tolerant; attractive flowers
Native: south-central Dade County, Florida, Bahamas, Cuba, Jamaica, and Dominican Republic
Notes: marvelous large shrub or small tree native to southern Florida; will survive full sun but prefers partial shade; fruits are edible and birds are very fond of them

Botanical name: *Tilia tomentosa*
Common name: Silver Linden
Hardiness range: 4B to 7B
Mature size: 50–75 feet tall by 35–50 feet wide
Light requirement: partial shade to full sun
Leaf persistence: deciduous
Flower: yellow; fragrant and showy in summer
Soil moisture: tolerates drought
Soil pH tolerance: acid to slightly alkaline
Uses: screen; street tree; specimen; parking lot
Attributes: attracts birds; urban tough
Native: Southeast Asia
Notes: similar to the American Basswood except the foliage is silvery and hairy on the undersides; more shade tolerant than many other large trees; sprouts often appear at the base of the trunk

Botanical name: *Ulmus alata*
Common name: Winged Elm
Hardiness range: 6A to 9B
Mature size: 35–50 feet tall by 40–50 feet wide
Light requirement: partial shade to full sun
Leaf persistence: deciduous
Flower: green; inconspicuous in spring
Soil moisture: tolerates drought
Soil pH tolerance: acid to alkaline
Uses: street tree; specimen; parking lot
Attributes: attracts birds; urban tough
Native: southeastern United States, from southern Illinois to eastern Texas to central Florida
Notes: well suited for planting in parking lot islands, along streets, or as a yard shade tree; must be pruned regularly at an early age to eliminate multiple trunks

Botanical name: *Ulmus americana*
Common name: American Elm, Gray Elm, Water Elm, White Elm
Hardiness range: 3A to 9B
Mature size: 50–90 feet tall by 50–60 feet wide
Light requirement: partial shade to full sun
Leaf persistence: deciduous
Flower: green; inconspicuous in spring
Soil moisture: tolerates drought and flooding
Soil pH tolerance: acid to alkaline
Uses: street tree; specimen; parking lot
Attributes: attractive fall color; fabulous form
Native: central and eastern North America to south-central Florida
Notes: should be monitored for symptoms of Dutch elm disease; some cultivars ('Valley Forge,' 'New Harmony,' and 'Princeton') are reported to be resistant to the disease

Botanical name: *Ulmus americana* var. *floridana*
Common name: Florida Elm
Hardiness range: 8A to 10A
Mature size: 50–75 feet tall by 50–60 feet wide
Light requirement: partial shade to full sun
Leaf persistence: deciduous
Flower: green; inconspicuous in spring
Soil moisture: tolerates some drought and flooding
Soil pH tolerance: acid to alkaline
Uses: street tree; specimen; parking lot
Attributes: urban tough; great street tree
Native: North America
Notes: adapts to a wide variety of soils; symmetrical, with a medium texture and moderately dense crown; requires regular pruning in the early years to develop a dominant trunk

Botanical name: *Ulmus crassifolia*
Common name: Cedar Elm
Hardiness range: 6B to 9A
Mature size: 40–50 feet tall by 50–60 feet wide
Light requirement: partial shade to full sun
Leaf persistence: deciduous
Flower: green; inconspicuous in fall
Soil moisture: tolerates drought and flooding
Soil pH tolerance: acid to alkaline
Uses: street tree; specimen; parking lot
Attributes: attractive fall color
Native: south-central United States to Suwannee county in Florida
Notes: commonly planted in Texas as a street tree; tolerates alkaline and wet soils; susceptible to Dutch elm disease

Botanical name: *Ulmus parvifolia*
Common name: Chinese Elm, Lacebark Elm
Hardiness range: 5B to 10A
Mature size: 40–65 feet tall by 45–65 feet wide
Light requirement: partial shade to full sun
Leaf persistence: deciduous and semievergreen
Flower: green; inconspicuous in spring
Soil moisture: tolerates drought and occasional wetness
Soil pH tolerance: acid to alkaline
Uses: street tree; pollarding; specimen; parking lot
Attributes: tolerates urban heat
Native: China, Japan
Notes: very suitable as a street tree and adapts to parking lot islands; 'Allee' and 'Bosck' are more upright and suited for streets and other urban landscapes

Botanical name: *Ulmus pumila*
Common name: Siberian Elm
Hardiness range: 4A to 9A
Mature size: 50–75 feet tall by 35–50 feet wide
Light requirement: full sun
Leaf persistence: deciduous
Flower: green; inconspicuous in spring
Soil moisture: tolerates drought and flooding
Soil pH tolerance: acid to alkaline
Uses: reclamation; grows where no other trees will grow
Attributes: breaks apart fairly easily
Native: eastern China, and from northern China to Turkistan
Notes: wood is fairly brittle and subject to damage during storms; most urban tree managers and horticulturists do not recommend planting this tree; has a place in tough regions where little else will grow

Botanical name: *Vitex agnus-castus*
Common name: Chastetree, Vitex
Hardiness range: 7B to 9B
Mature size: 10–25 feet tall and wide
Light requirement: partial shade to full sun
Leaf persistence: deciduous
Flower: blue, lavender, and white; showy in summer
Soil moisture: tolerates drought
Soil pH tolerance: acid to alkaline
Uses: containers; border; espalier; pollarding; specimen
Attributes: attracts butterflies
Native: southern Europe
Notes: prefers a loose, well-drained soil; often suffers from dieback in organic, mucky, or other soil that is kept too moist; could escape cultivation; select a cultivar for best flowering

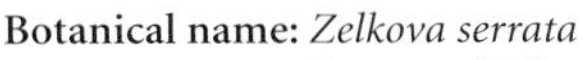

Botanical name: *Zelkova serrata*
Common name: Japanese Zelkova, Saw-Leafed Zelkova
Hardiness range: 5A to 8A
Mature size: 75–80 feet tall by 50–60 feet wide
Light requirement: full sun
Leaf persistence: deciduous
Flower: inconspicuous in spring
Soil moisture: tolerates drought and occasional wetness
Soil pH tolerance: acid to alkaline
Uses: street tree; specimen; parking lot
Attributes: pest tolerant; attractive fall color; urban tough
Native: Japan
Notes: wonderful street and shade tree; almost pest free; grows to be quite large; requires regular pruning first 20 years after planting to develop good structure

Slightly Salt-Tolerant Trees

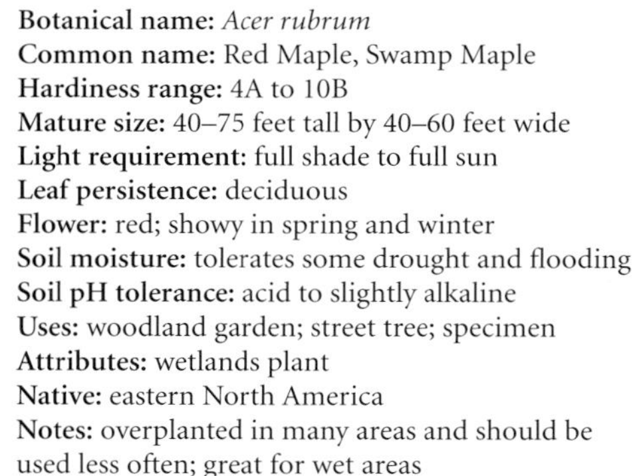

Botanical name: *Acer rubrum*
Common name: Red Maple, Swamp Maple
Hardiness range: 4A to 10B
Mature size: 40–75 feet tall by 40–60 feet wide
Light requirement: full shade to full sun
Leaf persistence: deciduous
Flower: red; showy in spring and winter
Soil moisture: tolerates some drought and flooding
Soil pH tolerance: acid to slightly alkaline
Uses: woodland garden; street tree; specimen
Attributes: wetlands plant
Native: eastern North America
Notes: overplanted in many areas and should be used less often; great for wet areas

Botanical name: *Albizia julibrissin*
Common name: Mimosa, Mimosa Tree, Silk Tree
Hardiness range: 6B to 9A
Mature size: 15–25 feet tall by 25–35 feet wide
Light requirement: full sun
Leaf persistence: deciduous
Flower: pink; fragrant and very showy in spring and summer
Soil moisture: tolerates drought and occasional wetness
Soil pH tolerance: acid to slightly alkaline
Uses: invasive
Attributes: attracts hummingbirds; weedy
Native: Iran to Japan
Notes: grows best in full sun; leaf chlorosis occurs if soil is too alkaline; roots are capable of forming nodules that fix nitrogen; typically short-lived but not before dispersing seeds to further spread this weed

Botanical name: *Albizia lebbeck*
Common name: Siris Tree, Woman's Tongue
Hardiness range: 10A to 11
Mature size: 25–50 feet tall by 35–50 feet wide
Light requirement: full sun
Leaf persistence: deciduous
Flower: white; showy in spring
Soil moisture: tolerates drought and occasional wetness
Soil pH tolerance: acid to alkaline
Uses: invasive
Attributes: pest tolerant
Native: tropical Asia
Notes: tends to naturalize in subtropical and tropical landscapes; probably best left in its natural habitat in Asia

Botanical name: *Averrhoa carambola*
Common name: Starfruit, Carambola
Hardiness range: 10B to 11
Mature size: 25–50 feet tall by 25–35 feet wide
Light requirement: partial shade to full sun
Leaf persistence: evergreen
Flower: pink; showy in spring through fall
Soil moisture: tolerates some drought
Soil pH tolerance: acid to slightly alkaline
Uses: specimen; fruit tree
Attributes: attractive flowers; edible greenish to yellow fruit
Native: Malay region
Notes: fruits have longitudinal ribs that give them a star-shaped appearance when sliced; flavor of fruit can vary considerably from plant to plant; fruit is best when picked yellow

Botanical name: *Bauhinia* spp.
Common name: Orchid Tree
Hardiness range: 9B to 11
Mature size: 25–50 feet tall by 25–35 feet wide
Light requirement: partial shade to full sun
Leaf persistence: evergreen and semievergreen
Flower: pink, purple, red, white, and yellow; very showy year-round
Soil moisture: tolerates drought
Soil pH tolerance: acid to slightly alkaline
Uses: *Bauhinia variegata* is invasive; seedless varieties like *B. blakeana* make nice street or parking lot trees; specimen
Attributes: pest tolerant
Native: pantropical
Notes: will show interveinal chlorosis on the leaves when grown in alkaline soils; types that produce seeds can become invasive; potassium, magnesium, and micronutrient deficiencies are common

Botanical name: *Brugmansia* spp.
Common name: Angel's Trumpet
Hardiness range: 8B to 10B
Mature size: 10–15 feet tall and wide
Light requirement: partial shade to full sun
Leaf persistence: evergreen
Flower: orange, pink, yellow, and white; fragrant and very showy in spring through fall
Soil moisture: will grow in moist soil
Soil pH tolerance: acid to slightly alkaline
Uses: standard; specimen
Attributes: attractive and fragrant flowers
Native: South America
Notes: flowers drape the plant for a number of weeks one or more times annually; the plant is killed to the ground in zone 8B; one time known as *Datura;* all parts are poisonous

Botanical name: *Carica papaya*
Common name: Papaya
Hardiness range: 9B to 11
Mature size: 10–15 feet by 3–6 feet wide
Light requirement: partial shade to full sun
Leaf persistence: evergreen
Flower: yellow; showy in spring and winter
Soil moisture: tolerates occasional wetness
Soil pH tolerance: acid to slightly alkaline
Uses: border; specimen
Attributes: delicious fruit
Native: lowland South America, cultivated throughout tropics
Notes: enormous simple, lobed leaves combine with a single trunk and delicious fruit to make this a desirable plant for many landscapes; can be grown farther north if winter temperatures remain warm

Botanical name: *Cassia fistula* (syn. *Cassia excelsa*)
Common name: Golden Shower Tree
Hardiness range: 10B to 11
Mature size: 25–50 feet tall by 25–35 feet wide
Light requirement: full sun
Leaf persistence: deciduous
Flower: yellow; very showy in summer
Soil moisture: tolerates some drought
Soil pH tolerance: acid to alkaline
Uses: street tree; specimen; parking lot; shade
Attributes: pest tolerant; attracts butterflies
Native: India
Notes: sprouts may develop along the main branches in response to low temperature; fruit may be poisonous if ingested

Botanical name: *Cinnamomum camphora*
Common name: Camphor Tree
Hardiness range: 9B to 11
Mature size: 50–60 feet tall by 45–65 feet wide
Light requirement: partial shade to full sun
Leaf persistence: evergreen
Flower: yellow; inconspicuous in spring
Soil moisture: tolerates drought
Soil pH tolerance: acid to slightly alkaline
Uses: invasive
Attributes: pest tolerant; attracts butterflies
Native: China, Taiwan, Japan
Notes: allow plenty of room for its fast-growing, large habit; can develop minor element deficiencies (chlorosis) on alkaline soils and can thus look terrible; has escaped cultivation in Florida, Louisiana, and parts of coastal Texas

Botanical name: *Diospyros khaki*
Common name: Japanese Persimmon
Hardiness range: 7A to 9B
Mature size: 15–25 feet tall and wide
Light requirement: full sun
Leaf persistence: deciduous
Flower: white; inconspicuous in spring
Soil moisture: tolerates some drought
Soil pH tolerance: acid to alkaline
Uses: specimen; fruit tree
Attributes: pest tolerant
Native: Japan, China
Notes: since the fruits are big and messy, locate it where it can be viewed from a distance, away from walks, decks, and patios

Botanical name: *Diospyros virginiana*
Common name: American Persimmon
Hardiness range: 4B to 9B
Mature size: 25–50 feet tall by 15–25 feet wide
Light requirement: full sun
Leaf persistence: deciduous
Flower: white; inconspicuous in spring
Soil moisture: tolerates drought and flooding
Soil pH tolerance: acid to alkaline
Uses: fruit tree; specimen
Attributes: attracts birds and butterflies
Native: eastern United States through the Florida Keys
Notes: often forms thickets that crowd out other plants; resists browsing by deer; host for butterfly larvae

Botanical name: *Enterolobium cyclocarpa*
Common name: Elephant's Ear, Ear Pod Tree
Hardiness range: 9B to 11
Mature size: 60–100 feet tall by 70–100 feet wide
Light requirement: partial shade to full sun
Leaf persistence: evergreen
Flower: white; inconspicuous
Soil moisture: tolerates drought
Soil pH tolerance: acid to slightly alkaline
Uses: specimen
Attributes: naturalizing
Native: tropical America
Notes: truly a tree of huge proportion; only suited for parks and other enormous landscapes; has been reported to naturalize

Botanical name: *Erythrina crista-galli*
Common name: Cockspur Coral Tree
Hardiness range: 8B to 11
Mature size: 10–25 feet tall and wide
Light requirement: full sun
Leaf persistence: deciduous
Flower: orange-red; very showy in spring through fall
Soil moisture: tolerates drought
Soil pH tolerance: acid to alkaline
Uses: street tree; standard; specimen; pollarding
Attributes: pest tolerant
Native: South America
Notes: requires pruning to develop an upright or strong structure; lower branches eventually droop to the ground

Botanical name: *Euphorbia tirucalli*
Common name: Milkbush, Pencil Tree
Hardiness range: 10A to 11
Mature size: 20–30 feet tall by 12–20 feet wide
Light requirement: partial shade to full sun
Leaf persistence: evergreen
Flower: inconspicuous
Soil moisture: tolerates drought
Soil pH tolerance: acid to slightly alkaline
Uses: containers; rock garden; border; specimen
Attributes: rarely has leaves
Native: tropical and southern Africa, and India, east to Indonesia
Notes: place in full sun and allow plenty of space for this large plant; sap is a milky juice

Botanical name: *Fagus grandifolia*
Common name: American Beech
Hardiness range: 4A to 8B
Mature size: 50–65 feet tall by 50–60 feet wide
Light requirement: partial shade to full sun
Leaf persistence: deciduous
Flower: inconspicuous in spring
Soil moisture: tolerates little drought due to shallow roots
Soil pH tolerance: acid to slightly alkaline
Uses: screen; specimen for large spaces
Attributes: pest tolerant
Native: eastern North America
Notes: grows slowly; prefers a sunny location and a moist, light soil; grows poorly in restricted soil spaces; many leaves remain brown through winter

Botanical name: *Fortunella margarita*
Common name: Oval Kumquat
Hardiness range: 8A to 9B
Mature size: 10–15 feet tall and wide
Light requirement: partial shade to full sun
Leaf persistence: evergreen
Flower: white; inconspicuous in spring
Soil moisture: tolerates some drought
Soil pH tolerance: acid to slightly alkaline
Uses: containers; border; specimen
Attributes: attractive, aromatic, and edible fruit
Native: southern China
Notes: place in full sun to partial shade in a moist spot for best growth; pollen causes few, if any, allergies; cute, small ornamental fruit tree for the patio or small garden spot

Botanical name: *Jacaranda mimosifolia* (syn. *Jacaranda acutifolia*)
Common name: Jacaranda
Hardiness range: 9B to 11
Mature size: 35–40 feet tall by 40–50 feet wide
Light requirement: full sun
Leaf persistence: deciduous
Flower: lavender and purple; fragrant and very showy in spring and summer
Soil moisture: tolerates drought
Soil pH tolerance: acid to alkaline
Uses: street tree; specimen; parking lot
Attributes: pest tolerant
Native: northwestern Argentina
Notes: heaviest flowering and fastest growth occurs in full sun; young trees require frequent pruning in the nursery and landscape to develop strong structure

Botanical name: *Liriodendron tulipifera*
Common name: Tulip Tree, Tulip Poplar, Yellow Poplar
Hardiness range: 4B to 9A
Mature size: 65–90 feet tall by 45–60 feet wide
Light requirement: full sun
Leaf persistence: deciduous
Flower: green and yellow; fragrant and showy in spring
Soil moisture: tolerates some drought and occasional wetness
Soil pH tolerance: acid to slightly alkaline
Uses: specimen; shade
Attributes: pest tolerant; attracts butterflies; grows rather quickly
Native: eastern North America
Notes: prefers well-drained, acid soil; drought conditions in summer often cause premature defoliation of interior leaves, which turn bright yellow and fall to the ground

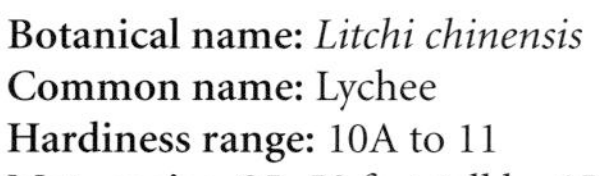

Botanical name: *Litchi chinensis*
Common name: Lychee
Hardiness range: 10A to 11
Mature size: 25–50 feet tall by 15–35 feet wide
Light requirement: full sun
Leaf persistence: evergreen
Flower: yellow; showy in spring
Soil moisture: tolerates some drought and occasional wetness
Soil pH tolerance: acid to slightly alkaline
Uses: specimen
Attributes: attractive flowers and fruit
Native: China
Notes: dense canopy can catch the wind, either blowing the tree over or breaking its branches; iron deficiency can show in alkaline soil

Botanical name: *Melia azederach*
Common name: Chinaberry, Pride of India
Hardiness range: 7A to 11
Mature size: 25–40 feet tall by 25–35 feet wide
Light requirement: partial shade to full sun
Leaf persistence: deciduous
Flower: lavender; fragrant and inconspicuous in spring
Soil moisture: tolerates drought
Soil pH tolerance: acid to alkaline
Uses: **invasive**
Attributes: fragrant flowers and attractive fruit
Native: Asia
Notes: considered a "weed" tree in the southeastern United States, so it is not usually available from nurseries; grows anywhere in any soil except wet; all parts of the plant are poisonous if ingested; branches break easily

Botanical name: *Morus rubra*
Common name: Red Mulberry
Hardiness range: 5A to 9B
Mature size: 40–70 feet tall by 35–45 feet wide
Light requirement: partial shade to full sun
Leaf persistence: deciduous
Flower: green and yellow; inconspicuous in spring
Soil moisture: tolerates drought and occasional wetness
Soil pH tolerance: acid to slightly alkaline
Uses: pollarding; shade; park
Attributes: attracts butterflies
Native: eastern United States to southern Florida
Notes: adapts to any soil and has naturalized in many parts of the world; well suited for planting as a quick shade tree in a park or other open area; the fruit (on female trees) can create a mess

Botanical name: *Ravenala madagascariensis*
Common name: Traveler's Tree
Hardiness range: 10A to 11
Mature size: 15–25 feet tall and wide
Light requirement: partial shade to full sun
Leaf persistence: evergreen
Flower: white; showy in spring, summer, and fall
Soil moisture: tolerates some drought
Soil pH tolerance: acid to slightly alkaline
Uses: border; specimen
Attributes: attractive flowers and trunk
Native: Madagascar
Notes: will produce best growth in full sun, though young plants may be grown in shade; should be grown on fertile soil, with ample organic matter, and routinely watered and fertilized

Botanical name: *Schefflera actinophylla* (syn. *Brassaia actinophylla*)
Common name: Schefflera, Octopus Plant, Queensland Umbrella Tree
Hardiness range: 10A to 11
Mature size: 25–35 feet tall by 10–15 feet wide
Light requirement: partial shade to full sun
Leaf persistence: evergreen
Flower: red; very showy in summer
Soil moisture: tolerates some drought and occasional wetness
Soil pH tolerance: acid to alkaline
Uses: invasive
Attributes: attracts birds
Native: India to Malay Peninsula, Philippines, northeastern Australia, and Hawaii
Notes: seeds spread by birds; puts significant leaf litter onto ground; often topped as desired to create multilevel masses of foliage; naturalized in some parts of southern Florida and Hawaii

Botanical name: *Spathodea campanulata*
Common name: African Tuliptree
Hardiness range: 10B to 11
Mature size: 50–75 feet tall by 35–50 feet wide
Light requirement: full sun
Leaf persistence: evergreen
Flower: orange or yellow; very showy in spring and winter
Soil moisture: tolerates some drought
Soil pH tolerance: acid to slightly alkaline
Uses: invasive
Attributes: attractive flowers
Native: tropical Africa
Notes: a beautiful tree that grows to a large size; damaged in hurricanes more than many other tropical trees

Botanical name: *Taxodium distichum*
Common name: Bald Cypress, Common Bald Cypress
Hardiness range: 4A to 10B
Mature size: 50–75 feet tall by 25–35 feet wide
Light requirement: partial shade to full sun
Leaf persistence: deciduous
Flower: brown; inconspicuous in spring
Soil moisture: tolerates drought and flooding
Soil pH tolerance: acid to slightly alkaline
Uses: screen; street tree; parking lot
Attributes: pest tolerant; wetlands plant; attracts butterflies
Native: eastern North America
Notes: ideal for wet locations but will grow remarkably well on almost any soil, including heavy, compacted, or poorly drained muck, except alkaline soils with a pH above 7.5

Salt-Tolerant Shrubs

Highly Salt-Tolerant Shrubs

Botanical name: *Acrostichum danaeifolium*
Common name: Giant Leather Fern
Hardiness range: 9A to 11
Mature size: 4–8 feet tall by 3–6 feet wide
Light requirement: full shade to full sun
Leaf persistence: evergreen
Flower: none
Soil moisture: thrives when flooded or in standing water
Soil pH tolerance: acid to slightly alkaline
Uses: woodland garden; foundation planting; massing; specimen
Attributes: wetlands plant; provides a continual green mass of foliage
Native: Florida, Central and South America, West Indies
Notes: beautiful fern native to Florida; grows larger than many other ferns, becoming 4 to 8 feet tall

Botanical name: *Agave americana*
Common name: Century Plant
Hardiness range: 8B to 11
Mature size: 8–12 feet tall and wide
Light requirement: partial shade to full sun
Leaf persistence: evergreen
Flower: white; very showy and rare
Soil moisture: tolerates drought
Soil pH tolerance: acid to alkaline
Uses: containers; rock garden; massing; specimen
Attributes: attracts birds
Native: Mexico
Notes: after 10 years or more (not a century), a lofty flower spike is produced, sometimes reaching a height of 20 feet, with terminal panicles of pale yellow to white blooms, after which the plant dies; remove sharp leaf tips to protect people and pets

Botanical name: *Agave angustifolia* 'Marginata'
Common name: Variegated Caribbean Agave
Hardiness range: 10A to 11
Mature size: 2–4 feet tall by 3–6 feet wide
Light requirement: partial shade to full sun
Leaf persistence: evergreen
Flower: yellow; very showy and rare
Soil moisture: tolerates drought
Soil pH tolerance: acid to alkaline
Uses: containers; rock garden; massing; specimen
Attributes: attracts birds
Native: tropical America
Notes: not common in cultivation; has green leaves with marginal bands of bright white; the sharp spine at the tips of its toothed leaves is often removed to protect people and pets

Botanical name: *Agave attenuata*
Common name: Foxtail Agave, Spineless Century Plant
Hardiness range: 9B to 11
Mature size: 2–4 feet tall by 3–6 feet wide
Light requirement: partial shade to full sun
Leaf persistence: evergreen
Flower: white; very showy year-round
Soil moisture: tolerates drought
Soil pH tolerance: acid to alkaline
Uses: containers; rock garden; seashore planting; massing; specimen; ground cover
Attributes: attracts birds; leaves spineless
Native: central Mexico
Notes: foliage is a soft, light, yellow-green with gray overtones; leaves do not terminate in a spine; can be included in gardens frequented by children

Botanical name: *Agave bovicornuta*
Common name: Century Plant
Hardiness range: 9A to 11
Mature size: 2–4 feet tall by 6 feet wide
Light requirement: partial shade to full sun
Leaf persistence: evergreen
Flower: yellow; very showy and rare
Soil moisture: tolerates some drought
Soil pH tolerance: acid to alkaline
Uses: containers; rock garden; seashore planting; border; massing; specimen
Attributes: attracts birds
Native: southern Mexico
Notes: after 12 to 18 years or more, a lofty flower spike is produced, sometimes reaching a height of 20 feet, with terminal panicles of pale yellow blooms

Botanical name: *Agave decipiens*
Common name: Century Plant
Hardiness range: 9A to 11
Mature size: 4–8 feet tall by 6–8 feet wide
Light requirement: partial shade to full sun
Leaf persistence: evergreen
Flower: yellow; very showy and rare
Soil moisture: tolerates drought
Soil pH tolerance: acid to alkaline
Uses: containers; rock garden; seashore planting; massing; specimen
Attributes: attracts birds
Native: Florida
Notes: after 10 years or more (though not a century), a lofty flower spike is produced, sometimes reaching a height of 20 feet; plant dies after blooming, but offsets arise from mother plant

Botanical name: *Agave guiengola*
Common name: Century Plant
Hardiness range: 9A to 11
Mature size: 6–8 feet tall and wide
Light requirement: partial shade to full sun
Leaf persistence: evergreen
Flower: yellow; very showy and rare
Soil moisture: tolerates drought
Soil pH tolerance: acid to alkaline
Uses: containers; rock garden; border; specimen
Attributes: attracts birds
Native: Mexico
Notes: due to its large size, most residences only need one of these; larger commercial landscapes have room for multiple mass plantings that can create a dramatic impact

Botanical name: *Agave parryi* var. *truncata*
Common name: Mescal, Parry's Agave
Hardiness range: 9A to 11
Mature size: 1–2 feet tall and wide
Light requirement: partial shade to full sun
Leaf persistence: evergreen
Flower: white; showy and rare
Soil moisture: tolerates drought
Soil pH tolerance: acid to alkaline
Uses: containers; rock garden; border; foundation planting; massing; specimen; ground cover
Attributes: attracts birds
Native: Arizona, New Mexico, Mexico
Notes: typically used in residences as a freestanding specimen, not planted in mass; looks very much like an artichoke

Botanical name: *Ardisia escallonioides*
Common name: Japanese Ardisia, Marbleberry, Marlberry
Hardiness range: 10A to 11
Mature size: 10–15 feet tall by 6–10 feet wide
Light requirement: partial shade to full sun
Leaf persistence: evergreen
Flower: white; fragrant and showy year-round
Soil moisture: tolerates some drought
Soil pH tolerance: acid to alkaline
Uses: screen; specimen
Attributes: attracts butterflies
Native: central and southern Florida into the Keys
Notes: occurs naturally with *Sabal* palms, stoppers, and other tropicals; flowers are borne at intervals throughout the year but do not last very long; small purple fruit are borne in the spring

Botanical name: *Capparis cynophallophora*
Common name: Jamaica Caper
Hardiness range: 10A to 11
Mature size: 10–18 feet tall by 10–15 feet wide
Light requirement: partial shade to full sun
Leaf persistence: evergreen
Flower: pink and white; showy in spring
Soil moisture: tolerates drought
Soil pH tolerance: acid to slightly alkaline
Uses: border; screen; street tree; standard; specimen
Attributes: attracts butterflies
Native: Florida
Notes: related to the plant producing edible capers; flowers have very showy, two-inch-long, purple stamens, white anthers, and white petals

Botanical name: *Carissa macrocarpa* (syn. *Carissa grandiflora*)
Common name: Natal Plum
Hardiness range: 9B to 11
Mature size: 6–10 feet tall and wide
Light requirement: partial shade to full sun
Leaf persistence: evergreen
Flower: white; fragrant and showy in summer
Soil moisture: tolerates drought
Soil pH tolerance: acid to alkaline
Uses: containers; border; screen; foundation planting; hedge; massing; erosion control
Attributes: attractive foliage, flowers, and fruit
Native: South Africa
Notes: has small, dark green, leathery, egg-shaped leaves that are accompanied by sharp, forked spines about 1 1/2 inches long; flowers are solitary, fragrant, and have overlapping petals

Botanical name: *Casasia clusiifolia*
Common name: Seven-Year Apple
Hardiness range: 10B to 11
Mature size: 10–15 feet tall and wide
Light requirement: partial shade to full sun
Leaf persistence: evergreen
Flower: white; fragrant and showy and appearing periodically throughout the year
Soil moisture: tolerates drought
Soil pH tolerance: acid to alkaline
Uses: border; screen; specimen
Attributes: sweet, heavy, and fragrant flowers
Native: southern Florida
Notes: one of Florida's most exceptional native drought- and salt-tolerant plants; grows up to the first dune near the ocean

Botanical name: *Cassia bahamensis*
Common name: Bahama Senna, Bahama Cassia
Hardiness range: 10B to 11
Mature size: 3–9 feet tall by 6–10 feet wide
Light requirement: partial shade to full sun
Leaf persistence: evergreen
Flower: yellow; very showy in fall and winter
Soil moisture: tolerates drought
Soil pH tolerance: acid to alkaline
Uses: containers; seashore planting; border; massing; specimen
Attributes: attracts butterflies
Native: Florida Keys
Notes: covered with little yellow flowers in the fall; pollen can cause allergies in certain people

Botanical name: *Chrysobalanus icaco*
Common name: Cocoplum
Hardiness range: 10A to 11
Mature size: 10–15 feet tall and wide
Light requirement: partial shade to full sun
Leaf persistence: evergreen
Flower: white; inconspicuous in spring
Soil moisture: tolerates drought
Soil pH tolerance: acid to alkaline
Uses: border; screen; espalier; hedge; pollarding; standard; specimen
Attributes: pest tolerant
Native: Cape Canaveral to Key West and Sanibel Island, Florida
Notes: tolerates urban conditions and performs well as a street tree; small edible fruit could make a mess on walks and patios; used most often as a clipped hedge

Botanical name: *Cortaderia selloana*
Common name: Pampas Grass
Hardiness range: 7B to 11
Mature size: 6–10 feet tall and wide
Light requirement: partial shade to full sun
Leaf persistence: evergreen
Flower: pink and white; showy in summer and fall
Soil moisture: tolerates drought
Soil pH tolerance: acid to alkaline
Uses: containers; massing; specimen
Attributes: attracts birds; suitable for cut flowers and for dried flowers
Native: South America
Notes: female plants have more showy plumes; male plants are not commonly offered for sale; foliage is sharp-edged and can be a hazard; reportedly has escaped cultivation in certain regions

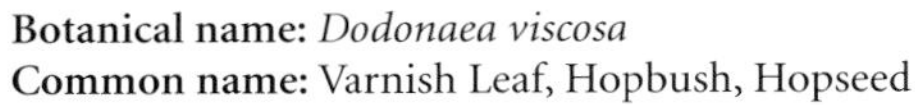

Botanical name: *Dodonaea viscosa*
Common name: Varnish Leaf, Hopbush, Hopseed Bush
Hardiness range: 9A to 11
Mature size: 10–15 feet tall and wide
Light requirement: full sun
Leaf persistence: evergreen
Flower: green and yellow; inconspicuous spring through fall
Soil moisture: tolerates drought well
Soil pH tolerance: acid to alkaline
Uses: border; screen; espalier; hedge; standard; specimen
Attributes: pest tolerant
Native: southern Florida, South Africa, Australia, Hawaii, and Mexico
Notes: used as a specimen plant due to its nice fruit display; makes a nice hedge or background plant; leaves have a resinous coating that protects against water loss

Botanical name: *Elaeagnus pungens*
Common name: Pungent Elaeagnus, Thorny Elaeagnus, Oleaster, Silverthorn
Hardiness range: 6B to 10A
Mature size: 10–15 feet tall and wide
Light requirement: partial shade to full sun
Leaf persistence: evergreen and semievergreen
Flower: white; fragrant and inconspicuous in spring and winter
Soil moisture: tolerates drought and occasional wetness
Soil pH tolerance: acid to alkaline
Uses: invasive
Attributes: fast growing
Native: China and Japan
Notes: especially effective as a hedge but requires frequent pruning because of its rampant growth; do not plant unless prepared to prune regularly; reportedly naturalizes under certain circumstances

Botanical name: *Eugenia foetida*
Common name: Boxleaf Stopper, Spanish Stopper
Hardiness range: 10A to 11
Mature size: 15–20 feet tall by 15–25 feet wide
Light requirement: partial shade to full sun
Leaf persistence: evergreen
Flower: white; inconspicuous in summer
Soil moisture: tolerates drought and occasional wetness
Soil pH tolerance: acid to alkaline
Uses: screen; street tree; standard; specimen
Attributes: pest tolerant
Native: southern Florida
Notes: grows in southern Florida on limestone soils in hardwood hammocks as an understory plant; several stems arise from the lower part of the plant, forming multiple trunks

Botanical name: *Eugenia rhombea*
Common name: Red Stopper
Hardiness range: 10B to 11
Mature size: 10–15 feet tall and wide
Light requirement: partial shade to full sun
Leaf persistence: evergreen
Flower: white; inconspicuous year-round
Soil moisture: tolerates drought and occasional wetness
Soil pH tolerance: acid to alkaline
Uses: screen; street tree; standard
Attributes: pest tolerant
Native: southern Florida
Notes: grows in southern Florida on limestone soils in coastal uplands as an understory plant; however, it is perfectly adapted to more open, sunny locations

Botanical name: *Euphorbia ingens*
Common name: Cactus Euphorbia, Naboom
Hardiness range: 10A to 11
Mature size: 20–30 feet tall by 10–15 feet wide
Light requirement: partial shade to full sun
Leaf persistence: deciduous
Flower: yellow; inconspicuous in winter
Soil moisture: tolerates drought
Soil pH tolerance: acid to alkaline
Uses: specimen
Attributes: coarse texture
Native: South Africa
Notes: the milky sap of euphorbias is highly irritating to the skin and can cause severe inflammation when in contact with the eyes or open wounds

Botanical name: *Euphorbia milii*
Common name: Crown of Thorns
Hardiness range: 10A to 11
Mature size: 1–5 feet tall and wide
Light requirement: partial shade to full sun
Leaf persistence: evergreen
Flower: pink, red, white, and yellow; showy year-round
Soil moisture: tolerates drought
Soil pH tolerance: acid to neutral
Uses: containers; rock garden; foundation planting; specimen; ground cover
Attributes: attractive foliage
Native: Madagascar
Notes: excellent for oceanfront plantings and is common in rock gardens; cultivars are available that grow in a spreading fashion and can be used as a ground cover

Botanical name: *Forestiera segregata*
Common name: Wild Olive, Ink Bush, Florida Privet
Hardiness range: 8B to 11
Mature size: 10–15 feet tall by 6–10 feet wide
Light requirement: partial shade to full sun
Leaf persistence: evergreen and semievergreen
Flower: green and white; inconspicuous in spring and winter
Soil moisture: tolerates drought and flooding
Soil pH tolerance: acid to alkaline
Uses: woodland garden; border; screen; hedge; massing; small shade tree
Attributes: pest tolerant; wetlands plant; attracts butterflies
Native: coastal Florida and Georgia
Notes: shrub or small tree that is densely foliated with small, evergreen leaves; bark of older plants roughened by many small, raised lenticels

Botanical name: *Ilex vomitoria* 'Nana'
Common name: Dwarf Yaupon Holly
Hardiness range: 7A to 10A
Mature size: 4–7 feet tall by 6–10 feet wide
Light requirement: full shade to full sun
Leaf persistence: evergreen
Flower: white; inconspicuous in spring
Soil moisture: tolerates drought and flooding
Soil pH tolerance: acid to slightly alkaline
Uses: bonsai; foundation planting; mass planting; hedge
Attributes: good evergreen dwarf shrub
Native: eastern North America to central Florida
Notes: stays dense but requires yearly pruning to keep within bounds

Botanical name: *Jacquinia keyensis*
Common name: Joewood
Hardiness range: 10B to 11
Mature size: 6–20 feet tall and wide
Light requirement: partial shade to full sun
Leaf persistence: evergreen
Flower: pale yellow; fragrant and showy year-round
Soil moisture: tolerates drought
Soil pH tolerance: acid to alkaline
Uses: containers; border; espalier; specimen
Attributes: fragrant, attractive flowers
Native: Florida Keys into the Caribbean
Notes: listed as a threatened species in Florida; bark of this plant is an attractive dark brown or blue-gray and is commonly mottled on older plants

Botanical name: *Juniperus × media* (many cultivars)
Common name: Juniper
Hardiness range: 5A to 10A
Mature size: 2–3 feet tall by 8–15 feet wide
Light requirement: partial shade to full sun
Leaf persistence: evergreen
Flower: brown and yellow; inconspicuous in spring
Soil moisture: tolerates drought
Soil pH tolerance: acid to alkaline
Uses: border; foundation planting; massing; ground cover; erosion control
Attributes: attractive foliage
Native: China, Mongolia, Japan
Notes: tolerates alkaline soil and is quite drought-tolerant, but root regeneration is slow after transplanting from a field nursery

Botanical name: *Lantana camara*
Common name: Yellow Sage, Lantana, Shrub Verbena
Hardiness range: 8B to 11
Mature size: 4–6 feet tall by 3–6 feet wide
Light requirement: partial shade to full sun
Leaf persistence: evergreen
Flower: orange, pink, red, salmon, white, and yellow; very showy year-round
Soil moisture: tolerates drought
Soil pH tolerance: acid to alkaline
Uses: invasive
Attributes: attracts birds and butterflies
Native: tropical America, naturalized from Florida to Texas
Notes: survives on poor soil and hot, dry, sunny locations; may produce fewer blooms if given too much water and fertilizer; the cultivar 'New Gold' is considered noninvasive because it does not produce viable seed

Botanical name: *Lantana montevidensis*
Common name: Purple Lantana, Trailing Lantana, Weeping Lantana
Hardiness range: 8B to 11
Mature size: 2–3 feet tall by 6–10 feet wide
Light requirement: full sun
Leaf persistence: evergreen
Flower: lavender; very showy in fall and winter
Soil moisture: tolerates drought
Soil pH tolerance: acid to alkaline
Uses: containers; border; massing; specimen; ground cover
Attributes: attracts birds and butterflies
Native: South America
Notes: once-a-year pruning in the spring can keep the plant as a lower ground cover and eliminates the woody growth; originally available only in lavender, now there is a white cultivar called 'Monma' (trade name is White Lightning) and a pink-and-white cultivar called 'Monswee'

Botanical name: *Ligustrum japonicum*
Common name: Waxleaf Privet, Japanese Ligustrum, Waxleaf Ligustrum, Japanese Privet
Hardiness range: 7B to 11B
Mature size: 12–18 feet tall by 15–25 feet wide
Light requirement: partial shade to full sun
Leaf persistence: evergreen
Flower: white; showy in spring and summer
Soil moisture: tolerates some drought
Soil pH tolerance: acid to slightly alkaline
Uses: containers; rock garden; border; screen; specimen; hedge; small shade tree
Attributes: pest tolerant
Native: Japan, Korea
Notes: grows in a wide range of soil types, including clay, as long as soils drain well after a rain

Botanical name: *Mallotonia gnaphalodes*
Common name: Sea Lavender
Hardiness range: 10B to 11
Mature size: 2–4 feet tall by 6–10 feet wide
Light requirement: full sun
Leaf persistence: evergreen
Flower: white; showy in fall and winter
Soil moisture: tolerates drought
Soil pH tolerance: acid to alkaline
Uses: massing; erosion control
Attributes: attractive flowers
Native: Florida
Notes: one of the best adapted small shrubs or tall ground covers for the seaside landscape; will grow in the first dune; small white flowers are produced year-round among the developing leaves

Botanical name: *Nerium oleander*
Common name: Oleander, Rose Bay
Hardiness range: 8B to 11
Mature size: 10–15 feet tall and wide
Light requirement: full sun
Leaf persistence: evergreen
Flower: orange, pink, red, white, or yellow; fragrant and very showy year-round
Soil moisture: tolerates drought
Soil pH tolerance: acid to alkaline
Uses: containers; border; screen; foundation planting; street tree; standard; massing; specimen
Attributes: attractive flowers
Native: Mediterranean region to Japan
Notes: can grow in slightly brackish water but needs all-day full sun for best growth, form, and flowering; all parts are poisonous; dwarf cultivars grow slowly

Botanical name: *Opuntia* spp.
Common name: Prickly Pear Cactus
Hardiness range: 3B to 11
Mature size: 2–10 feet tall by 1–10 feet wide
Light requirement: full sun
Leaf persistence: deciduous
Flower: orange, red, and yellow; showy in summer
Soil moisture: tolerates drought and salt
Soil pH tolerance: neutral to slightly alkaline
Uses: containers; border; specimen
Attributes: attractive flowers
Native: North and South America
Notes: forms irregular clumps of shrublike mounds and has a very coarse texture; leaves are inconspicuous; however, platelike sections of the stem are often thought of as leaves

Botanical name: *Phormium tenax*
Common name: New Zealand Flax, Coastal Flax, New Zealand Hemp
Hardiness range: 8A to 10B
Mature size: 4–7 feet tall by 4–6 feet wide
Light requirement: partial shade to full sun
Leaf persistence: evergreen
Flower: red; showy in spring and summer
Soil moisture: tolerates some drought
Soil pH tolerance: acid to neutral
Uses: containers; border; foundation planting; massing; specimen
Attributes: dramatic structure and form
Native: New Zealand
Notes: has woody, beanlike fruit which appears once blooming has ceased; many cultivars and hybrids are available with variations in leaf color and size

Botanical name: *Pithecellobium bahamensis*
Common name: Blackbead
Hardiness range: 10A to 11
Mature size: 10–15 feet tall and wide
Light requirement: full sun
Leaf persistence: evergreen
Flower: pink and white; showy in summer
Soil moisture: tolerates drought
Soil pH tolerance: acid to alkaline
Uses: border; screen; massing; specimen
Attributes: pest tolerant; attracts butterflies; attractive fruit
Native: Florida and West Indies
Notes: shrub or small spreading tree that is found in pinelands, hammocks, and dunes in southern Florida and the Keys; flowers are followed by showy, reddish brown fruits

Botanical name: *Pittosporum tobira*
Common name: Japanese Pittosporum, Australian Laurel
Hardiness range: 8A to 11
Mature size: 6–15 feet tall by 10–30 feet wide
Light requirement: partial shade to full sun
Leaf persistence: evergreen
Flower: white; fragrant and inconspicuous in spring
Soil moisture: tolerates some drought, but not wet soil
Soil pH tolerance: acid to alkaline
Uses: containers; border; screen; massing; hedge; small tree
Attributes: attractive foliage
Native: China, Japan
Notes: rapid growth when young makes this a fairly high-maintenance shrub, requiring frequent pruning; growth does slow with age as the plant reaches about 15 feet tall; careful training and pruning can create an ornamental small tree form; declines in wet soil; thrives along coasts

Botanical name: *Rhaphiolepis decourii* 'Majestic Beauty'
Common name: Indian Hawthorn, 'Majestic Beauty'
Hardiness range: 8A to 10A
Mature size: 10–12 feet tall and wide
Light requirement: partial shade to full sun
Leaf persistence: evergreen
Flower: pink; fragrant and showy in spring
Soil moisture: tolerates drought
Soil pH tolerance: acid to alkaline
Uses: specimen; patio tree
Attributes: attractive flowers
Native: Japan
Notes: high salt tolerance makes this plant especially useful for seaside plantings; deer appear to enjoy the foliage

Botanical name: *Rhaphiolepis indica* (syn. *Raphiolepsis indica*)
Common name: Indian Hawthorn
Hardiness range: 8A to 11
Mature size: 4–10 feet tall by 3–10 feet wide
Light requirement: partial shade to full sun
Leaf persistence: evergreen
Flower: pink and white; fragrant and showy in spring
Soil moisture: tolerates some drought; but not wet soil
Soil pH tolerance: acid to alkaline
Uses: border; foundation planting; massing; ground cover; erosion control
Attributes: attractive flowers and fruit
Native: southern China
Notes: select from disease-resistant cultivars and plant in full sun to avoid serious foliage disease; great shrub for the coast

Botanical name: *Rhus integrifolia*
Common name: Lemonade Berry
Hardiness range: 8B to 10B
Mature size: 3–20 feet tall by 5–15 feet wide
Light requirement: partial shade to full sun
Leaf persistence: evergreen
Flower: pink and white; showy in spring
Soil moisture: tolerates drought
Soil pH tolerance: acid to slightly alkaline
Uses: screen; hedge; massing; erosion control
Attributes: good roadside plant
Native: southern California
Notes: can be trained into hedges and espaliers; pollen can cause significant allergies

Botanical name: *Robinia hispida*
Common name: Moss Locust, Bristly Locust
Hardiness range: 5A to 8A
Mature size: 5–7 feet tall by 10–15 feet wide
Light requirement: partial shade to full sun
Leaf persistence: deciduous
Flower: pink and red; very showy in spring
Soil moisture: tolerates drought
Soil pH tolerance: acid to alkaline
Uses: massing; ground cover; erosion control
Attributes: attractive flowers
Native: southeastern United States
Notes: spreads by stolons, forming a thicket; makes a good reclamation plant for a landfill or mine site

Botanical name: *Scaevola frutescens*
Common name: Beach Naupaka, Hawaiian Beach Berry, Scaevola
Hardiness range: 10A to 11
Mature size: 6–12 feet tall by 4–10 feet wide
Light requirement: partial shade to full sun
Leaf persistence: evergreen
Flower: white; fragrant and inconspicuous in summer
Soil moisture: tolerates drought well
Soil pH tolerance: acid to alkaline
Uses: invasive
Attributes: attractive foliage
Native: islands and coasts of Indian and Pacific Oceans
Notes: has fleshy, bright green leaves that are densely clustered at the tips of the branches; fruits are white, fleshy, oval, and attractive; was used for erosion control but has become invasive

Botanical name: *Scaevola plumieri*
Common name: Inkberry
Hardiness range: 10A to 11
Mature size: 2–4 feet tall by 3–6 feet wide
Light requirement: partial shade to full sun
Leaf persistence: evergreen
Flower: white; inconspicuous in summer
Soil moisture: tolerates drought
Soil pH tolerance: acid to alkaline
Uses: border; foundation planting; massing; erosion control
Attributes: provides excellent cover for many birds
Native: Florida, West Indies, South America
Notes: foliage is clustered toward the tips of the branches and is thick, fleshy, and a glossy, medium green; the fruits are black, glossy, smooth, and fairly prominent among the foliage; exceptionally salt tolerant

Botanical name: *Senna polyphylla* (syns. *Cassia marginata; Cassia polyphylla*)
Common name: Senna
Hardiness range: 10A to 11
Mature size: 6–10 feet tall and wide
Light requirement: partial shade to full sun
Leaf persistence: evergreen
Flower: yellow; showy in spring, summer, and fall
Soil moisture: tolerates drought
Soil pH tolerance: acid to slightly alkaline
Uses: border; massing; specimen; containers
Attributes: pest tolerant; attracts butterflies
Native: Virgin Islands
Notes: cascading habit

Botanical name: *Sophora tomentosa*
Common name: Silver Bush, Necklace Pod, Hairy Sophora
Hardiness range: 10A to 11
Mature size: 6–10 feet tall and wide
Light requirement: full sun
Leaf persistence: evergreen
Flower: yellow; showy and appearing periodically throughout the year
Soil moisture: tolerates drought
Soil pH tolerance: acid to alkaline
Uses: seashore planting; border; massing; specimen; containers
Attributes: pest tolerant; attracts butterflies; attractive flowers
Native: southern Florida, West Indies, South America
Notes: the evergreen foliage of this plant is a wonderful silvery green color; flowers open from the base to the elongating tip of the flower spike; best to locate it where it will not need to be pruned; can be trained to a small tree

Botanical name: *Suriana maritima*
Common name: Bay Cedar
Hardiness range: 10B to 11
Mature size: 6–10 feet tall and wide
Light requirement: full sun
Leaf persistence: evergreen
Flower: yellow; inconspicuous and appearing periodically throughout the year
Soil moisture: tolerates drought
Soil pH tolerance: acid to alkaline
Uses: border; massing; specimen; erosion control
Attributes: attracts butterflies; attractive silvery foliage
Native: southern Florida, Caribbean, Central America, Bahamas
Notes: commonly found growing in thickets on sand dunes and rocky shores, often just behind the high-tide line; has a sturdy, branched trunk that has beautiful, dark brown, rough, flaky bark

Botanical name: *Syzygium paniculatum*
Common name: Brush Cherry
Hardiness range: 10A to 11
Mature size: 10–15 feet tall and wide
Light requirement: partial shade to full sun
Leaf persistence: evergreen
Flower: white; inconspicuous in summer
Soil moisture: tolerates drought
Soil pH tolerance: acid to slightly alkaline
Uses: border; screen; hedge; massing; specimen
Attributes: edible fruit
Native: Australia
Notes: small leaves, year-round growth, and a compact habit make this plant well suited for hedges, espaliers, and topiaries

Botanical name: *Tamarix ramosissima*
Common name: Tamarisk, Salt Cedar
Hardiness range: 2A to 9A
Mature size: 10–15 feet tall and wide
Light requirement: full sun
Leaf persistence: deciduous
Flower: pink; showy in spring and summer
Soil moisture: tolerates drought
Soil pH tolerance: acid to slightly alkaline
Uses: invasive
Native: eastern Europe to central and eastern Asia
Attributes: attractive flowers
Notes: grows too large for most residential landscapes; invasive and has covered more than 1 million acres in the Southwest—do not plant it

Botanical name: *Tecomaria capensis*
Common name: Cape Honeysuckle
Hardiness range: 9B to 11
Mature size: 6–10 feet tall and wide
Light requirement: full sun
Leaf persistence: evergreen
Flower: orange or yellow; very showy year-round
Soil moisture: tolerates some drought
Soil pH tolerance: acid to alkaline
Uses: border; specimen; possible hedge; containers; arbor; trellis
Attributes: pest tolerant; attractive flowers
Native: South Africa
Notes: beautiful when grown on an arbor or fence; Cape Honeysuckle can also be trained into a single-trunk small tree; habit is a viny shrub

Botanical name: *Thevetia peruviana*
Common name: Bestill Tree, Yellow Oleander, Lucky Nut
Hardiness range: 10A to 11
Mature size: 15–30 feet tall and wide
Light requirement: full sun
Leaf persistence: evergreen
Flower: yellow or peach-colored; fragrant and showy in summer
Soil moisture: tolerates some drought
Soil pH tolerance: acid to alkaline
Uses: screen; pollarding; massing; specimen; small tree
Attributes: attractive fruit
Native: tropical America
Notes: nice large shrub for tropical and subtropical landscapes; may escape cultivation; all parts of the plant are poisonous

Botanical name: *Viburnum suspensum*
Common name: Sandankwa Viburnum
Hardiness range: 8B to 10B
Mature size: 6–10 feet tall by 3–6 feet wide
Light requirement: partial shade to full sun
Leaf persistence: evergreen
Flower: white; inconspicuous in winter and spring
Soil moisture: tolerates some drought and occasional wetness
Soil pH tolerance: acid to alkaline
Uses: border; screen; foundation planting; hedge; massing
Attributes: leaves have sour bacon odor
Native: Japan; Ryukyu Islands
Notes: will tolerate full sun if given sufficient moisture; needs pruning to rejuvenate after 5–10 years; makes a great hedge, even on the dunes

Botanical name: *Yucca aloifolia*
Common name: Spanish Bayonet, Dagger Plant, Yucca
Hardiness range: 8A to 10A
Mature size: 10–15 feet tall by 3–6 feet wide
Light requirement: partial shade to full sun
Leaf persistence: evergreen
Flower: white; showy in spring and summer
Soil moisture: tolerates drought
Soil pH tolerance: acid to alkaline
Uses: containers; border; massing; specimen
Attributes: attracts butterflies
Native: southern United States, West Indies, Mexico
Notes: leaf margins on Spanish Dagger *(Y. gloriosa)* are smooth and leaf tips droop, whereas margins on Spanish Bayonet *(Y. aloifolia)* are rough and tips are sharp and stiff

Botanical name: *Yucca elata*
Common name: Soapweed Yucca, Soapweed
Hardiness range: 9A to 11
Mature size: 10–15 feet wide by 3–6 feet wide
Light requirement: full shade to full sun
Leaf persistence: evergreen
Flower: green and white; showy in spring and summer
Soil moisture: tolerates drought
Soil pH tolerance: acid to alkaline
Uses: border; specimen; massing; accent
Attributes: mostly nonallergenic; tolerates nearly full shade
Native: western Texas, Arizona, New Mexico
Notes: does well on any well-drained soil and should be watered sparingly, if at all

Botanical name: *Yucca filamentosa* (syn. *Yucca concave*)
Common name: Adam's Needle, Desert Candle, Needle Palm, Spanish Bayonet, Yucca
Hardiness range: 6A to 10A
Mature size: 2–3 feet tall by 3–6 feet wide
Light requirement: partial shade to full sun
Leaf persistence: evergreen
Flower: white; showy in spring
Soil moisture: tolerates drought
Soil pH tolerance: acid to alkaline
Uses: containers; rock garden; border; foundation planting; massing; specimen; ground cover; erosion control
Attributes: attracts butterflies
Native: southeastern United States
Notes: leaf terminates in a sharp spine and margins are filamentous; plants stay small; in summer, a tall, showy flower spike emerges from the center of the plant and displays prominently for several weeks

Botanical name: *Yucca gloriosa*
Common name: Spanish Dagger, Mound Lily Yucca
Hardiness range: 6A to 11
Mature size: 6–10 feet tall by 6–10 feet wide
Light requirement: partial shade to full sun
Leaf persistence: evergreen
Flower: white; very showy in spring and summer
Soil moisture: tolerates drought
Soil pH tolerance: acid to alkaline
Uses: massing; specimen
Attributes: attracts butterflies
Native: North Carolina to Florida
Notes: with the sharp-needled tips removed with shears, Spanish Dagger makes a wonderful accent at entryways or in a shrub border, and plants eventually form attractive clumps

Botanical name: *Zamia furfuracea*
Common name: Cardboard Cycad, Cardboard Plant
Hardiness range: 9B to 11
Mature size: 2–6 feet tall and 4–6 feet wide
Light requirement: partial shade to full sun
Leaf persistence: evergreen
Flower: no flowers
Soil moisture: tolerates drought
Soil pH tolerance: acid to alkaline
Uses: containers; foundation planting; massing; specimen; ground cover
Attributes: naturalizing in some locales
Native: West Indies, Mexico
Notes: slow growing; adapts easily to being a houseplant

Moderately Salt-Tolerant Shrubs

Botanical name: *Acalypha wilkesiana*
Common name: Copperleaf, Jacob's Coat
Hardiness range: 10B to 11
Mature size: 10–15 feet tall by 6–8 feet wide
Light requirement: partial shade or partial sun
Leaf persistence: evergreen
Flower: red; inconspicuous in summer
Soil moisture: tolerates some drought and occasional wetness
Soil pH tolerance: acid to slightly alkaline
Uses: containers; border; screen; foundation planting; massing; specimen
Attributes: attractive coppery red foliage
Native: South Pacific Islands
Notes: best grown in a subtropical landscape or in containers with a well-draining soil mix

Botanical name: *Acca sellowiana* (syn. *Feijoa sellowiana*)
Common name: Pineapple Guava, Feijoa
Hardiness range: 8A to 11
Mature size: 10–15 feet tall and wide
Light requirement: partial shade to full sun
Leaf persistence: evergreen
Flower: red and white; showy in spring
Soil moisture: tolerates drought and salt well; will grow in dry soil
Soil pH tolerance: acid to slightly alkaline
Uses: screen; standard; massing
Attributes: pest tolerant; great small tree
Native: southern Brazil, Paraguay, Uruguay, and northern Argentina
Notes: can be pruned to form a hedge or a small tree; bark on small tree is quite showy; pollen can cause mild allergies

Botanical name: *Aloe chabaudii*
Common name: Aloe
Hardiness range: 9A to 11
Mature size: 2–4 feet tall by 4–10 feet wide
Light requirement: partial shade to full sun
Leaf persistence: evergreen
Flower: red; showy in winter
Soil moisture: tolerates drought
Soil pH tolerance: acid to slightly alkaline
Uses: containers; rock garden; massing; ground cover
Attributes: drought tolerant
Native: South Africa
Notes: easy to grow in very well-drained soil; protect when temperature drops below 29 degrees F; sterile, so propagate it by division

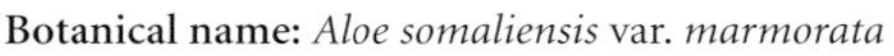

Botanical name: *Aloe somaliensis* var. *marmorata*
Common name: Aloe
Hardiness range: 9A to 11
Mature size: 2–3 feet tall by 1–2 feet wide
Light requirement: full shade to full sun
Leaf persistence: evergreen
Flower: red; showy in winter
Soil moisture: tolerates drought
Soil pH tolerance: acid to slightly alkaline
Uses: containers; rock garden; border; massing; ground cover
Attributes: drought tolerant
Native: Somali Republic
Notes: easy to grow in well-drained soil; protect when temperature drops below 29 degrees F; sterile, so propagate it by division

Botanical name: *Aloe ukambensis*
Common name: Aloe
Hardiness range: 9A to 11
Mature size: 2–3 feet tall and wide
Light requirement: full shade to full sun
Leaf persistence: evergreen
Flower: orange; showy in winter
Soil moisture: tolerates drought
Soil pH tolerance: acid to slightly alkaline
Uses: containers; rock garden; border; specimen; ground cover
Attributes: drought tolerant
Native: eastern Africa
Notes: easy to grow in well-drained soil; protect when temperature drops below 29 degrees F; sterile, so propagate it by division

Botanical name: *Alpinia zerumbet*
Common name: Shellflower Ginger, Ginger Lily
Hardiness range: 7B to 10A
Mature size: 6–7 feet tall by 3–4 feet wide
Light requirement: partial shade to full sun
Leaf persistence: evergreen
Flower: pink and white; fragrant and showy in summer
Soil moisture: tolerates some drought and occasional wetness
Soil pH tolerance: acid to slightly alkaline
Uses: containers; woodland garden; border; massing; specimen
Attributes: suitable for cut flowers
Native: eastern Asia
Notes: herbaceous perennial that is used in the landscape for its attractive foliage and shell-like flowers; leaves of variegated cultivars are green and yellow and are quite striking; white-and-pink fragrant flowers of variegated cultivars are borne in drooping clusters toward the stem ends

Botanical name: *Ananas comosus*
Common name: Pineapple
Hardiness range: 10A to 11
Mature size: 2–3 feet tall by 3–6 feet wide
Light requirement: partial shade to full sun
Leaf persistence: evergreen
Flower: purple and red; showy in summer
Soil moisture: tolerates drought
Soil pH tolerance: acid to slightly alkaline
Uses: containers; border; massing; specimen; ground cover for large areas
Attributes: attractive leaves and fruit
Native: Brazil
Notes: attractive as an ornamental; spineless cultivars, including 'Smooth Cayenne,' are recommended for planting in residential and commercial landscapes; can flower and produce fruit into zone 9A

Botanical name: *Annona glabra*
Common name: Pond Apple, Alligator Apple
Hardiness range: 10A to 11
Mature size: 15–25 feet tall and wide
Light requirement: partial shade to full sun
Leaf persistence: evergreen
Flower: yellowish white; fragrant and inconspicuous in spring
Soil moisture: tolerates some drought and flooding
Soil pH tolerance: acid to alkaline
Uses: screen; specimen
Attributes: pest tolerant; wetlands plant; attracts butterflies
Native: central and southern Florida, Caribbean, tropical America
Notes: large shrub or small tree found in wet, swampy areas in southern Florida; dull yellow fruit edible, but it is not planted for its fruit

Botanical name: *Baccharis halimifolia*
Common name: Groundselbush, Saltbush
Hardiness range: 4B to 9A
Mature size: 6–10 feet tall by 10–15 feet wide
Light requirement: full sun
Leaf persistence: deciduous
Flower: white; showy in fall
Soil moisture: tolerates some drought and flooding
Soil pH tolerance: acid to slightly alkaline
Uses: seashore planting
Attributes: wetlands plant; beautiful in fall in flower
Native: eastern and south-central United States, Mexico, West Indies
Notes: native to coastal and interior wetlands; often seen in its native habitat with Wax Myrtle; seeds are poisonous

Botanical name: *Baccharis salicina*
Common name: Baccharis
Hardiness range: 7B to 10A
Mature size: 3–4 feet tall by 2–4 feet wide
Light requirement: full sun
Leaf persistence: deciduous
Flower: white; showy in summer and fall
Soil moisture: tolerates some drought
Soil pH tolerance: acid to slightly alkaline
Uses: seashore planting
Attributes: attractive flowers; tolerates high soil salt
Native: south-central United States
Notes: grows best in full sun and well-drained soils; can be pruned back rather severely

Botanical name: *Bambusa* spp.
Common name: Bamboo
Hardiness range: 8A to 11
Mature size: 10–40 feet tall by 5–10 feet wide
Light requirement: partial shade to full sun
Leaf persistence: evergreen
Flower: inconspicuous
Soil moisture: tolerates some drought and occasional wetness; will grow in moist to wet soil
Soil pH tolerance: acid to slightly alkaline
Uses: containers; screen; specimen
Attributes: fast growing; potentially invasive
Native: southern China
Notes: grows about any place it is planted; can escape cultivation and become a pest in natural areas; place a root barrier constructed of steel, hard plastic, or fabric around the edge of the area where you want the plant contained; clumping types are less invasive

Botanical name: *Berberis julianae*
Common name: Wintergreen Barberry
Hardiness range: 6A to 9A
Mature size: 4–6 feet tall by 3–6 feet wide
Light requirement: partial shade to full sun
Leaf persistence: evergreen
Flower: white or yellow; showy in spring
Soil moisture: tolerates some drought
Soil pH tolerance: acid to alkaline
Uses: border; foundation planting; hedge; massing; erosion control
Attributes: pest tolerant; spiny foliage
Native: China
Notes: looks its best when grown on rich, somewhat moist soil in full sun or light, shifting shade; requires some pruning to maintain its best form; the center of the plant becomes thick with dead and living stems massed together

Botanical name: *Brunfelsia grandiflora*
Common name: Yesterday Today and Tomorrow
Hardiness range: 9B to 11
Mature size: 8–10 feet tall by 4–8 feet wide
Light requirement: partial shade to full sun
Leaf persistence: evergreen
Flower: blue, lavender, purple, and white; fragrant and showy spring through fall
Soil moisture: tolerates some drought
Soil pH tolerance: acid to alkaline
Uses: border; foundation planting; massing; specimen
Attributes: flowers change color from blue to purple to white
Native: western South America and Venezuela to Bolivia
Notes: one of the most beautiful landscaping plants; usually causes no allergies

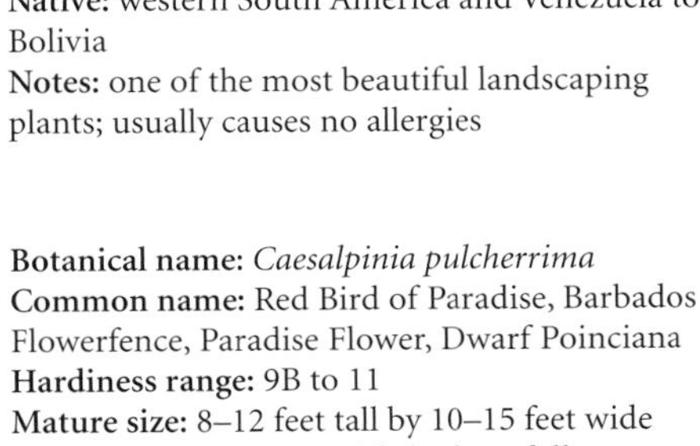

Botanical name: *Caesalpinia pulcherrima*
Common name: Red Bird of Paradise, Barbados Flowerfence, Paradise Flower, Dwarf Poinciana
Hardiness range: 9B to 11
Mature size: 8–12 feet tall by 10–15 feet wide
Light requirement: partial shade to full sun
Leaf persistence: evergreen
Flower: orange, red, and yellow; very showy and appearing periodically throughout the year
Soil moisture: tolerates drought
Soil pH tolerance: acid to alkaline
Uses: specimen
Attributes: pest tolerant; naturalizing; attracts butterflies
Native: West Indies
Notes: full sun is required for good flowering, but some shade is tolerated; pollen causes significant allergies in certain people

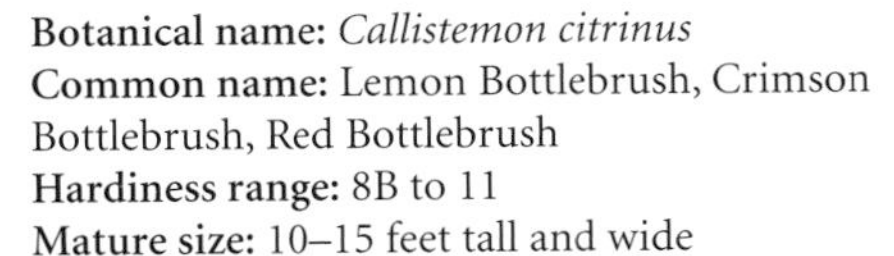

Botanical name: *Callistemon citrinus*
Common name: Lemon Bottlebrush, Crimson Bottlebrush, Red Bottlebrush
Hardiness range: 8B to 11
Mature size: 10–15 feet tall and wide
Light requirement: partial shade to full sun
Leaf persistence: evergreen
Flower: red; very showy in spring and summer
Soil moisture: tolerates drought
Soil pH tolerance: acid to slightly alkaline
Uses: containers; border; screen; espalier; pollarding; specimen
Attributes: attracts birds and butterflies; makes a nice small tree
Native: southeastern Australia
Notes: good choice for a sunny spot where you want flowers for the entire warm season; chlorotic plants in alkaline soil can often be greened up with regular applications of iron chelate

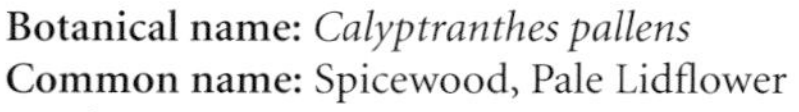

Botanical name: *Calyptranthes pallens*
Common name: Spicewood, Pale Lidflower
Hardiness range: 10B to 11
Mature size: 10–15 feet tall by 6–10 feet wide
Light requirement: partial shade to full sun
Leaf persistence: evergreen
Flower: white; fragrant and inconspicuous spring through fall
Soil moisture: tolerates some drought and occasional wetness
Soil pH tolerance: acid to alkaline
Uses: screen
Attributes: unique spicy fragrance; makes a nice small tree
Native: Miami to Key West, Florida
Notes: fruits change from green to orange, red, yellow, and then black; tree and fruits are appealing to many species of birds; smaller birds use the tree as cover

Botanical name: *Cereus uruguayanus* (syn. *Cereus peruvianus*)
Common name: Column Cactus, Curiosity Plant, Giant Club, Peruvian Apple
Hardiness range: 9A to 11
Mature size: 13–20 feet tall by 3–4 feet wide
Light requirement: full sun
Leaf persistence: evergreen
Flower: white; showy and lightly fragrant in summer
Soil moisture: tolerates drought; will grow in moist soil
Soil pH tolerance: neutral to slightly alkaline
Uses: containers; rock garden; specimen
Attributes: upright habit
Native: southeastern South America
Notes: needs shelter from wind; flowers occur when plant reaches maturity

Botanical name: *Chiococca alba*
Common name: West Indian Snowberry
Hardiness range: 10A to 11
Mature size: 4–6 feet tall by 6–10 feet wide
Light requirement: partial shade to full sun
Leaf persistence: evergreen
Flower: white and yellow; showy and appearing periodically throughout the year
Soil moisture: tolerates drought
Soil pH tolerance: acid to alkaline
Uses: woodland garden; specimen; trellis; espalier
Attributes: attractive flowers and fruit
Native: southern Florida and West Indies
Notes: common name used for this shrub refers to the large, ovoid, sparkling white fruits that follow the delightful flowers

Botanical name: *Clethra alnifolia*
Common name: Summer Sweet, Sweet Pepperbush
Hardiness range: 4A to 8B
Mature size: 3–8 feet tall by 3–6 feet wide
Light requirement: partial shade to full sun
Leaf persistence: deciduous
Flower: white; fragrant and showy in summer
Soil moisture: tolerates some drought and flooding
Soil pH tolerance: acid to slightly alkaline
Uses: screen; massing; specimen; foundation planting
Attributes: pest tolerant; wetlands plant; attracts butterflies
Native: eastern North America
Notes: great plant for wet, shaded, or sunny locations; flowers smell of spice and attract many bees; strong aroma may bother some people

Botanical name: *Cordyline terminalis*
Common name: Hawaiian Ti Plant, Good Luck Plant, Red Dracaena
Hardiness range: 10B to 11
Mature size: 4–6 feet tall by 1–3 feet wide
Light requirement: partial shade to full sun
Leaf persistence: evergreen
Flower: red, white, and yellow; inconspicuous in spring
Soil moisture: tolerates some drought
Soil pH tolerance: acid to slightly alkaline
Uses: containers; border; massing; specimen; indoor plant
Attributes: colorful foliage
Native: eastern Asia
Notes: grows well as a houseplant in a sunny location; for best leaf color, grow in partial shade

Botanical name: *Cotinus coggygria*
Common name: Smoke Tree, Smoke Bush, Wig Tree
Hardiness range: 5A to 8A
Mature size: 10–15 feet tall by 15–25 feet wide
Light requirement: full sun
Leaf persistence: deciduous
Flower: pink and white; showy in spring and summer
Soil moisture: tolerates drought
Soil pH tolerance: acid to alkaline
Uses: containers; border; screen; pollarding; massing; specimen
Attributes: attractive flowers
Native: southern Europe to Asia
Notes: useful in dry, rocky soil where there is no irrigation; grows in a wide range of soil pH; probably lives only 20 to 30 years or so in most situations

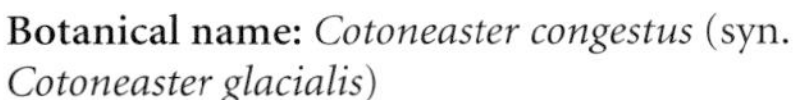

Botanical name: *Cotoneaster congestus* (syn. *Cotoneaster glacialis*)
Common name: Cotoneaster
Hardiness range: 6B to 9A
Mature size: 2–3 feet tall and wide
Light requirement: partial shade to full sun
Leaf persistence: evergreen and semievergreen
Flower: white; showy in spring
Soil moisture: tolerates drought
Soil pH tolerance: acid to alkaline
Uses: containers; rock garden; foundation planting; cascade; massing; ground cover; erosion control
Attributes: attractive fruit
Native: Himalayas
Notes: can be clipped easily into a variety of shapes

Botanical name: *Crassula ovata* (syn. *Crassula argentea*)
Common name: Jade Tree, Chinese Rubber Plant, Jade Plant
Hardiness range: 10A to 11
Mature size: 2–4 feet tall by 1–3 feet wide
Light requirement: full shade to partial sun
Leaf persistence: evergreen
Flower: pink and white; showy in spring
Soil moisture: tolerates drought and some salt
Soil pH tolerance: acid to slightly alkaline
Uses: containers; rock garden; indoor plant
Attributes: slow growing; thick leaves
Native: Africa
Notes: fast-draining soil is a necessity; water infrequently and only when the soil is very dry

Botanical name: *Cycas revoluta*
Common name: King Sago Palm, Japanese Sago Palm, Sago Palm
Hardiness range: 8B to 11
Mature size: 6–10 feet tall by 3–6 feet wide
Light requirement: partial shade to full sun
Leaf persistence: evergreen
Flower: no flowers
Soil moisture: tolerates drought
Soil pH tolerance: acid to slightly alkaline
Uses: containers; border; massing; specimen
Attributes: palmlike foliage
Native: southern Japan, Ryukyu Islands
Notes: performs very well in shade, part shade, or full sun and requires infrequent watering once established; foliage turns brown when temperatures dips to the low 20s

Botanical name: *Cyperus papyrus*
Common name: Papyrus, Egyptian Paper Plant, Egyptian Papyrus
Hardiness range: 9A to 11
Mature size: 6–10 feet tall and wide
Light requirement: partial shade to full sun
Leaf persistence: evergreen and semievergreen
Flower: green; showy year-round
Soil moisture: tolerates flooding and standing water
Soil pH tolerance: acid to slightly alkaline
Uses: **invasive**
Attributes: wetlands plant; grows submerged
Native: northern and tropical Africa
Notes: large sedge with strong, vertical canes; the delicate inflorescence sits atop a stout 3-angled cane and gives this plant a fine texture

Botanical name: *Euonymus japonicus*
Common name: Spindle Tree, Evergreen Euonymus, Japanese Euonymus
Hardiness range: 6B to 9A
Mature size: 6–12 feet tall by 3–8 feet wide
Light requirement: full shade to full sun
Leaf persistence: evergreen and semievergreen
Flower: green and white; inconspicuous in spring and summer
Soil moisture: will grow in moist, well-drained soil
Soil pH tolerance: acid to slightly alkaline
Uses: containers; woodland garden; border; screen; foundation planting; massing; specimen
Attributes: attractive fruit
Native: Japan
Notes: large shrub; showy, red-orange fruit is borne in the fall; dark green, deciduous foliage changes to showy bright red in the fall

Botanical name: *Fatsia japonica*
Common name: Japanese Fatsia, Japanese Aralia, False Castor-Oil Plant
Hardiness range: 8A to 11
Mature size: 4–6 feet tall by 5–8 feet wide
Light requirement: full shade to partial sun
Leaf persistence: evergreen
Flower: white; showy in fall
Soil moisture: tolerates some drought
Soil pH tolerance: acid to slightly alkaline
Uses: containers; massing; specimen
Attributes: coarse texture; attracts bees when flowering
Native: Japan
Notes: although tough and leathery in appearance, the leaves of Japanese Fatsia cannot tolerate sunny locations; an old plant becomes thin at the bottom and quite wide without pruning; cut large canes to the ground when the plant grows too large

Botanical name: *Hamelia patens*
Common name: Firebush, Scarlet Bush
Hardiness range: 9A to 11
Mature size: 6–15 feet tall by 5–15 feet wide
Light requirement: partial shade to full sun
Leaf persistence: evergreen
Flower: orange and red; showy year-round
Soil moisture: tolerates some drought and occasional wetness
Soil pH tolerance: acid to alkaline
Uses: containers; border; foundation planting; massing; specimen; possible hedge
Attributes: attracts birds and butterflies
Native: Florida, West Indies, south to Bolivia and Paraguay
Notes: can be found growing naturally in a variety of situations in the southern United States; can take heat and drought, but a strong wind can cause some leaf browning; killed to the ground in zone 8B in some winters, but it grows back and flowers

Botanical name: *Hibiscus syriacus*
Common name: Rose of Sharon, Althaea, Shrub Althea
Hardiness range: 5B to 9A
Mature size: 10–15 feet tall by 6–10 feet wide
Light requirement: partial shade to full sun
Leaf persistence: deciduous
Flower: blue, lavender, pink, purple, red, and white; very showy in summer
Soil moisture: tolerates some drought and occasional wetness
Soil pH tolerance: acid to slightly alkaline
Uses: containers; border; specimen
Attributes: attracts hummingbirds and butterflies
Native: China
Notes: plant in the perennial garden for the abundance of colorful flowers; too much or too little water, or overfertilization, could cause buds to drop from this plant; seeds often germinate in the landscape

Botanical name: *Ilex cornuta* 'Burfordii Nana'
Common name: Dwarf Burford Holly, Compact Burford Holly
Hardiness range: 7A to 9A
Mature size: 6–15 feet tall and wide
Light requirement: partial shade to full sun
Leaf persistence: evergreen
Flower: white; inconspicuous in spring; attracts bees
Soil moisture: tolerates drought, occasional wetness, and some salt
Soil pH tolerance: acid to alkaline
Uses: border; screen; foundation planting; hedge
Attributes: pest tolerant
Notes: watch for scale insects; foliage has sharp spine at tip

Botanical name: *Ilex cornuta* 'Rotunda'
Common name: Chinese Holly, Horned Holly
Hardiness range: 7A to 9A
Mature size: 4–6 feet tall by 6–10 feet wide
Light requirement: partial shade to full sun
Leaf persistence: evergreen
Flower: white; inconspicuous in spring
Soil moisture: tolerates drought; will grow in very dry to occasionally wet soil
Soil pH tolerance: acid to alkaline
Uses: border; foundation planting; massing; ground cover; erosion control
Attributes: pest tolerant
Native: eastern China
Notes: a common hedge plant for the south; sharp spines on foliage can limit usefulness in some locations

Botanical name: *Ilex crenata*
Common name: Japanese Holly, Box-Leaved Holly
Hardiness range: 6A to 8B
Mature size: 6–10 feet tall and wide
Light requirement: partial shade to full sun
Leaf persistence: evergreen
Flower: green and white; inconspicuous in spring
Soil moisture: tolerates drought
Soil pH tolerance: acid to slightly alkaline
Uses: border; foundation planting; espalier; hedge; massing
Attributes: compact habit; slow growing
Native: Japan
Notes: best used in mass groups as low shrubs, low hedges, or tall ground covers; eventually, the crowns grow completely together forming a sea of green; many cultivars available with different foliage characteristics, plant form, and size; very susceptible to damage by nematodes

Botanical name: *Ilex glabra*
Common name: Gallberry Holly, Inkberry Holly
Hardiness range: 5A to 10A
Mature size: 6–10 feet tall and wide
Light requirement: partial shade to full sun
Leaf persistence: evergreen
Flower: white; inconspicuous in spring
Soil moisture: tolerates some drought and flooding
Soil pH tolerance: acid to slightly alkaline
Uses: border; screen; foundation planting; hedge; massing
Attributes: pest tolerant; wetlands plant; attracts butterflies
Native: Nova Scotia to Florida and Texas
Notes: valued for its foliage and fruit; becomes somewhat open with age and often loses its small lower branches; female plants have berrylike black drupes that occur from September to May

Botanical name: *Ixora coccinea*
Common name: Ixora; Flame of the Woods, Jungle Geranium
Hardiness range: 10A to 11
Mature size: 6–10 feet tall by 3–6 feet wide
Light requirement: partial shade to full sun
Leaf persistence: evergreen
Flower: orange, pink, red, white, and yellow; very showy year-round
Soil moisture: tolerates some drought
Soil pH tolerance: acid to neutral
Uses: containers; border; screen; hedge; specimen
Attributes: attracts birds and butterflies; attractive flowers
Native: India
Notes: foliage turns yellow from manganese and iron deficiency in alkaline soil, especially along walks and foundations; a combination of potassium and phosphorus deficiency causes leaf spotting in sandy soils in Florida

Botanical name: *Juniperus chinensis*
Common name: Chinese Juniper, Juniper
Hardiness range: 4A to 10A
Mature size: 1–40 feet tall, depending on cultivar
Light requirement: full sun
Leaf persistence: evergreen
Flower: brown and yellow; inconspicuous in spring
Soil moisture: tolerates drought
Soil pH tolerance: acid to alkaline
Uses: screen; ground cover; erosion control
Attributes: drought tolerant
Native: China, Japan
Notes: grows best in full sun; needs well-drained soil or it will decline from root rot; cultivars of this species rule the marketplace

Botanical name: *Leucophyllum frutescens* (syn. *Leucophyllum texanum*)
Common name: Texas Sage, Silverleaf
Hardiness range: 7B to 10A
Mature size: 4–8 feet tall by 3–6 feet wide
Light requirement: full sun
Leaf persistence: evergreen
Flower: lavender, pink, purple, or white; showy in spring and summer
Soil moisture: tolerates drought
Soil pH tolerance: acid to alkaline
Uses: containers; screen; hedge; massing
Attributes: attractive silvery foliage and colorful flowers
Native: Texas, Mexico
Notes: root rot can set in and kill plants in soil kept too moist; once the plant is established, do not water it except in extended drought

Botanical name: *Mahonia aquifolium*
Common name: Oregon Grape, Oregon Holly Grape, Oregon Holly
Hardiness range: 4B to 8A
Mature size: 4–6 feet tall by 3–6 feet wide
Light requirement: full shade to full sun
Leaf persistence: evergreen
Flower: yellow; fragrant and showy in spring and winter
Soil moisture: tolerates some drought
Soil pH tolerance: acid to slightly alkaline
Uses: woodland garden; border; foundation planting; massing; specimen
Attributes: pest tolerant; attractive flowers and fruit
Native: northwestern North America
Notes: hollylike leaves, blue fruits, and striking yellow flowers; grows moderately fast; spreads slowly by the suckering root system

Botanical name: *Mahonia bealei*
Common name: Leatherleaf Mahonia
Hardiness range: 6B to 9A
Mature size: 7–10 feet tall by 5–10 feet wide
Light requirement: full shade to full sun
Leaf persistence: evergreen
Flower: yellow; fragrant and showy in spring
Soil moisture: tolerates some drought; will grow in dry soil
Soil pH tolerance: acid to slightly alkaline
Uses: rock garden; woodland garden; border; foundation planting; massing
Attributes: pest tolerant; attractive fruit
Native: Asia, Central America
Notes: performs best when given partial shade and well-drained soil; regular pruning is not required due to slow growth rate; flowers open over a 2- to 3-week period

Botanical name: *Malpighia coccigera*
Common name: Miniature Holly, Dwarf Holly, Singapore Holly
Hardiness range: 10B to 11
Mature size: 1–2 feet tall by 3–6 feet wide
Light requirement: partial shade to full sun
Leaf persistence: evergreen
Flower: pink; showy in spring and summer
Soil moisture: tolerates some drought
Soil pH tolerance: acid to alkaline
Uses: containers; rock garden; border; ground cover; erosion control
Attributes: compact habit
Native: West Indies
Notes: dwarf evergreen shrub that is valued for its compact habit and glossy green leaves; makes a dense ground cover as well as an interesting addition to the front of a shrub border

Botanical name: *Malpighia glabra*
Common name: Barbados Cherry
Hardiness range: 9B to 11
Mature size: 10–15 feet tall and wide
Light requirement: partial shade to full sun
Leaf persistence: evergreen
Flower: pink; showy in summer
Soil moisture: tolerates drought
Soil pH tolerance: acid to slightly alkaline
Uses: border; screen; specimen; fruit tree
Attributes: edible fruit
Native: Texas, south to northern South America, West Indies
Notes: well-suited as a foundation planting for larger buildings or used in the rear of the shrubbery border; often planted on residential property for the edible fruit

Botanical name: *Malvaviscus arboreus*
Common name: Turk's Cap, Wax Mallow, Scotch Purse
Hardiness range: 9A to 11
Mature size: 6–10 feet tall by 10–15 feet wide
Light requirement: partial shade to full sun
Leaf persistence: evergreen
Flower: red, pink, or white; showy year-round
Soil moisture: tolerates drought and occasional wetness
Soil pH tolerance: acid to slightly alkaline
Uses: containers; border; massing; specimen
Attributes: attractive flowers
Native: Mexico to Peru and Brazil
Notes: flowers best in full sun but will also flower nicely in partial shade, and any soil is acceptable; there are selections with white flowers and some with variegated foliage; grows fine in zone 8B even though the stems are occasionally killed in winter

Botanical name: *Podocarpus macrophyllus*
Common name: Chinese Podocarpus, Chinese Yew-Pine, Japanese Yew
Hardiness range: 8B to 11
Mature size: 15–25 feet tall by 8–15 feet wide
Light requirement: full shade to full sun
Leaf persistence: evergreen
Flower: yellow; inconspicuous in spring
Soil moisture: tolerates drought
Soil pH tolerance: acid to slightly alkaline
Uses: containers; border; screen; espalier; hedge; specimen; street tree
Attributes: pest tolerant; attracts birds
Native: central and southwestern Japan
Notes: versatile plant often used for hedges but can be trained into a nice small tree; do not plant in wet soils; magnesium deficiency can occur on excessively well-drained soils

Botanical name: *Polyscias balfouriana* 'Marginata' (syn. *Polyscias scutellaria*)
Common name: Ming Aralia, Balfour Aralia
Hardiness range: 10A to 11
Mature size: 4–8 feet tall by 3–6 feet wide
Light requirement: full shade to partial sun
Leaf persistence: evergreen
Flower: white; inconspicuous year-round
Soil moisture: tolerates drought and occasional wetness
Soil pH tolerance: acid to slightly alkaline
Uses: containers; border; screen; massing; specimen
Attributes: attractive foliage
Native: New Caledonia
Notes: well suited for containers placed indoors or out; its fine texture gives it a grace and elegance unmatched by other small tropical plants; leaves of the cultivar 'Marginata' have white edges

Botanical name: *Prunus laurocerasus*
Common name: Common Cherry Laurel, English Laurel
Hardiness range: 6A to 8B
Mature size: 12–20 feet tall and wide
Light requirement: full shade to full sun
Leaf persistence: evergreen
Flower: white; fragrant and showy in spring
Soil moisture: tolerates drought
Soil pH tolerance: acid to slightly alkaline
Uses: border; screen; specimen
Attributes: attractive foliage
Native: southeastern Europe, southwestern Asia
Notes: a fast-growing shrub that can reach a mature height of 12 to 20 feet but is smaller under cultivation; tolerates wet soil for only a short period of time; often pruned as a tall hedge or screen

Botanical name: *Psychotria nervosa*
Common name: Wild Coffee
Hardiness range: 10B to 11
Mature size: 6–10 feet tall by 3–6 feet wide
Light requirement: full shade to full sun
Leaf persistence: evergreen
Flower: white; inconspicuous in spring and summer
Soil moisture: tolerates drought
Soil pH tolerance: acid to alkaline
Uses: border; screen; foundation planting; hedge; massing; specimen
Attributes: pest tolerant; attracts butterflies
Native: southern Florida and West Indies
Notes: fruit resembles the true coffee bean; green, wrinkled, shiny foliage gives a rich texture to any landscape

Botanical name: *Pyracantha coccinea*
Common name: Firethorn, Pyracantha
Hardiness range: 6A to 9A
Mature size: 6–15 feet tall by 10–15 feet wide
Light requirement: partial shade to full sun
Leaf persistence: semievergreen
Flower: white; showy in spring
Soil moisture: tolerates drought and occasional wetness
Soil pH tolerance: acid to alkaline
Uses: espalier; erosion control
Attributes: attractive fruit
Native: southeastern Europe and Asia
Notes: flowers are borne on previous year's wood, so prune after flowering in the spring; sometimes grown as an espalier; fruit eaten by birds; without pruning, a messy-looking, open shrub

Botanical name: *Rosa* spp.
Common name: Rose
Hardiness range: 2B to 10B
Mature size: 5–10 feet tall and wide
Light requirement: full sun
Leaf persistence: deciduous
Flower: orange, pink, purple, red, white, or yellow; fragrant and very showy in summer and fall
Soil moisture: will grow in well-drained soil
Soil pH tolerance: acid to slightly alkaline
Uses: containers; rock garden; woodland garden; massing; specimen
Attributes: attracts birds and butterflies; suitable for cut flowers and for dried flowers
Native: throughout the northern hemisphere
Notes: requires full sun with good air circulation to minimize foliage diseases; it is best to plant resistant cultivars

Botanical name: *Russelia equisetiformis*
Common name: Firecracker Plant, Coral Plant, Fountain Bush
Hardiness range: 9B to 11
Mature size: 4–6 feet tall by 6–10 feet wide
Light requirement: full sun
Leaf persistence: evergreen
Flower: red; very showy year-round
Soil moisture: tolerates drought
Soil pH tolerance: acid to alkaline
Uses: containers; border; cascade; massing; specimen; erosion control
Attributes: attracts butterflies and hummingbirds
Native: Mexico
Notes: weeping shrub that, when in full bloom, looks as if it is raining flowers; fruits are small, inconspicuous, and hang in clusters; has escaped from cultivation in some areas

Botanical name: *Senna pendula* (syn. *Cassia pendula*)
Common name: Butterfly Bush
Hardiness range: 8B to 11
Mature size: 10–13 feet tall by 6–10 feet wide
Light requirement: partial shade to full sun
Leaf persistence: semievergreen
Flower: yellow; very showy in fall
Soil moisture: tolerates some drought
Soil pH tolerance: acid to slightly alkaline
Uses: **invasive**
Attributes: attracts butterflies and caterpillars
Native: China
Notes: tolerates many soil conditions; needs full sun for best growth and flowering; often falls over or leans to one side

Botanical name: *Sophora davidii*
Common name: Sophora
Hardiness range: 5B to 8B
Mature size: 8–12 feet tall by 10–12 feet wide
Light requirement: partial shade to full sun
Leaf persistence: deciduous
Flower: blue, lavender, and white; fragrant and showy in spring
Soil moisture: tolerates drought
Soil pH tolerance: neutral to alkaline
Uses: specimen
Attributes: showy trunk and flowers
Native: China
Notes: will tolerate hot, windy conditions and alkaline or wet soils

Botanical name: *Triphasia trifolia*
Common name: Limeberry
Hardiness range: 9B to 11
Mature size: 6–10 feet tall and wide
Light requirement: partial shade to full sun
Leaf persistence: evergreen
Flower: white; inconspicuous in spring through fall
Soil moisture: tolerates drought
Soil pH tolerance: acid to alkaline
Uses: hedge
Attributes: fragrant flowers; attractive fruit
Native: Southeast Asia
Notes: once used as a hedge or screen but is not popular now; has escaped cultivation in some areas

Botanical name: *Viburnum odoratissimum*
Common name: Sweet Viburnum
Hardiness range: 8B to 10A
Mature size: 15–25 feet tall and wide
Light requirement: full shade to full sun
Leaf persistence: evergreen
Flower: white; fragrant and showy in spring
Soil moisture: tolerates drought
Soil pH tolerance: acid to alkaline
Uses: border; screen; specimen; hedge; small tree
Attributes: attractive and fragrant flowers
Native: Himalayas to Japan
Notes: suitable as a small tree; flowers are followed by small, showy red berries that are highly ornamental and turn black when ripe

Botanical name: *Vitex trifolia*
Common name: Vitex
Hardiness range: 9B to 11
Mature size: 10–15 feet tall by 6–10 feet wide
Light requirement: full sun
Leaf persistence: evergreen and semievergreen
Flower: blue, lavender, or purple; showy in summer
Soil moisture: tolerates some drought
Soil pH tolerance: acid to alkaline
Uses: screen; specimen; small tree
Attributes: fragrant foliage
Native: Asia to Australia
Notes: fast-growing shrub; is popular for its delicate foliage and pretty blue flowers

Botanical name: *Zingiber zerumbet*
Common name: Pinecone Ginger, Shampoo Ginger, Pinecone Lily
Hardiness range: 9A to 11
Mature size: 6–7 feet tall by 3–6 feet wide
Light requirement: partial shade to full sun
Leaf persistence: semievergreen
Flower: yellow; showy in summer and fall
Soil moisture: tolerates some drought and occasional wetness
Soil pH tolerance: acid to slightly alkaline
Uses: border; massing; specimen
Attributes: attractive variegated foliage
Native: India and Malay Peninsula
Notes: short, braced inflorescence, resembling red pine cones, appear from the ground on 10-inch-tall stalks in autumn and are much-favored for use in floral arrangements; will usually grow back from roots even if the plant is killed back in winter in zone 8B

Slightly Salt-Tolerant Shrubs

Botanical name: *Abelia grandiflora*
Common name: Glossy Abelia
Hardiness range: 5B to 9A
Mature size: 6–10 feet tall and wide
Light requirement: partial shade to full sun
Leaf persistence: evergreen
Flower: pink; fragrant and showy spring through fall
Soil moisture: tolerates some drought
Soil pH tolerance: acid to slightly alkaline
Uses: border; screen; hedge; massing; specimen; erosion control
Attributes: pest tolerant; attracts butterflies
Native: unknown
Notes: variegated and dwarf cultivars available; often pruned into a hedge, but poorly suited for this purpose; best pruned by reduction (not hedged)

Botanical name: *Berberis thunbergii*
Common name: Japanese Barberry
Hardiness range: 4A to 8A
Mature size: 3–6 feet tall by 4–6 feet wide
Light requirement: full shade to full sun
Leaf persistence: semievergreen
Flower: yellowish white; inconspicuous in spring
Soil moisture: tolerates some drought
Soil pH tolerance: acid to alkaline
Uses: rock garden; woodland garden; border; foundation planting; hedge; erosion control
Attributes: pest tolerant
Native: eastern Asia
Notes: thorny, so it can be used as a barrier; purple-leafed cultivars turn green in shade; can be sheared and used as a hedge

Botanical name: *Breynia nivosa* (syn. *Breynia distacha*)
Common name: Snow Bush
Hardiness range: 9B to 11
Mature size: 4–6 feet tall by 3–6 feet wide
Light requirement: partial shade to full sun
Leaf persistence: evergreen
Flower: white; showy in summer and fall
Soil moisture: tolerates some drought
Soil pH tolerance: acid to slightly alkaline
Uses: containers; border; screen; hedge; specimen
Attributes: attractive foliage
Native: Pacific Islands and other tropics
Notes: vase-shaped to rounded plant has variegated leaves with white, green, and red coloration; dwarf cultivars are better suited for landscape than the parent species

Botanical name: *Buddleia* spp.
Common name: Butterfly Bush
Hardiness range: 6A to 10B
Mature size: 6–12 feet tall and wide
Light requirement: partial shade to full sun
Leaf persistence: deciduous and semievergreen
Flower: pink, red, white, or purple; showy in spring and summer
Soil moisture: tolerates some drought and occasional wetness
Soil pH tolerance: acid to alkaline
Uses: containers; rock garden; border; specimen
Attributes: attracts hummingbirds, birds, and butterflies; suitable for cut flowers
Native: hybrid
Notes: becomes a tangled, woody mess after a couple of years and needs to be cut back; cultivars are available in a variety of flower colors; often cut back each spring; has become invasive in some regions

Botanical name: *Buxus microphylla*
Common name: Littleleaf Box, Boxwood
Hardiness range: 6A to 10A
Mature size: 3–6 feet tall and wide
Light requirement: partial shade to full sun
Leaf persistence: evergreen
Flower: green; inconspicuous in spring
Soil moisture: tolerates some drought
Soil pH tolerance: acid to slightly alkaline
Uses: containers; foundation planting; hedge; border
Attributes: tolerates shearing exceptionally well
Native: Japan
Notes: best grown where the root zone can be mulched and left undisturbed; requires a well-drained soil; often clipped, but can be reduction pruned as well

Botanical name: *Calliandra haematocephala* (syn. *Calliandra inaequilatera*)
Common name: Powderpuff
Hardiness range: 9B to 11
Mature size: 10–15 feet tall and wide
Light requirement: partial shade to full sun
Leaf persistence: evergreen
Flower: pink or red; slightly fragrant and showy year-round
Soil moisture: tolerates drought
Soil pH tolerance: acid to slightly alkaline
Uses: containers; espalier; specimen
Attributes: attracts butterflies
Native: Bolivia
Notes: may be used as a tall flowering hedge with regular clipping, or as a flowering tree with the lower branches removed; suckers often appear from the base of the plant; has whitefly and scale problems

Botanical name: *Camellia japonica*
Common name: Japanese Camellia
Hardiness range: 7A to 9B
Mature size: 10–15 feet tall by 6–10 feet wide
Light requirement: partial shade to full sun
Leaf persistence: evergreen
Flower: lavender, orange, pink, red, white, or yellow; very showy in winter to spring
Soil moisture: tolerates some drought
Soil pH tolerance: acid to slightly alkaline
Uses: containers; border; espalier; specimen
Attributes: attractive flowers
Native: coasts of Japan, South Korea, Taiwan
Notes: it is natural for some flower buds to drop, and it should not cause too much concern because camellias sometimes set more buds than they can open; sometimes bud drop can be caused by overwatering, but even more by underwatering, especially during summer

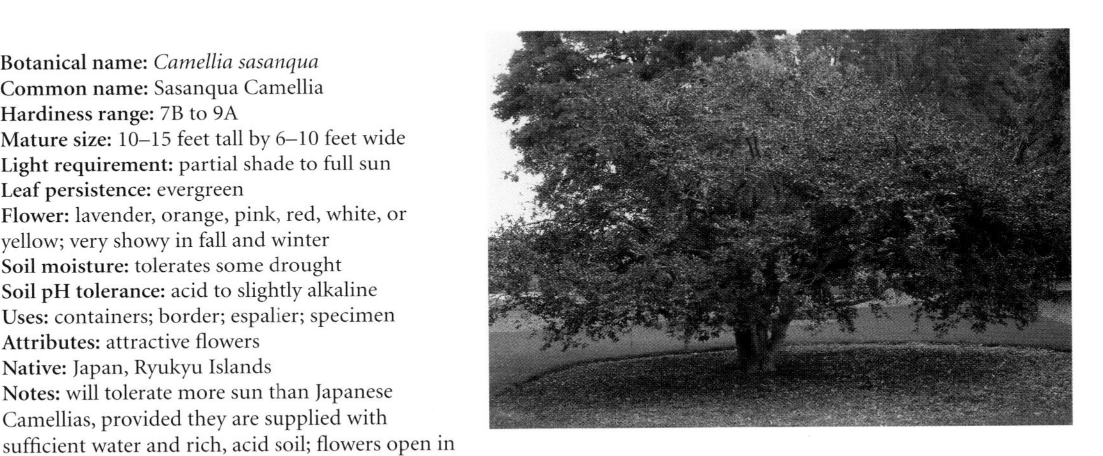

Botanical name: *Camellia sasanqua*
Common name: Sasanqua Camellia
Hardiness range: 7B to 9A
Mature size: 10–15 feet tall by 6–10 feet wide
Light requirement: partial shade to full sun
Leaf persistence: evergreen
Flower: lavender, orange, pink, red, white, or yellow; very showy in fall and winter
Soil moisture: tolerates some drought
Soil pH tolerance: acid to slightly alkaline
Uses: containers; border; espalier; specimen
Attributes: attractive flowers
Native: Japan, Ryukyu Islands
Notes: will tolerate more sun than Japanese Camellias, provided they are supplied with sufficient water and rich, acid soil; flowers open in fall before *C. japonica*

Botanical name: *Codiaeum variegatum*
Common name: Croton
Hardiness range: 10B to 11
Mature size: 4–6 feet tall by 3–6 feet wide
Light requirement: partial shade to full sun
Leaf persistence: evergreen
Flower: white; inconspicuous
Soil moisture: tolerates drought
Soil pH tolerance: acid to alkaline
Uses: containers; border; foundation planting; massing; specimen
Attributes: attracts butterflies; attractive variegated foliage
Native: Malay Peninsula and Pacific Islands
Notes: develops best leaf color when grown in full sun but can tolerate light, dappled shade; available in a great variety of beautiful leaf colors and shapes

Botanical name: *Duranta erecta* (syn. *Duranta repens*)
Common name: Golden Dewdrop, Pigeonberry, Sky Flower
Hardiness range: 9B to 11
Mature size: 10–15 feet tall and wide
Light requirement: partial shade to full sun
Leaf persistence: evergreen
Flower: lavender, purple, or white; fragrant and showy spring through fall
Soil moisture: tolerates drought
Soil pH tolerance: acid to slightly alkaline
Uses: border; espalier; cascade; massing; specimen; erosion control
Attributes: attracts butterflies; attractive orange fruit
Native: tropical America, possibly Florida
Notes: large, fast-growing, multistemmed shrub is popular as a screen or background planting, but is too vigorous and tall to use against the foundation or in small areas; clips into a hedge or espalier

Botanical name: *Erythrina herbacea*
Common name: Coral Bean, Cherokee Bean, Cardinal Spear, Eastern Coral Bean
Hardiness range: 8A to 11
Mature size: 4–6 feet tall by 6–10 feet wide
Light requirement: partial shade to full sun
Leaf persistence: evergreen and semievergreen
Flower: red; showy in spring and summer
Soil moisture: tolerates drought
Soil pH tolerance: acid to alkaline
Uses: woodland planting; specimen
Attributes: attractive flowers and showy fruit; attracts hummingbirds
Native: southern United States
Notes: stems are armed with short, backwardly curved spines; scarlet, tubular flowers are borne in 2-foot-long terminal spikes; seedpods split in the fall to reveal beautiful scarlet seeds

Botanical name: *Eugenia uniflora*
Common name: Surinam Cherry, Stopper
Hardiness range: 9B to 11
Mature size: 8–15 feet tall by 6–10 feet wide
Light requirement: full sun
Leaf persistence: evergreen
Flower: white; fragrant and showy in spring
Soil moisture: tolerates some drought and occasional wetness
Soil pH tolerance: acid to alkaline
Uses: invasive
Attributes: has been used as a hedge for decades; attractive orange fruit
Native: tropical America
Notes: has interesting tan, thin, peeling bark and multiple stems, which made it a good candidate for training into a small tree

Botanical name: *Euphorbia pulcherrima*
Common name: Poinsettia, Christmas Flower
Hardiness range: 9A to 10B
Mature size: 6–9 feet tall and wide
Light requirement: partial shade to full sun
Leaf persistence: evergreen
Flower: green; inconspicuous in winter
Soil moisture: will grow in moist soil
Soil pH tolerance: acid to slightly alkaline
Uses: containers; specimen
Attributes: very attractive modified leaves (bracts)
Native: western Mexico
Notes: unlike most Euphorbias, this plant is not considered poisonous; can be planted outdoors after enjoying indoors

Botanical name: *Galphimia glauca*
Common name: Thryallis, Rain of Gold
Hardiness range: 9B to 11
Mature size: 4–6 feet tall by 3–6 feet wide
Light requirement: full sun
Leaf persistence: evergreen
Flower: yellow; showy year-round
Soil moisture: tolerates some drought
Soil pH tolerance: acid to slightly alkaline
Uses: containers; border; foundation planting; massing; erosion control
Attributes: attractive flowers
Native: Mexico and Guatemala
Notes: full sun is needed for best appearance and flowering but it can tolerate some shade; killed to the ground at about 25 degrees F, but quickly regrows in the spring in zones 8B and 9

Botanical name: *Gardenia augusta* (syns. *Gardenia grandiflora, Gardenia jasminoides*)
Common name: Cape Jasmine, Gardenia
Hardiness range: 8A to 10A
Mature size: 4–8 feet tall by 5–8 feet wide
Light requirement: partial shade to full sun
Leaf persistence: evergreen
Flower: white; fragrant and showy in spring and summer
Soil moisture: tolerates some drought
Soil pH tolerance: acid to slightly alkaline
Uses: containers; border; screen; foundation planting; standard; specimen
Attributes: extremely fragrant flower; suitable for cut flowers
Native: China
Notes: has pure white flowers in late spring and early summer; dry soil, wet soil, insect infestation or root damage from digging, overfertilization, or nematodes can cause flower bud drop

Botanical name: *Hibiscus rosa-sinensis*
Common name: Chinese Hibiscus, Tropical Hibiscus
Hardiness range: 9A to 11
Mature size: 6–10 feet tall and wide
Light requirement: partial shade to full sun
Leaf persistence: evergreen
Flower: orange, pink, red, salmon, white, or yellow; very showy year-round
Soil moisture: tolerates some drought
Soil pH tolerance: acid to slightly alkaline
Uses: containers; border; specimen; standard; hedge
Attributes: attracts birds and butterflies
Native: tropical Asia
Notes: appreciates abundant watering and fertilization; attractive specimen plant when given enough room to allow development of its natural vase-shaped arching form; be sure to cut circling roots at planting

Botanical name: *Hibiscus schizopetalus*
Common name: Japanese Hibiscus, Japanese Lantern
Hardiness range: 9B to 11
Mature size: 6–10 feet tall and wide
Light requirement: partial shade to full sun
Leaf persistence: evergreen
Flower: orange, pink, red, salmon, white, or yellow; very showy year-round
Soil moisture: tolerates some drought
Soil pH tolerance: acid to slightly alkaline
Uses: containers; specimen
Attributes: attracts butterflies
Native: tropical Asia
Notes: flowers last for about one day, then close and drop from the plant; new ones usually emerge the next day

Botanical name: *Holmskioldia sanguinea*
Common name: Chinese Hat Plant
Hardiness range: 10B to 11
Mature size: 8–15 feet tall by 10–12 feet wide
Light requirement: partial shade to full sun
Leaf persistence: evergreen
Flower: orange and yellow; very showy year-round
Soil moisture: tolerates some drought
Soil pH tolerance: acid to slightly alkaline
Uses: border; specimen
Attributes: attractive flowers
Native: Himalayas
Notes: to some people, the bright orange flowers resemble a hat

Botanical name: *Jatropha integerrima*
Common name: Peregrina, Firecracker
Hardiness range: 10B to 11
Mature size: 10–15 feet tall and wide
Light requirement: partial shade to full sun
Leaf persistence: evergreen
Flower: red; very showy year-round
Soil moisture: tolerates some drought
Soil pH tolerance: acid to alkaline
Uses: containers; border; specimen
Attributes: pest tolerant; attracts birds and butterflies
Native: Cuba
Notes: flowers best in full sun; pollen causes severe allergies in some people; can be trained to a small tree

Botanical name: *Lagerstroemia indica*
Common name: Crape Myrtle
Hardiness range: 7A to 9B
Mature size: 6–25 feet tall and wide
Light requirement: full sun
Leaf persistence: deciduous
Flower: lavender, pink, purple, red, or white; very showy spring through fall
Soil moisture: tolerates some drought
Soil pH tolerance: acid to slightly alkaline
Uses: containers; border; street tree; pollarding; standard; massing; specimen
Attributes: attractive flowers and bark
Native: China
Notes: grows best in full sun with rich, moist soil but will tolerate less hospitable locations

Botanical name: *Michelia figo* (syn. *Michelia fuscata*)
Common name: Banana Shrub, Michelia
Hardiness range: 8A to 10A
Mature size: 12–20 feet tall by 12–15 feet wide
Light requirement: partial shade to full sun
Leaf persistence: evergreen
Flower: white; fragrant and showy in spring
Soil moisture: tolerates some drought
Soil pH tolerance: acid to slightly alkaline
Uses: border; specimen
Attributes: fragrant and attractive flowers
Native: China
Notes: flowers smell like ripening cantaloupes or bananas; this smell can be very pleasant but can also be overwhelming when these shrubs are massed together; typically infested with scales; can be trained to a small tree

Botanical name: *Murraya paniculata*
Common name: Orange Jasmine, Chalcas, Satinwood
Hardiness range: 9B to 11
Mature size: 6–10 feet tall and wide
Light requirement: partial shade to full sun
Leaf persistence: evergreen
Flower: white; fragrant and showy year-round
Soil moisture: tolerates drought
Soil pH tolerance: acid to alkaline
Uses: invasive
Attributes: fragrant white flowers
Native: Southeast Asia and Malay Peninsula
Notes: grows best in well-drained, nematode-free soil with moderate moisture

Botanical name: *Nandina domestica*
Common name: Heavenly Bamboo
Hardiness range: 6B to 9B
Mature size: 6–10 feet tall by 1–3 feet wide
Light requirement: partial shade to full sun
Leaf persistence: evergreen
Flower: white; showy in spring
Soil moisture: tolerates some drought
Soil pH tolerance: acid to alkaline
Uses: invasive
Attributes: attracts birds
Native: India to eastern Asia
Notes: has erect panicles of creamy white flowers in spring, followed by decorative bright red berries in fall and winter; berries are eaten by birds, and they can spread the seed to neighboring yards and woods

Botanical name: *Osmanthus fragrans*
Common name: Sweet Olive, Tea Olive
Hardiness range: 7B to 9A
Mature size: 15–25 feet tall and wide
Light requirement: partial shade to full sun
Leaf persistence: evergreen
Flower: white; fragrant and showy in spring and fall
Soil moisture: tolerates some drought
Soil pH tolerance: acid to slightly alkaline
Uses: containers; border; screen; specimen
Attributes: pest tolerant; outstanding flower fragrance
Native: eastern Asia
Notes: lustrous, medium-green leaves have paler undersides and are joined from October through March by a multitude of small but extremely fragrant white blossoms; makes a nice small tree

Botanical name: *Photinia × fraseri*
Common name: Fraser Photinia, Redtip Photinia
Hardiness range: 7B to 9A
Mature size: 15–25 feet tall by 10–20 feet wide
Light requirement: full sun
Leaf persistence: evergreen
Flower: white; very showy in summer
Soil moisture: tolerates drought
Soil pH tolerance: acid to slightly alkaline
Uses: screen; street tree in good soil; standard; specimen
Attributes: colorful foliage
Native: hybrid origin
Notes: requires good drainage and full sun to look its best; tolerates some shade and grows well unless infected with leaf spot; when planted in shaded landscapes often has severe leaf spot disease

Botanical name: *Plumbago auriculata* (syn. *Plumbago capensis*)
Common name: Cape Leadwort, Plumbago, Sky Flower
Hardiness range: 9A to 11
Mature size: 6–10 feet tall and wide
Light requirement: partial shade to full sun
Leaf persistence: evergreen
Flower: blue or white; slightly fragrant and very showy year-round
Soil moisture: tolerates some drought
Soil pH tolerance: acid to slightly alkaline
Uses: containers; border; foundation planting; cascade; massing; specimen; ground cover
Attributes: attracts butterflies; attractive flowers
Native: South Africa
Notes: needs full sun for best growth and flowering; leaves may yellow on soils with a high pH; responds well to an application or two of fertilizer during the growing season; the foliage can cause skin irritation in some people

Botanical name: *Spiraea cantoniensis*
Common name: Reeve's Spirea, Bridal Wreath
Hardiness range: 7A to 9A
Mature size: 4–6 feet tall by 4–8 feet wide
Light requirement: full sun
Leaf persistence: deciduous
Flower: white; fragrant and very showy in spring
Soil moisture: tolerates some drought
Soil pH tolerance: acid to slightly alkaline
Uses: border; screen; specimen
Attributes: attractive and fragrant flowers
Native: China
Notes: plants receiving less than 4 to 5 hours of direct sun become thin and flower poorly; flowers are produced on year-old growth, so pruning should be done just after flowering

Botanical name: *Tabernaemontana divaricata*
Common name: Crepe Jasmine, Butterfly Gardenia, Pinwheel Flower
Hardiness range: 10B to 11
Mature size: 6–10 feet tall and wide
Light requirement: partial shade to full sun
Leaf persistence: evergreen
Flower: white; showy year-round
Soil moisture: will grow in well-drained soil
Soil pH tolerance: acid to alkaline
Uses: containers; border; screen; foundation planting; massing; specimen
Attributes: pest tolerant
Native: India
Notes: requires frequent fertilization when in highly alkaline soils

Botanical name: *Tecoma stans*
Common name: Yellow Elder, Yellow Trumpet Flower, Yellow Bells
Hardiness range: 9B to 11
Mature size: 10–20 feet tall and wide
Light requirement: full sun
Leaf persistence: evergreen and semievergreen
Flower: yellow; very showy year-round
Soil moisture: tolerates drought
Soil pH tolerance: acid to alkaline
Uses: border; pollarding; specimen
Attributes: pest tolerant
Native: Mexico, south to South America
Notes: makes a nice addition to a deck or patio garden and is suited for planting in parking lot islands and street medians; often has a difficult time holding itself erect

Botanical name: *Ternstroemia gymnanthera* (syn. *Cleyera japonica*)
Common name: Cleyera
Hardiness range: 7B to 11
Mature size: 8–15 feet tall and wide
Light requirement: partial shade to full sun
Leaf persistence: evergreen
Flower: green and white; inconspicuous in summer
Soil moisture: tolerates some drought
Soil pH tolerance: acid to slightly alkaline
Uses: containers; massing; screen; hedge
Attributes: attractive foliage
Native: eastern Asia
Notes: requires full sun for best growth; makes a nice clipped hedge

Botanical name: *Tetrapanax papyriferus*
Common name: Rice Paper Plant, Chinese Rice Paper Plant
Hardiness range: 8B to 11
Mature size: 6–10 feet tall and wide
Light requirement: full shade to partial sun
Leaf persistence: evergreen
Flower: white; showy in fall
Soil moisture: tolerates some drought and occasional wetness
Soil pH tolerance: acid to slightly alkaline
Uses: containers; woodland garden; border; massing; specimen
Attributes: attractive flowers
Native: southern China, Taiwan
Notes: vigorous suckering habit makes it a bit too invasive for some gardeners; might be best in locations where its roots can be easily contained

Botanical name: *Thunbergia erecta*
Common name: Bush Clock Vine, King's Mantle
Hardiness range: 10A to 11
Mature size: 4–6 feet tall by 3–6 feet wide
Light requirement: partial shade to full sun
Leaf persistence: evergreen
Flower: purple; very showy year-round
Soil moisture: will grow in moist soil
Soil pH tolerance: acid to alkaline
Uses: containers; arbor; border; specimen; hedge
Attributes: attractive flowers and foliage
Native: tropical Africa
Notes: slightly fragrant, purple flowers have a yellow throat, grow to 1¼ inches long, and may appear singly or in small clusters, occurring year-round, especially in the summer

Botanical name: *Tibouchina granulosa*
Common name: Purple Glory Tree
Hardiness range: 10B to 11
Mature size: 15–20 feet tall and wide
Light requirement: full sun
Leaf persistence: evergreen
Flower: purple; very showy in spring, summer, and fall
Soil moisture: tolerates some drought
Soil pH tolerance: acid to slightly alkaline
Uses: border; pollarding; specimen; containers
Attributes: pest tolerant
Native: Brazil
Notes: ideal for a mixed shrubbery border or can be used in small groupings to compound the impact when in flower

Botanical name: *Tibouchina urvilleana*
Common name: Princess Flower
Hardiness range: 9B to 11
Mature size: 10–15 feet tall and wide
Light requirement: full sun
Leaf persistence: evergreen
Flower: purple; very showy year-round
Soil moisture: tolerates drought
Soil pH tolerance: acid to slightly alkaline
Uses: border; pollarding; specimen
Attributes: pest tolerant
Native: Brazil
Notes: canopy must be pruned regularly to keep lower branches from drooping to the ground

Botanical name: *Viburnum obovatum*
Common name: Walter Viburnum, Blackhaw, Small Viburnum
Hardiness range: 6B to 10A
Mature size: 12–20 feet tall by 6–15 feet wide
Light requirement: partial shade to full sun
Leaf persistence: evergreen and semievergreen
Flower: white; showy in spring and summer
Soil moisture: tolerates drought and occasional wetness
Soil pH tolerance: acid to alkaline
Uses: seashore planting; screen; espalier; hedge; massing; specimen
Attributes: pest tolerant; attracts butterflies
Native: Florida
Notes: best *Viburnum* for use in central and southern Florida; unfortunately, it is not widely available, but more nurseries are offering it every year; dwarf cultivars available

Botanical name: *Viburnum tinus*
Common name: Laurustinus Viburnum
Hardiness range: 8A to 9A
Mature size: 6–10 feet tall by 3–6 feet wide
Light requirement: partial shade to full sun
Leaf persistence: evergreen
Flower: pink and white; fragrant and showy in spring and winter
Soil moisture: tolerates some drought
Soil pH tolerance: acid to slightly alkaline
Uses: border; screen; massing; specimen
Attributes: attracts butterflies; attractive and fragrant flowers
Native: Mediterranean region
Notes: produces many pinkish white, fragrant, early spring flowers, followed by ornamental blue-black fruit; young shrub grows mostly upright, eventually spreading slightly to form a vase shape

Salt-Tolerant Vines and Ground Covers

Highly Salt-Tolerant Vines and Ground Covers

Botanical name: *Aloe vera* (syn. *Aloe barbadensis*)
Common name: Medicinal Aloe, Barbados Aloe
Hardiness range: 9A to 11
Mature size: 1–2 feet tall by 1–3 feet wide
Light requirement: full shade to full sun
Leaf persistence: evergreen
Flower: orange and yellow; showy year-round
Soil moisture: tolerates drought
Soil pH tolerance: acid to slightly alkaline
Uses: containers; rock garden; ground cover
Attributes: drought tolerant; medicinal properties
Native: Mediterranean region, Barbados, Jamaica, Mexico, Peru, Bolivia, and Mexico
Notes: the clear sap derived from the plant's succulent foliage is useful in making medicines and cosmetics; frequently used as a soothing and healing gel for cuts, burns, insect bites, and sunburns

Botanical name: *Aptenia cordifolia*
Common name: Baby Sunrose
Hardiness range: 10A to 11
Mature size: 3–4 inches tall by 2–3 feet wide
Light requirement: full sun
Leaf persistence: evergreen
Flower: red; spring through fall
Soil moisture: tolerates drought
Soil pH tolerance: acid to slightly alkaline
Uses: containers; rock garden; ground cover; hanging basket
Attributes: bright red, asterlike flowers
Native: South Africa
Notes: spectacular flowering hanging basket or ground cover for small, exposed, well-drained gardens; moderately thick, succulent stems crawl along the ground, forming a tight, almost clipped appearance

Botanical name: *Borrichia arborescens*
Common name: Silver Sea Oxeye, Tall Sea Oxeye Daisy
Hardiness range: 10A to 11
Mature size: 2–4 feet tall by 1–3 feet wide
Light requirement: full sun
Leaf persistence: evergreen
Flower: yellow; showy year-round
Soil moisture: tolerates some drought and flooding
Soil pH tolerance: acid to alkaline
Uses: seashore planting in salt water; massing
Attributes: wetlands plant; attracts butterflies
Native: Florida
Notes: an upright to somewhat round shrub that grows near brackish water; produces fruits that are small, sharp, and needlelike

Botanical name: *Canavalia maritima*
Common name: Bay Bean, Beach Bean
Hardiness range: 10B to 11
Mature size: 6–12 inches tall and spreading
Light requirement: full sun
Leaf persistence: evergreen
Flower: purple; showy year-round
Soil moisture: tolerates drought
Soil pH tolerance: acid to slightly alkaline
Uses: massing; ground cover; erosion control
Attributes: attractive flowers
Native: Florida
Notes: a dense ground cover that is commonly found in the coastal sands; robust, woody pods follow the beautiful pink to purple flowers

Botanical name: *Carpobrotus edulis*
Common name: Hottentot Fig, Ice Plant
Hardiness range: 8B to 11
Mature size: 18–24 inches tall and spreading
Light requirement: full sun
Leaf persistence: evergreen
Flower: yellow; showy in summer
Soil moisture: tolerates drought
Soil pH tolerance: acid to slightly alkaline
Uses: containers; ground cover; erosion control
Attributes: attractive flowers
Native: South Africa
Notes: grows well in full sun in hot conditions; stays low to the ground or will cascade over a retaining wall; fruit is inconspicuous; keep it on the dry side and on sloping ground for best performance

Botanical name: *Cynodon dactylon*
Common name: Bermuda Grass, Bahama Grass
Hardiness range: 7B to 11
Mature size: 1–6 inches tall and spreading
Light requirement: full sun
Leaf persistence: evergreen
Flower: inconspicuous
Soil moisture: tolerates drought
Soil pH tolerance: acid to alkaline
Uses: lawns; athletic fields
Attributes: rapid growth; tolerates pollution; excellent wear tolerance
Native: Europe, Asia, Australia
Notes: place in full sun and cut with a reel mower; regular edging is required to keep it out of adjacent shrub beds; uses less water than cool-season grasses

Botanical name: *Epipremnum pinnatum* 'Aureum' (syns. *Epipremnum aureum; Pothos aureus; Scindapsus aureus*)
Common name: Golden Pothos, Devil's Ivy, Taro Vine
Hardiness range: 10A to 11
Mature size: 10–40 feet tall and spreading
Light requirement: full shade to partial sun
Leaf persistence: evergreen
Flower: green; inconspicuous year-round
Soil moisture: tolerates drought and occasional wetness
Soil pH tolerance: acid to slightly alkaline
Uses: invasive
Attributes: attractive foliage
Native: Solomon Islands
Notes: vining habit makes it unsuitable for planting in and around a shrub border, since stems will grow up into the shrub; frequent trimming is required along the edges of this ground cover

Botanical name: *Euonymus fortunei*
Common name: Wintercreeper, Wintercreeper Euonymus
Hardiness range: 4B to 8B
Mature size: 1–2 feet tall and spreading
Light requirement: full shade to full sun
Leaf persistence: semievergreen
Flower: green and white; inconspicuous in summer
Soil moisture: tolerates drought
Soil pH tolerance: acid to alkaline
Uses: containers; massing; ground cover; erosion control
Attributes: attractive foliage
Native: central and western China
Notes: can be a trailing vinelike plant or an upright shrub, depending on the cultivar; can be sheared to keep it neat; can climb up into shrubs

Botanical name: *Evolvulus glomeratus*
Common name: Blue Daze
Hardiness range: 8B to 11
Mature size: 6–12 inches tall by 1–3 feet wide
Light requirement: partial shade to full sun
Leaf persistence: semievergreen
Flower: blue; showy year-round
Soil moisture: tolerates some drought
Soil pH tolerance: acid to slightly alkaline
Uses: containers; rock garden; massing; ground cover
Attributes: attractive flowers
Native: tropical America
Notes: becomes a gray-green, carpetlike cover accented with a profusion of clear blue flowers; flowers close in the afternoon and new flowers open in the morning; used as an annual in the northern states

Botanical name: *Ficus pumila*
Common name: Creeping Fig
Hardiness range: 7B to 11
Mature size: 2 inches to 40 feet tall by 10–100 feet wide
Light requirement: full shade to full sun
Leaf persistence: evergreen
Flower: green; inconspicuous in spring
Soil moisture: tolerates drought and occasional wetness
Soil pH tolerance: acid to slightly alkaline
Uses: containers; arbor; ground cover
Attributes: attracts birds
Native: eastern Asia, from Japan to northern Vietnam
Notes: a favorite vine to grow on walls; needs no support to adhere to a wall; makes a low, dense ground cover only one or two inches high; adult foliage is much larger than juvenile

Botanical name: *Gaillardia pulchella* (syn. *Gaillardia drummondii*)
Common name: Blanket Flower, Fire Wheels, Indian Blanket
Hardiness range: 8B to 11
Mature size: 1–2 feet tall by 1–3 feet wide
Light requirement: full sun
Leaf persistence: semievergreen
Flower: red and yellow; showy in summer and fall
Soil moisture: tolerates drought well
Soil pH tolerance: acid to slightly alkaline
Uses: containers; border; massing
Attributes: attracts butterflies; suitable for cut flowers
Native: eastern and south-central United States
Notes: does well in heat and humidity and is perfectly suited to coastal gardens; many cultivars have been selected for flower color

Botanical name: *Helianthus debilis*
Common name: Beach Sunflower, Dune Sunflower
Hardiness range: 8B to 11
Mature size: 1–2 feet tall by 3–6 feet wide
Light requirement: full sun
Leaf persistence: evergreen and semievergreen
Flower: yellow; showy throughout the year
Soil moisture: tolerates drought
Soil pH tolerance: acid to alkaline
Uses: containers; massing; ground cover; erosion control
Attributes: suitable for cut flowers and for dried flowers
Native: Alabama, Florida, and Louisiana
Notes: a spreading perennial that has attractive, small, sunflower-like flower heads throughout the year

Botanical name: *Hemerocallis* hybrids and cultivars
Common name: Daylily
Hardiness range: 4A to 10A
Mature size: 18–24 inches tall and wide
Light requirement: partial shade or partial sun
Leaf persistence: deciduous
Flower: yellow, orange, red, pink, and purple; showy in summer
Soil moisture: tolerates some drought
Soil pH tolerance: neutral to slightly alkaline
Uses: containers; woodland garden; massing; ground cover
Attributes: attracts butterflies; suitable for cut flowers
Native: Europe, Asia
Notes: tolerates a wide range of soil conditions and full sun; however, if it shows sun scald, move to an area where protected from afternoon sun

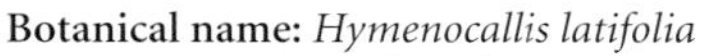

Botanical name: *Hymenocallis latifolia*
Common name: Spider Lily
Hardiness range: 10A to 11
Mature size: 2–3 feet tall by 3–6 feet wide
Light requirement: partial shade to full sun
Leaf persistence: evergreen
Flower: white; fragrant and showy in summer
Soil moisture: thrives with plentiful soil moisture
Soil pH tolerance: acid to alkaline
Uses: foundation planting; massing; specimen; ground cover
Attributes: wetlands plant
Native: Florida, West Indies
Notes: popular for its exceptional foliage and snow white flowers; large, ovoid capsules that produce viable seeds appear on this plant after flowering has ceased

Botanical name: *Ipomoea pes-caprae*
Common name: Beach Morning Glory, Goat's Foot Vine, Railroad Vine
Hardiness range: 10B to 11
Mature size: 3–12 inches tall and spreading
Light requirement: full sun
Leaf persistence: evergreen
Flower: purple; showy in summer and fall
Soil moisture: tolerates drought
Soil pH tolerance: acid to alkaline
Uses: arbor; ground cover
Attributes: attractive flowers
Native: Florida to Texas and Georgia, on seashores
Notes: stems may creep along the ground to a length of 75 feet; flowers open in the early morning and close before noon each day

Botanical name: *Ipomoea stolonifera*
Common name: Fiddleleaf Morning Glory
Hardiness range: 8A to 11
Mature size: 4–6 inches tall and spreading
Light requirement: full sun
Leaf persistence: evergreen
Flower: white; showy in summer and fall
Soil moisture: tolerates drought
Soil pH tolerance: acid to alkaline
Uses: arbor; ground cover
Attributes: vine that spreads very rapidly
Native: southeastern United States
Notes: herbaceous vine that spreads very rapidly; flowers open in the early morning and close before noon each day

Botanical name: *Juniperus conferta* cultivars
Common name: Shore Juniper
Hardiness range: 6A to 10A
Mature size: 1–2 feet tall by 6–10 feet wide
Light requirement: full sun
Leaf persistence: evergreen
Flower: no flowers
Soil moisture: tolerates drought
Soil pH tolerance: acid to alkaline
Uses: containers; cascading over a wall; massing; ground cover; erosion control
Attributes: soft, gray-green foliage
Native: Sakhalin, Japan
Notes: very susceptible to the foliage fungus blight that kills many plantings; place in full sun for best performance

Botanical name: *Liriope spicata*
Common name: Creeping Lilyturf, Lilyturf, Creeping Liriope
Hardiness range: 4B to 10A
Mature size: 8–12 inches tall by 1–3 feet wide
Light requirement: full shade to full sun
Leaf persistence: evergreen
Flower: lavender; inconspicuous in summer
Soil moisture: tolerates some drought
Soil pH tolerance: acid to alkaline
Uses: containers; rock garden; woodland garden; massing; ground cover; erosion control
Attributes: suitable for cut flowers
Native: China, Japan
Notes: forms a dense, uniform cover, unlike *L. muscari,* which forms clumps until well established, several years after planting; spreads quickly by rhizomes and can invade adjacent turf or other ground covers

Botanical name: *Monarda punctata*
Common name: Beebalm, Horsemint
Hardiness range: 4A to 9A
Mature size: 1–2 feet tall by 1–3 feet wide
Light requirement: full sun
Leaf persistence: deciduous
Flower: pink, red, and white; showy in summer
Soil moisture: tolerates some drought
Soil pH tolerance: acid to slightly alkaline
Uses: rock garden; massing; ground cover; erosion control
Attributes: attracts butterflies
Native: Long Island, south to Florida and Louisiana
Notes: cultivars will not come true from seed; should be planted in areas with good air circulation in full sun; attracts pollinators

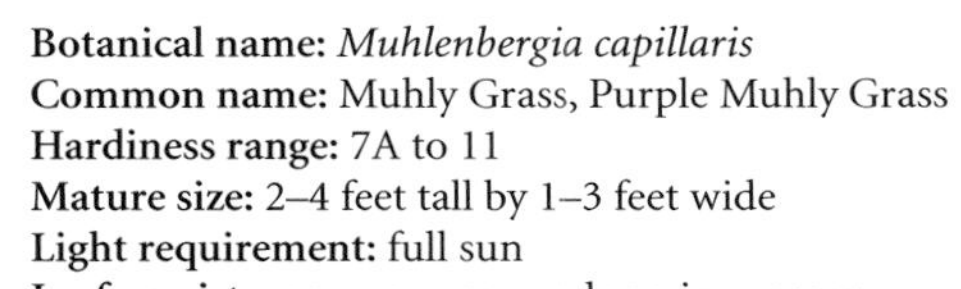

Botanical name: *Muhlenbergia capillaris*
Common name: Muhly Grass, Purple Muhly Grass
Hardiness range: 7A to 11
Mature size: 2–4 feet tall by 1–3 feet wide
Light requirement: full sun
Leaf persistence: evergreen and semievergreen
Flower: pink; showy in fall
Soil moisture: tolerates drought and flooding
Soil pH tolerance: acid to slightly alkaline
Uses: ground cover; dune stabilization; foundation planting
Attributes: attractive foliage and fall colors
Native: Florida
Notes: upright habit makes this markedly different from many other grasses; delicate pink to purple flowers emerge in fall

Botanical name: *Ophiopogon japonicus*
Common name: Dwarf Lilyturf, Mondo Grass, Monkey Grass
Hardiness range: 7A to 11
Mature size: 6–8 inches tall by 6–12 inches wide
Light requirement: full shade to partial sun
Leaf persistence: evergreen
Flower: white; inconspicuous in summer
Soil moisture: tolerates some drought
Soil pH tolerance: acid to slightly alkaline
Uses: rock garden; woodland garden; massing; ground cover for shaded location
Attributes: forms a dense mat
Native: Japan
Notes: can be invasive; best to mow to the ground in early March to get rid of unsightly foliage; dwarf and black-leaved forms are available

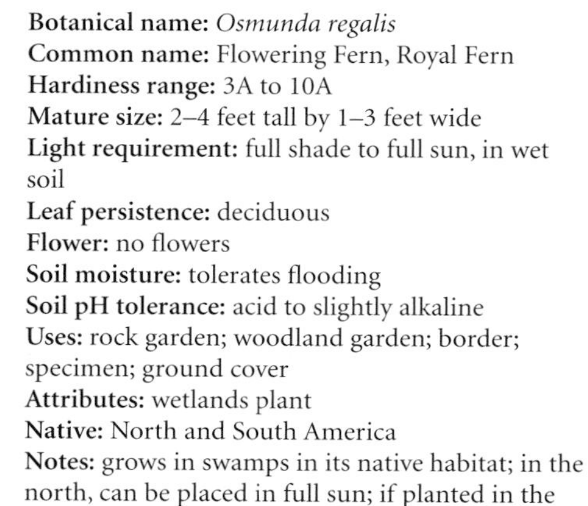

Botanical name: *Osmunda regalis*
Common name: Flowering Fern, Royal Fern
Hardiness range: 3A to 10A
Mature size: 2–4 feet tall by 1–3 feet wide
Light requirement: full shade to full sun, in wet soil
Leaf persistence: deciduous
Flower: no flowers
Soil moisture: tolerates flooding
Soil pH tolerance: acid to slightly alkaline
Uses: rock garden; woodland garden; border; specimen; ground cover
Attributes: wetlands plant
Native: North and South America
Notes: grows in swamps in its native habitat; in the north, can be placed in full sun; if planted in the sun, will need a moist to wet soil

Botanical name: *Parthenocissus quinquefolia*
Common name: Virginia Creeper, Woodbine
Hardiness range: 3B to 10A
Mature size: 40–60 feet tall and wide
Light requirement: full shade to full sun
Leaf persistence: deciduous
Flower: green; inconspicuous in spring
Soil moisture: tolerates drought and occasional wetness
Soil pH tolerance: acid to slightly alkaline
Uses: woodland garden; arbor
Attributes: fall color; fast growing
Native: northeastern United States to Florida, Texas, and Mexico
Notes: deciduous, high-climbing vine will grow on walls, fences, and arbors and is found growing up into trees in the wild; can be invasive

Botanical name: *Pyrostegia venusta* (syn. *Pyrostegia ignea*)
Common name: Flame Vine
Hardiness range: 9A to 11
Mature size: 7–30 feet tall and spreading
Light requirement: partial shade to full sun
Leaf persistence: evergreen
Flower: orange; showy in fall and winter
Soil moisture: tolerates drought
Soil pH tolerance: acid to slightly alkaline
Uses: containers; arbor or fence; specimen
Attributes: attracts birds; attractive flowers
Native: Brazil, Paraguay
Notes: grows rapidly; climbing by tendrils, this vigorous evergreen vine makes a brilliant fall and winter display of reddish orange flowers; has escaped cultivation in much of central Florida and is often seen in flower during the winter and spring growing in trees

Botanical name: *Smilax* spp.
Common name: Greenbrier
Hardiness range: 4A to 9A
Mature size: depends on support
Light requirement: partial shade to full sun
Leaf persistence: semievergreen
Flower: green, white, and yellow; showy in summer
Soil moisture: will grow in moist soil
Soil pH tolerance: acid to alkaline
Uses: trellis; arbor; considered a terrible weed by most people
Attributes: attractive foliage
Native: eastern United States, Nova Scotia to Georgia, west to Minnesota, Illinois, and Texas
Notes: considered a weed in some parts of the United States

Botanical name: *Spartina alternifolia*
Common name: Cordgrass, Marsh Grass
Hardiness range: 8B to 11
Mature size: 2–4 feet tall by 3–6 feet wide
Light requirement: partial shade to full sun
Leaf persistence: evergreen
Flower: brown; showy in fall
Soil moisture: tolerates flooding
Soil pH tolerance: acid to slightly alkaline
Uses: massing; ground cover; riverbank stabilization
Attributes: wetlands plant; grows submerged
Native: Florida
Notes: will grow well on the margins of sand ponds and freshwater marshes; tolerates saline water and often grows in coastal saltwater marshes

Botanical name: *Spartina bakeri*
Common name: Sand Cordgrass, Marsh Grass
Hardiness range: 8B to 11
Mature size: 2–4 feet tall by 3–6 feet wide
Light requirement: partial shade to full sun
Leaf persistence: evergreen
Flower: brown; showy in fall
Soil moisture: tolerates drought and flooding
Soil pH tolerance: acid to slightly alkaline
Uses: border; massing; specimen; ground cover; erosion control
Attributes: wetlands plant
Native: Florida
Notes: a robust ornamental grass that can form wide clumps; its fine-textured, wiry leaves form a fountain spray pattern

Botanical name: *Stenotaphrum secundatum*
Common name: St. Augustine Grass, Buffalo Grass
Hardiness range: 7B to 11
Mature size: 2–6 inches tall and spreading
Light requirement: partial shade to full sun
Leaf persistence: semievergreen in north, evergreen in south
Flower: green; inconspicuous spring through fall
Soil moisture: will grow in moist soil
Soil pH tolerance: acid to slightly alkaline
Uses: lawns
Attributes: forms a dense, attractive lawn
Native: tropical America, western Africa, Pacific Islands
Notes: very tolerant to salt air but will not tolerate regular foot traffic; thins in drought without irrigation; can invade adjacent property

Botanical name: *Uniola paniculata*
Common name: Sea Oats Grass
Hardiness range: 7B to 11
Mature size: 6–10 feet tall by 1–3 feet wide
Light requirement: full sun
Leaf persistence: evergreen
Flower: brown; showy in summer
Soil moisture: tolerates drought
Soil pH tolerance: acid to slightly alkaline
Uses: dune stabilization; ground cover; erosion control
Attributes: naturalizing; controls beach erosion
Native: southeastern United States to the West Indies
Notes: once blanketed the coastal landscape along the southeastern United States from North Carolina to southern Florida; now it is endangered due to development

Botanical name: *Wedelia trilobata*
Common name: Wedelia
Hardiness range: 8B to 11
Mature size: 6–12 inches tall and spreading
Light requirement: partial shade to full sun
Leaf persistence: evergreen and semievergreen
Flower: yellow; showy year-round
Soil moisture: tolerates drought and flooding
Soil pH tolerance: acid to alkaline
Uses: invasive
Attributes: attractive flowers
Native: tropical America
Notes: will cover rough, rocky ground or wet drainage ditches, and even tolerates some degree of foot traffic; invasive, especially in wet areas

Botanical name: *Zamia floridana*
Common name: Coontie, Florida Arrowroot
Hardiness range: 8B to 11
Mature size: 2–4 feet tall by 3–6 feet wide
Light requirement: partial shade to full sun
Leaf persistence: evergreen
Flower: no flowers
Soil moisture: tolerates drought
Soil pH tolerance: acid to alkaline
Uses: containers; border; foundation planting; massing; specimen; ground cover
Attributes: attracts butterflies
Native: Florida
Notes: water with moderation, once established; provides a tropical effect; all parts are poisonous; susceptible to scale infestation

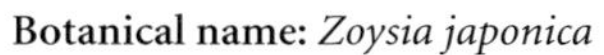

Botanical name: *Zoysia japonica*
Common name: Zoysia Grass, Korean Grass
Hardiness range: 7B to 11
Mature size: 1–2 inches tall and spreading
Light requirement: partial shade to full sun
Leaf persistence: evergreen
Flower: inconspicuous
Soil moisture: tolerates some drought; will grow in moist soil
Soil pH tolerance: acid to alkaline
Uses: ground cover; erosion control; lawns
Attributes: forms an extremely dense sod
Native: Japan
Notes: excellent wear tolerance; establishes very slowly, but once established it makes a great lawn; very sensitive to soil nematodes

Moderately Salt-Tolerant Vines and Ground Covers

Botanical name: *Agapanthus africanus*
Common name: African Lily, Lily of the Nile
Hardiness range: 8B to 10A
Mature size: 18 inches to 3 feet tall and spreading
Light requirement: partial shade to full sun
Leaf persistence: evergreen
Flower: blue; showy in summer and fall
Soil moisture: tolerates drought
Soil pH tolerance: neutral to slightly alkaline
Uses: containers; border; foundation planting; massing; specimen
Attributes: attracts butterflies; suitable for cut flowers
Native: South Africa
Notes: water well during growing season; cut back water in the winter; attractive foliage lasts year-round; flowers are gorgeous

Botanical name: *Allamanda cathartica*
Common name: Golden Trumpet Vine; Common Allamanda, Yellow Allamanda
Hardiness range: 9B to 11
Mature size: 4–15 feet tall and spreading
Light requirement: full sun
Leaf persistence: evergreen
Flower: yellow; fragrant and very showy in spring and summer
Soil moisture: tolerates drought
Soil pH tolerance: acid to alkaline
Uses: containers; arbor; fence; mailbox
Attributes: attractive and fragrant flowers
Native: South America
Notes: spiny, yellow-green fruit appears simultaneously with yellow, trumpet-shaped flowers; should be planted in frost-free locations

Botanical name: *Alternanthera ficoidea*
Common name: Joseph's Coat, Copperleaf
Hardiness range: 8B to 10A
Mature size: 2–3 feet tall by 2 feet wide
Light requirement: partial shade to full sun
Leaf persistence: evergreen
Flower: white; inconspicuous year-round in warm climates
Soil moisture: will grow in moist soil
Soil pH tolerance: neutral to slightly alkaline
Uses: containers; massing; ground cover
Attributes: attractive foliage
Native: Mexico, South America
Notes: often grown as an annual in cold climates; usually grown for the foliage

Botanical name: *Artemisia stelleriana* 'Silver Brocade'
Common name: Dusty Miller, Old Woman, Beach Wormwood
Hardiness range: 3A to 9A
Mature size: 6–20 inches tall by 18–24 inches wide
Light requirement: full sun
Leaf persistence: deciduous
Flower: yellow; showy in summer
Soil moisture: tolerates some drought
Soil pH tolerance: neutral to slightly alkaline
Uses: massing; ground cover
Attributes: suitable for dried flowers
Native: Asia
Notes: broader leaf form of *Artemisia;* allow these plants to slightly dry out between waterings, and fertilize sparingly

Botanical name: *Asparagus densiflorus* 'Myers'
Common name: Asparagus Fern, Foxtail Asparagus, Emerald Feather
Hardiness range: 9B to 11
Mature size: 1–2 feet tall by 1–3 feet wide
Light requirement: full shade to full sun
Leaf persistence: evergreen
Flower: white; inconspicuous and periodically during the year
Soil moisture: tolerates some drought
Soil pH tolerance: acid to slightly alkaline
Uses: containers; border; specimen; ground cover
Attributes: attractive foliage
Native: southern Africa
Notes: not known to be invasive like its relative 'Sprengeri'; 'Myers' Asparagus Fern is a spreading perennial herb that has a fine texture and a stiff, upright habit; bright red berries are quite showy

Botanical name: *Bougainvillea* spp.
Common name: Bougainvillea
Hardiness range: 9B to 11
Mature size: 15–25 feet tall by 25–35 feet wide
Light requirement: full sun
Leaf persistence: evergreen
Flower: lavender, orange, purple, red, and yellow; showy year-round
Soil moisture: tolerates drought
Soil pH tolerance: acid to slightly alkaline
Uses: containers; rock garden; arbor; espalier; cascade; pollarding; massing
Attributes: attracts butterflies
Native: South America
Notes: evergreen shrubby vine popular for its long-lasting, colorful flower bracts; pollen produces few if any allergies

Botanical name: *Catharanthus roseus*
Common name: Madagascar Periwinkle
Hardiness range: 9B to 11
Mature size: 1–2 feet tall by 1–3 feet wide
Light requirement: partial shade to full sun
Leaf persistence: deciduous
Flower: lavender, pink, and white; showy in summer and fall
Soil moisture: tolerates drought well
Soil pH tolerance: acid to slightly alkaline
Uses: containers; border; massing; specimen; ground cover
Attributes: attractive flowers
Native: Madagascar and India
Notes: often grown as an annual; prune new growth in spring to promote a bushy habit; spreads readily; easily killed by root disease—keep on the dry side to help prevent this problem

Botanical name: *Costus speciosus* 'Variegatus'
Common name: Spiral Ginger, Crepe Ginger
Hardiness range: 8B to 11
Mature size: 8–10 feet tall and spreading
Light requirement: full shade to full sun
Leaf persistence: evergreen
Flower: white; showy in summer and fall
Soil moisture: tolerates some drought
Soil pH tolerance: acid to slightly alkaline
Uses: containers; foundation planting; massing; specimen
Attributes: attracts birds
Native: East Indies
Notes: variegated leaves of this tropical evergreen are borne on red stems emerging directly from the ground; white flowers are produced in the warm months, appearing on conical heads at the tips of branches

Botanical name: *Crinum americanum*
Common name: Swamp Lily, String Lily
Hardiness range: 8B to 11
Mature size: 2–4 feet tall by 3–6 feet wide
Light requirement: partial shade to full sun
Leaf persistence: evergreen
Flower: white; fragrant and showy year-round
Soil moisture: will grow in wet soil
Soil pH tolerance: acid to slightly alkaline
Uses: border; massing; specimen; ground cover
Attributes: wetlands plant
Native: tropics and subtropics worldwide
Notes: best grown in soils that are moderately moist; water during dry weather; all parts are poisonous

Botanical name: *Cuphea hyssopifolia*
Common name: False Heather, Mexican Heather
Hardiness range: 8B to 11
Mature size: 1–2 feet tall by 1–3 feet wide
Light requirement: partial shade to full sun
Leaf persistence: evergreen
Flower: lavender, pink, purple, and white; showy spring through fall
Soil moisture: tolerates drought
Soil pH tolerance: acid to alkaline
Uses: containers; border; massing; ground cover; erosion control
Attributes: attractive flowers
Native: Mexico and Guatemala
Notes: ideal as a ground cover or as an edging; planted on 2-foot centers, a dense ground cover forms in several months; may self-seed and spread

Botanical name: *Dracaena thalioides*
Common name: Dwarf Dracaena, Lance Dracaena
Hardiness range: 10B to 11
Mature size: 1–2 feet tall by 1–3 feet wide
Light requirement: full shade to partial sun
Leaf persistence: evergreen
Flower: pink; inconspicuous year-round
Soil moisture: will grow in moist, well-drained soil
Soil pH tolerance: acid to slightly alkaline
Uses: containers; woodland garden; massing; ground cover; erosion control
Attributes: attractive foliage
Native: tropical Africa
Notes: has an upright habit and is used in the landscape for its attractive foliage; studies have demonstrated that these plants can clean up indoor air pollutants such as formaldehyde, carbon monoxide, and benzene

Botanical name: *Hedera canariensis*
Common name: Algerian Ivy, Canary Island Ivy
Hardiness range: 8B to 10A
Mature size: 6–12 inches tall and spreading
Light requirement: full shade to partial sun
Leaf persistence: evergreen
Flower: white; inconspicuous in fall
Soil moisture: tolerates some drought
Soil pH tolerance: acid to slightly alkaline
Uses: containers; woodland garden; arbor; cascading over a wall; massing; ground cover; erosion control
Attributes: attractive foliage
Native: Canary Islands and northern Africa
Notes: does best in some shade on moist but well-drained soils; more susceptible to cold damage than English Ivy

Botanical name: *Hedera helix*
Common name: English Ivy, Baltic Ivy
Hardiness range: 4B to 9A
Mature size: 6–12 inches tall and spreading
Light requirement: full shade to full sun
Leaf persistence: evergreen
Flower: white; inconspicuous in fall
Soil moisture: tolerates some drought
Soil pH tolerance: acid to slightly alkaline
Uses: containers; cascading over a wall; massing; ground cover; erosion control
Attributes: attractive foliage
Native: Europe, western Asia, northern Africa
Notes: benefits from some shade, especially when grown in the warmer climates; plant on 1-foot centers for quick establishment; invasive in some states but not reported as such in Florida

Botanical name: *Hedychium coronarium*
Common name: Butterfly Ginger, Garland Flower, Butterfly Lily
Hardiness range: 8B to 11
Mature size: 4–5 feet tall by 3–6 feet wide
Light requirement: partial sun to full sun, in wet soil
Leaf persistence: deciduous
Flower: white; very fragrant and showy in spring through fall
Soil moisture: tolerates some drought and occasional wetness
Soil pH tolerance: acid to slightly alkaline
Uses: containers; border; massing; ground cover
Attributes: attracts butterflies
Native: India
Notes: one of the nicest gingers for the home landscape because of its fragrance; each flower lasts about one day; spreads by underground rhizomes, often forming dense clumps of multiple stems; keep soil moist

Botanical name: *Hosta capitata* 'Naikaimo'
Common name: Hosta
Hardiness range: 4A to 9A
Mature size: 18–20 inches tall by 18–24 inches wide
Light requirement: full shade
Leaf persistence: deciduous
Flower: lavender; showy in summer and fall
Soil moisture: will grow in well-drained soil
Soil pH tolerance: acid to slightly alkaline
Uses: woodland garden; seashore planting; border; foundation planting; massing; specimen; ground cover
Attributes: attractive foliage
Native: Korea, Japan
Notes: will grow best in a fertile loamy soil in a woodland setting with filtered sunlight; variegated types like more sun than the green types; difficult to cultivate in zones 8–9

Botanical name: *Juniperus chinensis* var. *procumbens* 'Nana'
Common name: Chinese Juniper, Juniper
Hardiness range: 4A to 10A
Mature size: 2 feet tall and spreading
Light requirement: full sun
Leaf persistence: evergreen
Flower: brown and yellow; inconspicuous in spring
Soil moisture: tolerates drought
Soil pH tolerance: acid to alkaline
Uses: ground cover
Attributes: drought tolerant; attractive foliage
Native: eastern Asia
Notes: grows best in full sun; needs well-drained soil or will decline from root rot; attacked seriously by mites and *Phomopsis* blight

Botanical name: *Juniperus horizontalis* cultivars
Common name: Creeping Juniper
Hardiness range: 4A to 9A
Mature size: 1–3 feet tall by 10–20 feet wide
Light requirement: full sun
Leaf persistence: evergreen
Flower: inconspicuous
Soil moisture: tolerates drought
Soil pH tolerance: acid to alkaline
Uses: rock garden; cascading over a wall; massing; ground cover; erosion control
Attributes: quite drought tolerant
Native: North America
Notes: tolerates exposed sites and a wide range of soils; excellent for low-maintenance landscapes, as it requires virtually no pruning to maintain a tight habit

Botanical name: *Kalanchoe blossfeldiana*
Common name: Christmas Kalanchoe, Flaming Katy
Hardiness range: 10B to 11
Mature size: 1–2 feet tall by 1 foot wide
Light requirement: partial shade to full sun
Leaf persistence: evergreen
Flower: orange, pink, red, white, and yellow; showy in spring and winter
Soil moisture: tolerates drought
Soil pH tolerance: acid to slightly alkaline
Uses: containers; rock garden; ground cover
Attributes: attractive flowers
Native: Madagascar
Notes: often used as a houseplant, and its flowers may last up to eight weeks

Botanical name: *Lantana ovatifolia* var. *reclinata*
Common name: Dwarf Lantana, Gold Lantana
Hardiness range: 9A to 11
Mature size: 1–2 feet tall by 3–6 feet wide
Light requirement: full sun
Leaf persistence: evergreen
Flower: yellow; very showy year-round
Soil moisture: tolerates drought
Soil pH tolerance: acid to alkaline
Uses: containers; foundation planting; massing; ground cover; erosion control
Attributes: attracts butterflies
Native: Florida
Notes: flowering can be reduced with applications of too much water or fertilizer; although plants will be frozen back in winters when it reaches 20–30 degrees F, new growth quickly appears in spring

Botanical name: *Liriope muscari* (syn. *Liriope graminifolia* var. *densiflora*)
Common name: Lilyturf, Border Grass, Blue Lilyturf, Liriope, Big Blue Liriope
Hardiness range: 5A to 10A
Mature size: 6–12 inches tall by 1–3 feet wide
Light requirement: full shade to full sun
Leaf persistence: evergreen
Flower: lavender; inconspicuous in summer and fall
Soil moisture: tolerates some drought
Soil pH tolerance: acid to alkaline
Uses: containers; rock garden; woodland garden; border; massing; specimen; ground cover
Attributes: suitable for cut flowers
Native: China, Japan
Notes: unlike *Liriope spicata,* usually is slow spreading; should be mowed back with a sharp lawn mower blade in the early spring to enjoy a flush of new growth

Botanical name: *Lonicera japonica*
Common name: Japanese Honeysuckle, Hall's Honeysuckle
Hardiness range: 4A to 10A
Mature size: 10–50 feet tall and wide
Light requirement: full shade to full sun
Leaf persistence: semievergreen
Flower: white and yellow; fragrant and showy in spring and summer
Soil moisture: tolerates some drought
Soil pH tolerance: acid to alkaline
Uses: invasive
Attributes: fragrant and attractive flowers; invasive
Native: eastern Asia
Notes: will grow in the shade, but flowers poorly there; rampant vine that can easily grow out of control in the landscape; considered a weed and an invasive plant

Botanical name: *Lonicera sempervirens*
Common name: Trumpet Honeysuckle, Coral Honeysuckle
Hardiness range: 4A to 10A
Mature size: 3–20 feet tall and spreading
Light requirement: partial shade to full sun
Leaf persistence: deciduous and semievergreen
Flower: red or yellow; fragrant and showy in spring and summer
Soil moisture: tolerates some drought and occasional wetness
Soil pH tolerance: acid to alkaline
Uses: arbor; trellis; fence
Attributes: wetlands plant; attracts birds and butterflies
Native: eastern and southern United States
Notes: best suited for sunny locations; flowers poorly in the shade; does not spread out of control quite as easily as Japanese Honeysuckle; cultivars have flowers with colors ranging from yellow, orange, red, and pink; a very pretty plant worthy of wider cultivation

Botanical name: *Mandevilla splendens*
Common name: Pink Allamanda
Hardiness range: 10A to 11
Mature size: 3–18 feet tall and spreading
Light requirement: full sun
Leaf persistence: evergreen
Flower: pink; fragrant and very showy year-round
Soil moisture: tolerates some drought
Soil pH tolerance: acid to slightly alkaline
Uses: containers; arbor; cascading over a wall
Attributes: attractive flowers
Native: southeastern Brazil
Notes: needs well-drained soil and should receive ample moisture during the growing season; flowers appear in greatest abundance during the summer but some appear year-round

Botanical name: *Neoregelia compacta*
Common name: Bromeliad
Hardiness range: 10A to 11
Mature size: 6–12 inches tall by 1–2 feet wide
Light requirement: full shade to full sun
Leaf persistence: evergreen
Flower: center of plant turns bright red at flowering
Soil moisture: tolerates drought
Soil pH tolerance: acid to slightly alkaline
Uses: containers; rock garden; massing; ground cover
Attributes: attractive foliage
Native: Brazil
Notes: has a tendency to send up shoots readily from its stolons

Botanical name: *Neoregelia concentrica* 'Albo Marginata'
Common name: Bromeliad
Hardiness range: 10A to 11
Mature size: 6–12 inches tall by 1–3 feet wide
Light requirement: full shade to full sun
Leaf persistence: evergreen
Flower: purple; showy spring through fall
Soil moisture: tolerates drought
Soil pH tolerance: acid to slightly alkaline
Uses: containers; rock garden; massing; ground cover
Attributes: attractive foliage and flowers
Native: Brazil
Notes: tolerates full sun to deep shade; foliage will take on a bronze color when exposed to high light intensities

Botanical name: *Neoregelia spectabilis*
Common name: Painted Fingernail Bromeliad
Hardiness range: 10A to 11
Mature size: 6–12 inches tall by 1–3 feet wide
Light requirement: full shade to full sun
Leaf persistence: evergreen
Flower: red; showy in summer
Soil moisture: tolerates drought
Soil pH tolerance: acid to slightly alkaline
Uses: containers; rock garden; massing; ground cover
Attributes: attractive foliage and flowers
Native: Brazil
Notes: foliage will take on a bronze color when exposed to high light intensities; may be wired to tree branches with sphagnum moss around the roots; has pale green foliage and bright red tips at the end of each leaf

Botanical name: *Pentas lanceolata*
Common name: Pentas, Egyptian Star Flower
Hardiness range: 9A to 11
Mature size: 2–4 feet tall by 1–3 feet wide
Light requirement: partial shade to full sun
Leaf persistence: semievergreen
Flower: lavender, pink, purple, red, and white; showy spring through fall
Soil moisture: tolerates some drought
Soil pH tolerance: acid to slightly alkaline
Uses: containers; border; ground cover
Attributes: attracts butterflies; attractive flowers
Native: eastern tropical Africa to Saudi Arabia
Notes: prefers fertile, well-drained soil and regular moisture; and grows quickly in full sun or light shade; will flower fairly well with as little as 2 to 3 hours of sun each day; butterfly nectar source

Botanical name: *Pilea cadierei*
Common name: Aluminum Plant, Watermelon Pilea
Hardiness range: 10A to 11
Mature size: 6–12 inches tall and spreading
Light requirement: full shade to partial sun
Leaf persistence: evergreen
Flower: white; inconspicuous in summer
Soil moisture: tolerates occasional wetness
Soil pH tolerance: acid to slightly alkaline
Uses: containers; massing; ground cover; erosion control
Attributes: attractive foliage
Native: Vietnam
Notes: variegated foliage is unlike any other, with shiny silver, irregularly shaped markings parallel to the lateral leaf veins; could escape cultivation

Botanical name: *Portulaca grandiflora*
Common name: Garden Portulaca, Rose Moss, Sun Moss
Hardiness range: 9 to 11
Mature size: 6–8 inches tall by 6–12 inches wide
Light requirement: full sun
Leaf persistence: evergreen
Flower: yellow; showy spring through fall
Soil moisture: tolerates drought
Soil pH tolerance: neutral to alkaline
Uses: containers; rock garden; ground cover
Attributes: attractive flowers
Native: South America
Notes: seeds will germinate outdoors if planted in the spring; individual flowers only last one day; flowers close in the evening

Botanical name: *Pseudogynoxys chenopodioides* (syn. *Senecio confusus*)
Common name: Mexican Flamevine, Orangeglow Vine
Hardiness range: 10A to 11
Mature size: 10–20 feet tall and wide
Light requirement: full sun
Leaf persistence: evergreen
Flower: orange; fragrant and very showy year-round
Soil moisture: tolerates some drought
Soil pH tolerance: acid to alkaline
Uses: arbor; trellis
Attributes: attractive and fragrant flowers
Native: Colombia
Notes: plant in full sun for best growth and flowering

Botanical name: *Sansevieria trifasciata*
Common name: Snake Plant, Mother-in-Law's Tongue
Hardiness range: 9B to 11
Mature size: 2–4 feet tall by 1–3 feet wide
Light requirement: full shade to full sun
Leaf persistence: evergreen
Flower: green and white; fragrant and inconspicuous year-round
Soil moisture: tolerates drought
Soil pH tolerance: acid to slightly alkaline
Uses: containers
Attributes: stiff upright leaves
Native: Nigeria
Notes: much used for container culture; no plant could be more forgiving of poor light, little water, and general neglect; has the potential to naturalize; performs well indoors

Botanical name: *Trachelospermum asiaticum*
Common name: Asiatic Jasmine, Small-Leaf Confederate Jasmine
Hardiness range: 7B to 10A
Mature size: 1–2 feet tall and spreading
Light requirement: full shade to full sun
Leaf persistence: evergreen
Flower: yellow-white; fragrant; inconspicuous and rare in summer
Soil moisture: tolerates some drought
Soil pH tolerance: acid to alkaline
Uses: ground cover; erosion control
Attributes: pest tolerant; very aggressive plant once established, can invade adjacent landscapes
Native: Korea, Japan
Notes: pruning along sidewalks and other edges is necessary to control growth; plant only in an area confined by walks, curbs, or buildings to reduce the chance of invading adjacent areas

Botanical name: *Trachelospermum jasminoides*
Common name: Confederate Jasmine, Star Jasmine
Hardiness range: 8A to 10A
Mature size: depends on support
Light requirement: partial shade to full sun
Leaf persistence: evergreen
Flower: white; very fragrant and showy in summer
Soil moisture: tolerates some drought
Soil pH tolerance: acid to alkaline
Uses: containers; arbor
Attributes: pest tolerant; attracts butterflies; very fragrant flowers
Native: China
Notes: can take over a landscape if not kept in bounds; seedlings can appear near established plants; fragrance can be overpowering at close range

Botanical name: *Tradescantia pallida* (syn. *Setcreasea purpurea*)
Common name: Spiderwort, Spider-Lily
Hardiness range: 9B to 11
Mature size: 1–2 feet tall
Light requirement: partial shade to full sun
Leaf persistence: evergreen
Flower: pink; inconspicuous year-round
Soil moisture: will grow in moist, well-drained soil
Soil pH tolerance: acid to slightly alkaline
Uses: containers
Attributes: attractive foliage
Native: Mexico
Notes: makes a good houseplant and can be grown in containers outdoors; can escape cultivation, becoming a weed

Botanical name: *Tradescantia zebrina* (syn. *Zebrina pendula*)
Common name: Wandering Jew, Silvery Inch Plant, Zebra Plant
Hardiness range: 9A to 11
Mature size: 1 foot tall
Light requirement: full shade to partial sun
Leaf persistence: evergreen
Flower: pink; inconspicuous and appearing periodically throughout the year
Soil moisture: tolerates drought and occasional wetness
Soil pH tolerance: acid to slightly alkaline
Uses: containers
Attributes: attractive foliage
Native: Mexico
Notes: plant can spread into adjacent woods

Slightly Salt-Tolerant Vines and Ground Covers

Botanical name: *Aspidistra elatior*
Common name: Cast Iron Plant
Hardiness range: 7A to 11
Mature size: 1–2 feet tall by 1–3 feet wide
Light requirement: full shade to partial sun
Leaf persistence: evergreen
Flower: brown; inconspicuous year-round
Soil moisture: tolerates some drought
Soil pH tolerance: acid to slightly alkaline
Uses: containers; woodland garden; border; foundation planting; massing; specimen; ground cover
Attributes: very shade tolerant
Native: Japan
Notes: in exposed locations, the leaves are very susceptible to winter burn; full sun exposure for just a couple of hours will burn foliage

Botanical name: *Campsis radicans*
Common name: Trumpet Creeper, Trumpet Vine
Hardiness range: 4B to 10A
Mature size: climbs up to 40 feet or more
Light requirement: partial shade to full sun
Leaf persistence: deciduous
Flower: orange or yellow; showy in summer
Soil moisture: tolerates drought and occasional wetness
Soil pH tolerance: acid to alkaline
Uses: woodland garden; arbor
Attributes: attracts birds, hummingbirds, and butterflies
Native: Pennsylvania to Illinois, south to Texas and Florida
Notes: flowers best in full sun; climbs to 40 feet or more when given support; flowers are often visited by hummingbirds; the foliage causes skin inflammation in some people

Botanical name: *Clerodendrum thomsoniae*
Common name: Glory Bower, Bleeding Heart Vine
Hardiness range: 9B to 11
Mature size: 4–10 feet tall by 4–6 feet wide
Light requirement: partial shade to full sun
Leaf persistence: evergreen
Flower: white; showy spring through fall
Soil moisture: will grow in moist soil
Soil pH tolerance: neutral
Uses: containers; arbor; specimen
Attributes: attractive flowers
Native: tropical western Africa
Notes: this species has predominately white blossoms and a few crimson ones as well

Botanical name: *Cydista aequinoctialis*
Common name: Garlic Vine, Bejuco Colorado
Hardiness range: 10B to 11
Mature size: 10–30 feet tall by 20–30 feet or more wide
Light requirement: full sun
Leaf persistence: evergreen
Flower: lavender and pink; fragrant and very showy spring through fall
Soil moisture: tolerates drought
Soil pH tolerance: acid to slightly alkaline
Uses: arbor
Attributes: attractive flowers
Native: West Indies, Central America, south to Brazil
Notes: produces one of the prettiest flowers of any vine; all parts of the plant smell like garlic when injured

Botanical name: *Gerbera jamesonii*
Common name: African Daisy, Gerbera Daisy
Hardiness range: 8B to 11
Mature size: 18–24 inches tall by 12 inches wide
Light requirement: partial shade to partial sun
Leaf persistence: evergreen
Flower: orange, pink, purple, red, white, or yellow; showy most of the year
Soil moisture: will grow in dry soil
Soil pH tolerance: acid to slightly alkaline
Uses: containers; massing
Attributes: attracts butterflies; suitable for cut flowers
Native: South Africa
Notes: give some shade during hot summer afternoons; good drainage is a must; keep mulch away from leaves and stems to prevent rot

Botanical name: *Gloriosa superba* 'Rothschildiana'
Common name: Glory Lily, Gloriosa Lily
Hardiness range: 8B to 11
Mature size: 4–6 feet tall by 1–2 feet wide
Light requirement: partial shade to full sun
Leaf persistence: deciduous
Flower: red and yellow; showy summer and fall
Soil moisture: will grow in moist soil
Soil pH tolerance: neutral
Uses: containers; trellis
Attributes: unusual and colorful flowers
Native: tropical Africa and Asia
Notes: tubers should be planted in late winter for bloom in summer and fall

Botanical name: *Hoya carnosa*
Common name: Wax Plant, Hindu Rope Plant, Honey Plant, Wax Flower
Hardiness range: 10B to 11
Mature size: 3–4 feet tall and spreading
Light requirement: partial shade to full sun
Leaf persistence: evergreen
Flower: white with pink center; very fragrant and showy spring through fall
Soil moisture: tolerates drought
Soil pH tolerance: neutral
Uses: containers; arbor
Attributes: attractive foliage
Native: India, Myanmar (Burma), southern China
Notes: grows on a trellis or arbor; sensitive to frost and hot sun

Botanical name: *Mitchella repens*
Common name: Patridgeberry
Hardiness range: 4A to 9B
Mature size: 2–4 inches tall and spreading
Light requirement: full shade
Leaf persistence: evergreen
Flower: white; fragrant in summer
Soil moisture: will grow in moist soil
Soil pH tolerance: acid to slightly alkaline
Uses: rock garden; woodland garden; specimen; ground cover
Attributes: attractive red fruit, which is eaten by birds
Native: North America
Notes: stems will root wherever they touch ground; red berries are produced in fall and eaten by wildlife

Botanical name: *Petrea volubilis*
Common name: Queen's Wreath, Purple Wreath
Hardiness range: 10B to 11
Mature size: 30–40 feet tall by 40–50 feet wide
Light requirement: partial shade to full sun
Leaf persistence: evergreen
Flower: blue, lavender, purple, and white; showy in spring and summer
Soil moisture: tolerates some drought and occasional wetness
Soil pH tolerance: acid to alkaline
Uses: containers; arbor; specimen
Attributes: attractive flowers
Native: West Indies, Mexico, Central America
Notes: very showy display of purplish blue, star-shaped flowers arranged in foot-long, slender, hanging clusters; climbs trees

Botanical name: *Quisqualis indica*
Common name: Rangoon Creeper
Hardiness range: 9B to 11
Mature size: 10–40 feet tall by 15–30 feet wide
Light requirement: full shade to partial shade or partial sun
Leaf persistence: evergreen
Flower: red; showy and fragrant spring through fall
Soil moisture: tolerates some drought; will grow in dry soil
Soil pH tolerance: acid to slightly alkaline
Uses: arbor; border
Attributes: fast growing
Native: Myanmar (Burma), Philippine Islands, New Guinea
Notes: flowers emerge white, turn pink, then turn bright red; could invade natural areas

Botanical name: *Solenostemon scuttellarioides* (syn. *Coleus blumei*)
Common name: Coleus, Flame Nettle, Painted nettle
Hardiness range: 9B to 11
Mature size: 1–3 feet tall by 1–2 feet wide
Light requirement: full shade to full sun
Leaf persistence: evergreen
Flower: blue and white; inconspicuous spring and summer
Soil moisture: will grow in moist soil
Soil pH tolerance: acid to slightly alkaline
Uses: containers; border; foundation planting; massing; ground cover
Attributes: very attractive foliage
Native: Malaysia and Southeast Asia
Notes: usually grown as an annual in cooler zones, but can be perennial in frost-free areas; removing flowers will help maintain bright foliage; some cultivars tolerate sun in summer

Botanical name: *Thunbergia battiscombei*
Common name: Clock Vine
Hardiness range: 10B to 11
Mature size: 4–10 feet tall by 10–15 feet wide
Light requirement: partial shade to full sun
Leaf persistence: evergreen
Flower: blue and purple; very showy year-round
Soil moisture: will grow in well-drained soil; moderately drought tolerant
Soil pH tolerance: acid to slightly alkaline
Uses: arbor
Attributes: attractive flowers
Native: tropical Africa
Notes: water generously and protect from strong winds; can be maintained as a hedge

Botanical name: *Thunbergia grandiflora*
Common name: Clock Vine, Sky Flower, Blue Trumpet Vine
Hardiness range: 9B to 11
Mature size: 15–25 feet tall and spreading
Light requirement: partial shade to full sun
Leaf persistence: evergreen
Flower: blue and purple; showy in summer and fall
Soil moisture: tolerates some drought
Soil pH tolerance: acid to alkaline
Uses: containers; arbor; specimen
Attributes: attractive foliage and flowers
Native: northern India
Notes: prefers a fertile soil; takes a year to get started, then grows rapidly

Salt-Tolerant Palms

Highly Salt-Tolerant Palms

Botanical name: *Coccothrinax argentata*
Common name: Silver Palm, Thatch Palm
Hardiness range: 10B to 11
Mature size: 10–15 feet tall by 6–10 feet wide
Light requirement: full shade to full sun
Leaf persistence: evergreen
Flower: white; inconspicuous in summer
Soil moisture: will grow in moist soil
Soil pH tolerance: acid to alkaline
Uses: specimen; accent; border
Attributes: trunk is not showy; highly flammable
Native: Florida
Notes: will grow straight up and provide a beautiful blue accent; especially useful in coastal locations and for soils with a high pH

Botanical name: *Coccothrinax crinita*
Common name: Old Man Palm, Thatch Palm
Hardiness range: 10B to 11
Mature size: 10–15 feet tall by 6–10 feet wide
Light requirement: partial shade to full sun
Leaf persistence: evergreen
Flower: yellow; inconspicuous in summer
Soil moisture: tolerates some drought and occasional wetness
Soil pH tolerance: acid to alkaline
Uses: containers; border; specimen; accent
Attributes: pest tolerant
Native: Cuba
Notes: one Old Man Palm may be all that is needed in a small landscape, but they can be planted in mass if room and budget permit

Botanical name: *Coccothrinax miraguama*
Common name: Miraguama Palm
Hardiness range: 10B to 11
Mature size: 15–20 feet tall by 6–10 feet wide
Light requirement: partial shade to full sun
Leaf persistence: evergreen
Flower: yellow; inconspicuous in summer
Soil moisture: tolerates drought
Soil pH tolerance: acid to alkaline
Uses: border; massing; specimen; accent
Attributes: pest tolerant
Native: Cuba
Notes: one of the nicest *Coccothrinax* palm species; remains most healthy if all green foliage is left on the palm

Botanical name: *Coccothrinax proctorii*
Common name: Palm
Hardiness range: 10B to 11
Mature size: 10–15 feet tall by 6–10 feet wide
Light requirement: partial shade to full sun
Leaf persistence: evergreen
Flower: white; inconspicuous in summer
Soil moisture: tolerates drought
Soil pH tolerance: acid to slightly alkaline
Uses: specimen; accent
Attributes: highly flammable
Native: unknown
Notes: tolerates only slight alkalinity

Botanical name: *Cocos nucifera*
Common name: Coconut Palm
Hardiness range: 10B to 11
Mature size: 50–75 feet tall by 15–25 feet wide
Light requirement: full sun
Leaf persistence: evergreen
Flower: white; inconspicuous in spring
Soil moisture: tolerates drought
Soil pH tolerance: acid to alkaline
Uses: street tree; specimen
Attributes: attractive and edible fruit
Native: Melanesia; Pacific Islands
Notes: highly susceptible to lethal yellowing (varies with cultivar); 'Maypan,' a hybrid of 'Malayan' × 'Panama Tall,' has some resistance to lethal yellowing

Botanical name: *Hyophorbe lagenicaulis*
Common name: Bottle Palm, Pignut Palm
Hardiness range: 10A to 11
Mature size: 15–25 feet tall by 8–12 feet wide
Light requirement: partial shade to full sun
Leaf persistence: evergreen
Flower: cream; slightly showy in spring
Soil moisture: will grow in moist soil
Soil pH tolerance: acid to slightly alkaline
Uses: specimen; accent
Attributes: attractive fruit; unusually shaped and beautifully sculpted crownshaft (green pillarlike extension of the trunk in certain palms, formed by overlapping petiole bases of new leaves)
Native: Round Island (Mascarenes)
Notes: tolerates only slightly alkaline soils; trunk swells at base; makes a nice accent for the tropical landscape

Botanical name: *Hyophorbe verschaffeltii*
Common name: Spindle Palm, Bottle Palm
Hardiness range: 10B to 11
Mature size: 15–20 feet tall by 6–8 feet wide
Light requirement: partial shade to full sun
Leaf persistence: evergreen
Flower: white; showy in spring
Soil moisture: tolerates some drought
Soil pH tolerance: acid to alkaline
Uses: containers; specimen
Attributes: bright green foliage
Native: Rodrigues Island
Notes: nice palm for an accent in the landscape; trunk swelling is less prominent on this palm than *H. lagenicaulis;* slightly susceptible to lethal yellowing

Botanical name: *Sabal bermudana*
Common name: Bermuda Palmetto
Hardiness range: 8B to 11
Mature size: 25–50 feet tall by 10–15 feet wide
Light requirement: partial shade to full sun
Leaf persistence: evergreen
Flower: white; showy in summer
Soil moisture: tolerates drought and some flooding
Soil pH tolerance: acid to alkaline
Uses: massing; specimen; street tree
Attributes: attractive flowers
Native: Bermuda
Notes: exceptionally easy to transplant and will thrive in full sun or partial shade; will adapt to slightly brackish water as well as to dry, sandy locations; requires no special care once established

Botanical name: *Sabal blackburniana* (syn. *Sabal domingensis*)
Common name: Hispaniolan Palmetto
Hardiness range: 8B to 11
Mature size: 25–50 feet tall by 10–15 feet wide
Light requirement: partial shade to full sun
Leaf persistence: evergreen
Flower: white; showy in summer
Soil moisture: tolerates drought and flooding
Soil pH tolerance: acid to alkaline
Uses: street tree; standard; massing; specimen
Attributes: attractive flowers
Native: Bermuda
Notes: drought-tolerant, but not until it is well established in the landscape after transplanting; new transplants (particularly those receiving too little water) are particularly susceptible to the palm weevil, which kills the palm

Botanical name: *Sabal minor*
Common name: Dwarf Palmetto, Bush Palmetto
Hardiness range: 7B to 11
Mature size: 4–6 feet tall by 3–6 feet wide
Light requirement: partial shade to full sun
Leaf persistence: evergreen
Flower: white; fragrant and showy in spring
Soil moisture: tolerates drought; will grow in moist soil
Soil pH tolerance: acid to alkaline
Uses: specimen; ground cover
Attributes: attractive flowers; fruit is eaten by birds
Native: North Carolina to Florida, Texas, and Missouri
Notes: among the hardiest palms; occurs in the understory of woods across a broad swath of the southeastern United States; very rarely forming an aboveground trunk

Botanical name: *Sabal palmetto*
Common name: Cabbage Palmetto, Blue Palmetto, Common Palmetto
Hardiness range: 8B to 11
Mature size: 25–50 feet tall by 10–15 feet wide
Light requirement: partial shade to full sun
Leaf persistence: evergreen
Flower: white; showy in summer
Soil moisture: tolerates drought and flooding
Soil pH tolerance: acid to alkaline
Uses: street tree; standard; massing; specimen
Attributes: pest tolerant; attracts birds and butterflies
Native: Florida, Georgia, North and South Carolina
Notes: staple landscape plant in Florida and along the Gulf Coast; palms that receive little water following transplanting often perform best when most leaves are removed; those receiving regular irrigation following planting establish most quickly when all leaves remain on the palm

Botanical name: *Sabal rosei*
Common name: Palmetto
Hardiness range: 8B to 11
Mature size: 25–50 feet tall by 10–15 feet wide
Light requirement: partial shade to full sun
Leaf persistence: evergreen
Flower: white; showy in summer
Soil moisture: tolerates drought and flooding
Soil pH tolerance: acid to alkaline
Uses: street tree; standard; massing; specimen
Native: Bermuda
Notes: exceptionally easy to transplant and thrives in full sun or partial shade; adapts to slightly brackish water as well as dry, sandy locations and requires no special care once established

Botanical name: *Serenoa repens*
Common name: Saw Palmetto
Hardiness range: 8A to 11
Mature size: 4–8 feet tall by 6–10 feet wide
Light requirement: full shade to full sun
Leaf persistence: evergreen
Flower: white; inconspicuous in spring
Soil moisture: tolerates drought
Soil pH tolerance: acid to alkaline
Uses: woodland garden; border; massing; specimen; erosion control; small tree
Attributes: attracts butterflies
Native: coastal Carolinas to southern Florida
Notes: most have green leaves, but a form with blue leaves can be found along the southeastern coast of Florida; berries are an important food source for many mammals and birds and are used for making a prostate medication

Botanical name: *Thrinax morrisii* (syn. *Thrinax microcarpa*)
Common name: Key Thatch Palm
Hardiness range: 10B to 11
Mature size: 15–25 feet tall by 6–10 feet wide
Light requirement: partial shade to full sun
Leaf persistence: evergreen
Flower: white; inconspicuous in spring
Soil moisture: tolerates drought and occasional wetness
Soil pH tolerance: acid to alkaline
Uses: specimen; accent; screen
Attributes: pest tolerant
Native: Florida
Notes: small enough to be popular in small-scale landscapes, courtyards, and gardens; coarse texture makes this a good accent plant

Botanical name: *Thrinax radiata* (syn. *Thrinax excelsa*)
Common name: Florida Thatch Palm
Hardiness range: 10B to 11
Mature size: 15–25 feet tall by 6–10 feet wide
Light requirement: partial shade to full sun
Leaf persistence: evergreen
Flower: white; inconspicuous in summer
Soil moisture: tolerates drought and occasional wetness
Soil pH tolerance: acid to alkaline
Uses: specimen; accent; screen
Attributes: pest tolerant
Native: Florida
Notes: ideal for seaside applications; looks best planted in a mulched area or in a bed with a low-growing ground cover

Moderately Salt-Tolerant Palms

Botanical name: *Acoelorraphe wrightii*
Common name: Paurotis Palm, Saw Cabbage Palm, Silver Palm
Hardiness range: 9B to 11
Mature size: 15–25 feet tall by 10–15 feet wide
Light requirement: partial shade to full sun
Leaf persistence: evergreen
Flower: white and yellow; very showy in spring and summer
Soil moisture: tolerates some drought and flooding
Soil pH tolerance: acid to slightly alkaline
Uses: containers; border; screen; specimen
Attributes: pest tolerant; tolerates wet soil
Native: West Indies, southern Florida, Mexico, Central America
Notes: could decline and die without irrigation and without correct fertilization on dry, well-drained sites; new stems emerge regularly at the base of the plant

Botanical name: *Bismarckia nobilis*
Common name: Bismarck Palm
Hardiness range: 9B to 11
Mature size: 25–50 feet tall by 10–15 feet wide
Light requirement: partial shade to full sun
Leaf persistence: evergreen
Flower: white; inconspicuous in spring
Soil moisture: tolerates drought and occasional wetness
Soil pH tolerance: acid to slightly alkaline
Uses: specimen; street tree
Attributes: pest tolerant
Native: pantropical
Notes: has a striking blue color; cannot be transplanted until a trunk develops and is visible at the base of the plant; pollen from male plants can cause significant allergies in some people

Botanical name: *Butia capitata*
Common name: Pindo Palm, Jelly Palm
Hardiness range: 8B to 10B
Mature size: 15–25 feet tall by 10–15 feet wide
Light requirement: partial shade to full sun
Leaf persistence: evergreen
Flower: white; showy in spring
Soil moisture: tolerates drought
Soil pH tolerance: acid to alkaline
Uses: street tree; specimen
Attributes: pest tolerant
Native: Brazil to Argentina
Notes: large, showy clusters of orange-yellow, juicy, edible fruits, the size of large dates, are produced and are often used to make jams or jellies; these can also be eaten fresh

Botanical name: *Chamaerops humilis*
Common name: European Fan Palm, Dwarf Fan Palm, Hair Palm, Mediterranean Fan Palm
Hardiness range: 8B to 11
Mature size: 6–10 feet tall and wide
Light requirement: partial shade to full sun
Leaf persistence: evergreen
Flower: yellow; inconspicuous in spring
Soil moisture: tolerates drought
Soil pH tolerance: acid to alkaline
Uses: containers; border; massing; specimen
Attributes: pest tolerant
Native: Mediterranean region east from western Portugal and Morocco
Notes: often grown with several trunks for a clumping effect; growth is slow, so mature plants are considered extremely valuable

Botanical name: *Copernicia alba*
Common name: Wax Palm, Caranda Palm
Hardiness range: 10B to 11
Mature size: 20–25 feet tall by 6–10 feet wide
Light requirement: partial shade to full sun
Leaf persistence: evergreen
Flower: brown; very showy in spring
Soil moisture: tolerates drought
Soil pH tolerance: acid to alkaline
Uses: specimen
Attributes: pest tolerant
Native: Brazil to Argentina
Notes: palms that receive little water following transplanting often perform best when most leaves are removed; those receiving regular irrigation following planting establish most quickly when all leaves remain on the palm

Botanical name: *Copernicia baileyana*
Common name: Bailey Copernicia Palm, Wax Palm, Yarey Palm
Hardiness range: 10B to 11
Mature size: 30–40 feet tall by 6–10 feet wide
Light requirement: partial shade to full sun
Leaf persistence: evergreen
Flower: brown; very showy in spring
Soil moisture: tolerates drought
Soil pH tolerance: acid to alkaline
Uses: specimen
Attributes: pest tolerant
Native: Cuba
Notes: a thick trunk is characteristic of this imposing palm

Botanical name: *Copernicia ekmanii*
Common name: Wax Palm, Caranda Palm
Hardiness range: 10B to 11
Mature size: 30–40 feet tall by 6–10 feet wide
Light requirement: partial shade to full sun
Leaf persistence: evergreen
Flower: brown; very showy in spring
Soil moisture: tolerates drought
Soil pH tolerance: acid to alkaine
Uses: specimen
Attributes: pest tolerant
Native: unknown
Notes: place in full sun for best growth

Botanical name: *Copernicia hospita*
Common name: Cana Palm, Guano Palm, Hospita Palm
Hardiness range: 10B to 11
Mature size: 15–25 feet tall by 6–10 feet wide
Light requirement: full sun
Leaf persistence: evergreen
Flower: brown; fragrant and very showy in spring
Soil moisture: tolerates drought
Soil pH tolerance: acid to alkaline
Uses: specimen; accent
Attributes: pest tolerant
Native: Cuba
Notes: native to the open forests of Cuba; leaves form an erect crown of impressive dimensions on mature trees

Botanical name: *Dypsis lutescens* (syn. *Chrysalidocarpus lutescens*)
Common name: Yellow Butterfly Palm, Areca, Bamboo Palm, Golden Feather Palm
Hardiness range: 10A to 11
Mature size: 15–25 feet tall by 6–10 feet wide
Light requirement: full shade to full sun
Leaf persistence: evergreen
Flower: white; inconspicuous in spring
Soil moisture: tolerates drought and occasional wetness
Soil pH tolerance: acid to slightly alkaline
Uses: containers; border; screen; specimen
Attributes: pest tolerant
Native: Madagascar
Notes: can be used as a houseplant; requires regular fertilizer applications to maintain acceptable medium-green foliage; older leaves become chlorotic, frequently from a deficiency of potassium

Botanical name: *Gastrococos crispa*
Common name: Gastrococos
Hardiness range: 10A to 11
Mature size: 50–75 feet tall by 15–25 feet wide
Light requirement: partial shade to full sun
Leaf persistence: evergreen
Flower: yellow; showy in spring
Soil moisture: tolerates some drought
Soil pH tolerance: acid to slightly alkaline
Uses: specimen
Attributes: attractive flowers
Native: Cuba
Notes: not really suited for beachside planting; the old fronds should be removed before they drop since they can cause injury or damage to plants or property when allowed to fall

Botanical name: *Hyphaene thebaica*
Common name: Gingerbread Palm
Hardiness range: 10B to 11
Mature size: 15–40 feet tall by 10–20 feet wide
Light requirement: full sun
Leaf persistence: evergreen
Flower: purple and yellow; inconspicuous in spring
Soil moisture: tolerates drought
Soil pH tolerance: acid to alkaline
Uses: specimen
Attributes: branched trunks
Native: northern Africa
Notes: one of only a few palms with branched trunks; very tolerant of extended drought

Botanical name: *Jubaea chilensis*
Common name: Chilean Wine Palm, Honey Palm, Syrup Palm
Hardiness range: 9A to 10B
Mature size: 25–50 feet tall by 15–25 feet wide
Light requirement: full sun
Leaf persistence: evergreen
Flower: purple; inconspicuous in spring and winter
Soil moisture: tolerates drought
Soil pH tolerance: acid to alkaline
Uses: specimen
Attributes: attractive fruit
Native: China
Notes: damaged trees are susceptible to ganoderma butt rot; only prune the fronds that hang below the horizontal

Botanical name: *Latania loddigesii*
Common name: Palm, Blue Latan
Hardiness range: 10B to 11
Mature size: 25–30 feet tall by 10–15 feet wide
Light requirement: partial shade to full sun
Leaf persistence: evergreen
Flower: brownish green; inconspicuous in summer
Soil moisture: tolerates drought
Soil pH tolerance: acid to slightly alkaline
Uses: specimen
Attributes: trunk has no thorns; single trunk
Native: Mauritius Island
Notes: coarse-textured palm for a large landscape; tolerates only slight alkalinity; moderately susceptible to lethal yellowing

Botanical name: *Latania lontaroides*
Common name: Red Latan Palm
Hardiness range: 10B to 11
Mature size: 25–30 feet tall by 10–15 feet wide
Light requirement: partial shade to full sun
Leaf persistence: evergreen
Flower: white and yellow; inconspicuous in summer
Soil moisture: tolerates drought
Soil pH tolerance: acid to slightly alkaline
Uses: border; specimen
Attributes: symmetrical with a coarse texture and an open crown
Native: Reunion Island
Notes: reddish foliage on young plants; moderately susceptible to lethal yellowing

Botanical name: *Livistona australis*
Common name: Cabbage Palm, Australian Palm, Gippsland Palm
Hardiness range: 9A to 11
Mature size: 40–60 feet tall by 10–12 feet wide
Light requirement: partial shade to full sun
Leaf persistence: evergreen
Flower: yellow; inconspicuous in spring and summer
Soil moisture: tolerates some drought
Soil pH tolerance: acid to alkaline
Uses: street tree; specimen
Attributes: showy trunk
Native: eastern Australia
Notes: tolerates full sun; young specimens of this palm should be partially shaded; petioles have sharp teeth; root system tends to be slow to develop on young palms

Botanical name: *Livistona chinensis*
Common name: Chinese Fan Palm
Hardiness range: 9A to 11
Mature size: 25–50 feet tall by 10–15 feet wide
Light requirement: partial shade to full sun
Leaf persistence: evergreen
Flower: white; inconspicuous in spring and summer
Soil moisture: tolerates some drought
Soil pH tolerance: acid to alkaline
Uses: containers; street tree; specimen
Attributes: attractive foliage
Native: southern Japan and China
Notes: young specimens should be partially shaded; root system of young plants tends to be slow to develop; moderately susceptible to lethal yellowing and ganoderma butt rot

Botanical name: *Livistona decipiens*
Common name: Ribbon Fan Palm
Hardiness range: 9B to 11
Mature size: 30–35 feet tall by 10–12 feet wide
Light requirement: partial shade to full sun
Leaf persistence: evergreen
Flower: yellow; inconspicuous in spring and summer
Soil moisture: tolerates drought
Soil pH tolerance: acid to alkaline
Uses: street tree; specimen
Attributes: showy trunk; fine texture
Native: Australia
Notes: fast-growing fan palm comparable to growth rate on the Washingtonia Palm; leaflets are deeply divided and segments hang down, lending a delicate, fine texture to any landscape

Botanical name: *Livistona mariae*
Common name: Central Australian Fan Palm
Hardiness range: 10A to 11
Mature size: 40–60 feet tall by 15–20 feet wide
Light requirement: partial shade to full sun
Leaf persistence: evergreen
Flower: yellow; inconspicuous in spring and summer
Soil moisture: tolerates some drought
Soil pH tolerance: acid to alkaline
Uses: street tree; specimen
Attributes: showy trunk
Native: central Australia
Notes: leaves are larger than other fan palms, and tips hang with graceful elegance; root system tends to be slow to develop on young palms

Botanical name: *Livistona saribus*
Common name: Taraw Palm
Hardiness range: 10A to 11
Mature size: 40–60 feet tall by 10–15 feet wide
Light requirement: partial shade to full sun
Leaf persistence: evergreen
Flower: white and yellow; inconspicuous in spring and summer
Soil moisture: tolerates some drought
Soil pH tolerance: acid to alkaline
Uses: specimen
Attributes: no major pest problems
Native: Southeast Asia, Indonesia, Philippines
Notes: tolerates full sun; young specimens of this palm should be partially shaded; petioles are spiny; root system tends to be slow to develop on young palms

Botanical name: *Phoenix canariensis*
Common name: Canary Island Date Palm
Hardiness range: 8B to 11
Mature size: 25–40 feet tall by 15–25 feet wide
Light requirement: full sun
Leaf persistence: evergreen
Flower: white; inconspicuous in winter and spring
Soil moisture: tolerates drought
Soil pH tolerance: acid to alkaline
Uses: street tree; specimen
Attributes: formal aspect in a landscape
Native: Canary Islands
Notes: declines in wet soil, especially if planted too deep or irrigated regularly after it is established; locate the top portion of the root initiation zone several inches above the mulch layer; does well as a street or avenue tree, even in confined soil spaces; keep mulch away from the trunk; moderately susceptible to lethal yellowing

Botanical name: *Phoenix dactylifera*
Common name: Date Palm
Hardiness range: 8B to 11
Mature size: 50–75 feet tall by 15–30 feet wide
Light requirement: full sun
Leaf persistence: evergreen
Flower: white; inconspicuous in winter and spring
Soil moisture: tolerates drought
Soil pH tolerance: acid to alkaline
Uses: street tree; specimen
Attributes: attractive fruit
Native: western Asia, northern Africa
Notes: popular in southern California and Arizona and in other parts of the arid Southwest; suffers in many Louisiana and Florida landscapes because of humid conditions, frequent rainfall, and overirrigation after it is established; keep mulch away from trunk; moderately susceptible to lethal yellowing

Botanical name: *Phoenix reclinata*
Common name: Senegal Date Palm
Hardiness range: 9 to 11
Mature size: 25–40 feet tall by 15–25 feet wide
Light requirement: partial shade to full sun
Leaf persistence: evergreen
Flower: white; showy in spring and summer
Soil moisture: tolerates some drought
Soil pH tolerance: acid to alkaline
Uses: specimen
Attributes: attractive flowers and fruit
Native: tropical Africa
Notes: too large for all but the largest residential landscapes; large specimens command a high price; should receive adequate moisture during periods of drought; has sharp spines; forms clumping stems; slightly susceptible to lethal yellowing

Botanical name: *Phoenix rupicola*
Common name: Wild Date Palm, India Palm
Hardiness range: 10A to 11
Mature size: 20–30 feet tall by 20–25 feet wide
Light requirement: full sun
Leaf persistence: evergreen
Flower: white; showy in winter and spring
Soil moisture: tolerates drought
Soil pH tolerance: acid to slightly alkaline
Uses: specimen
Attributes: attractive flowers and fruit
Native: Himalayan India
Notes: does well as a street or avenue tree, even in confined spaces; requires pruning to remove old leaves; older leaves frequently become chlorotic from magnesium or potassium-deficiency

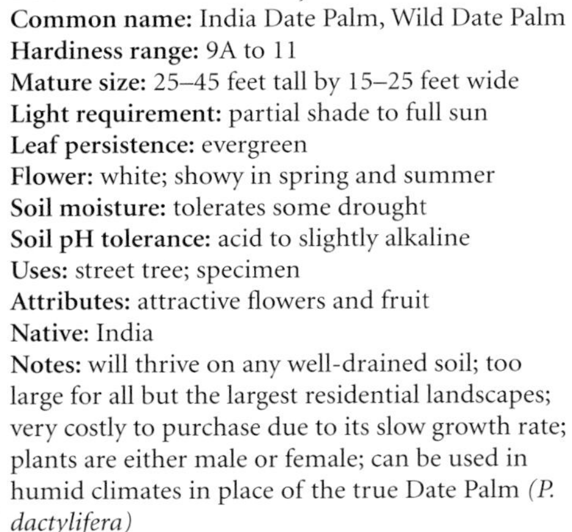

Botanical name: *Phoenix sylvestris*
Common name: India Date Palm, Wild Date Palm
Hardiness range: 9A to 11
Mature size: 25–45 feet tall by 15–25 feet wide
Light requirement: partial shade to full sun
Leaf persistence: evergreen
Flower: white; showy in spring and summer
Soil moisture: tolerates some drought
Soil pH tolerance: acid to slightly alkaline
Uses: street tree; specimen
Attributes: attractive flowers and fruit
Native: India
Notes: will thrive on any well-drained soil; too large for all but the largest residential landscapes; very costly to purchase due to its slow growth rate; plants are either male or female; can be used in humid climates in place of the true Date Palm *(P. dactylifera)*

Botanical name: *Pritchardia pacifica*
Common name: Fiji Fan Palm
Hardiness range: 10B to 11
Mature size: 20–25 feet tall by 8–10 feet wide
Light requirement: partial shade to full sun
Leaf persistence: evergreen
Flower: yellow; inconspicuous in spring
Soil moisture: tolerates some drought
Soil pH tolerance: acid to alkaline
Uses: street tree; specimen
Attributes: attractive foliage
Native: Tonga
Notes: popular in the Pacific Islands including Hawaii; root-balls of field-grown nursery plants or on palms dug and moved in the landscape should be as large as possible for best survival and health following transplanting; highly susceptible to lethal yellowing

Botanical name: *Raphia farinifera*
Common name: Raffia Palm
Hardiness range: 9B to 11
Mature size: 25–45 feet tall by 15–25 feet wide
Light requirement: full sun
Leaf persistence: evergreen
Flower: white; showy in spring
Soil moisture: tolerates some drought and occasional wetness
Soil pH tolerance: acid to slightly alkaline
Uses: specimen
Attributes: source of commercial raffia
Native: tropical Africa and Madagascar
Notes: remains most healthy if all green foliage is left on the palm; only remove those leaves that are completely dead; removing too much green foliage can slow growth and make the palm more susceptible to attack from pests

Botanical name: *Ravenea rivularis*
Common name: Majesty Palm
Hardiness range: 10A to 11
Mature size: 50–75 feet tall by 10–15 feet wide
Light requirement: partial shade to full sun
Leaf persistence: evergreen
Flower: white; inconspicuous in spring
Soil moisture: tolerates some drought
Soil pH tolerance: acid to slightly alkaline
Uses: containers; specimen
Attributes: pest tolerant
Native: Central America
Notes: best suited for dry climates; most widely used as an interior plant; *R. glauca,* a species not known to exceed 20 feet, is also available

Botanical name: *Rhapidophyllum hystrix*
Common name: Needle Palm
Hardiness range: 8A to 10A
Mature size: 4–6 feet tall by 6–10 feet wide
Light requirement: full shade to full sun
Leaf persistence: evergreen
Flower: red; inconspicuous in spring
Soil moisture: tolerates drought and occasional wetness
Soil pH tolerance: acid to slightly alkaline
Uses: border; foundation planting; massing; specimen; ground cover; erosion control
Attributes: pest tolerant
Native: southeastern United States into Florida
Notes: long spines on trunk can inflict severe pain; grows best in moist, fertile soil in a partially shaded location; a versatile, underused plant

Botanical name: *Rhapis excelsa*
Common name: Lady Palm, Bamboo Palm, Miniature Fan Palm
Hardiness range: 9 to 11
Mature size: 6–10 feet tall and wide
Light requirement: full shade to partial sun
Leaf persistence: evergreen
Flower: yellow; fragrant and inconspicuous in spring
Soil moisture: tolerates some drought
Soil pH tolerance: acid to alkaline
Uses: containers; border; screen; specimen
Attributes: multiple trunks
Native: southern China
Notes: needs partial to deep shade and fertile organic soil to look its best; performs well in foundation plantings facing north or in other shady locations

Botanical name: *Roystonea borinquena*
Common name: Puerto Rican Royal Palm
Hardiness range: 10A to 11
Mature size: 50–75 feet tall by 15–25 feet wide
Light requirement: partial shade to full sun
Leaf persistence: evergreen
Flower: yellow; fragrant and showy in spring
Soil moisture: tolerates some drought and occasional wetness
Soil pH tolerance: acid to slightly alkaline
Uses: street tree; specimen
Native: Puerto Rico
Notes: withstands strong winds and salt spray very well but some foliage injury will be evident when located next to the ocean; needs regular fertilization and irrigation in harsh sites

Botanical name: *Roystonea elata*
Common name: Royal Palm
Hardiness range: 10A to 11
Mature size: 50–75 feet tall by 15–25 feet wide
Light requirement: partial shade to full sun
Leaf persistence: evergreen
Flower: yellow; fragrant and showy in spring
Soil moisture: tolerates occasional wetness
Soil pH tolerance: acid to slightly alkaline
Uses: street tree; specimen
Attributes: wetlands plant
Native: Dade and Collier Counties, Florida
Notes: endangered in Florida; often declines when planted in highway medians and other low-maintenance areas; needs regular fertilization and irrigation in harsh sites

Botanical name: *Roystonea princeps*
Common name: Morass Royal Palm
Hardiness range: 10A to 11
Mature size: 50–75 feet tall by 15–25 feet wide
Light requirement: partial shade to full sun
Leaf persistence: evergreen
Flower: yellow; fragrant and showy in spring
Soil moisture: tolerates some drought and occasional wetness
Soil pH tolerance: acid to slightly alkaline
Uses: street tree; specimen
Attributes: wetlands plant
Native: Jamaica
Notes: grows quite rapidly when given an abundance of water and fertilizer in full sun or dappled shade; needs regular fertilization and irrigation in harsh sites

Botanical name: *Roystonea regia*
Common name: Cuban Royal Palm
Hardiness range: 9B to 11
Mature size: 50–75 feet tall by 15–25 feet wide
Light requirement: partial shade to full sun
Leaf persistence: evergreen
Flower: yellow; fragrant and showy in spring
Soil moisture: tolerates some drought
Soil pH tolerance: acid to slightly alkaline
Uses: street tree; specimen
Attributes: wetlands plant
Native: Cuba
Notes: withstands some strong winds and salt spray; not really suited for beachside planting; performs poorly in highway medians and other areas receiving little fertilizer and irrigation

Botanical name: *Sabal causiarum*
Common name: Hat Palm, Palmetto
Hardiness range: 8B to 11
Mature size: 40–50 feet tall by 10–15 feet wide
Light requirement: partial shade to full sun
Leaf persistence: evergreen
Flower: white; showy in summer
Soil moisture: tolerates some drought
Soil pH tolerance: acid to alkaline
Uses: street tree; massing; specimen
Attributes: pest tolerant; showy flowers; fruit eaten by birds
Native: Puerto Rico
Notes: palms receiving little water following transplanting often perform best when most leaves are removed; with regular irrigation, they establish most quickly when all leaves remain on the plant

Botanical name: *Syagrus coronata*
Common name: Licuri Palm
Hardiness range: 9B to 11
Mature size: 25–30 feet tall by 15–25 feet wide
Light requirement: full sun
Leaf persistence: evergreen
Flower: white; showy in spring
Soil moisture: tolerates some drought and occasional wetness
Soil pH tolerance: acid to slightly alkaline
Uses: specimen
Native: eastern Brazil
Notes: prefers acid, well-drained soils and will show severe mineral deficiencies in alkaline soil; is not affected by lethal yellowing disease

Botanical name: *Syagrus romanzoffianum* (syn. *Arecastrum romanzoffianum*)
Common name: Queen Palm
Hardiness range: 9B to 11
Mature size: 25–50 feet tall by 15–25 feet wide
Light requirement: partial shade to full sun
Leaf persistence: evergreen
Flower: white; showy in spring
Soil moisture: tolerates some drought and occasional wetness
Soil pH tolerance: acid
Uses: specimen
Attributes: attractive flowers and fruit
Native: South America
Notes: grows best in acid, well-drained soils and shows severe mineral deficiencies on alkaline soil; not affected by lethal yellowing disease; pollen can cause significant allergies; considered a junk palm by some

Botanical name: *Trachycarpus fortunei*
Common name: Windmill Palm
Hardiness range: 8A to 10B
Mature size: 15–25 feet tall by 6–10 feet wide
Light requirement: full shade to partial sun
Leaf persistence: evergreen
Flower: white and yellow; fragrant and inconspicuous in summer
Soil moisture: tolerates some drought
Soil pH tolerance: acid to slightly alkaline
Uses: containers; woodland garden; border; specimen
Attributes: very attractive lining an entry walk to a large building
Native: northern Myanmar (Burma), central and eastern China
Notes: should be grown in shade or partial shade on fertile soil to look its best, but may tolerate full sun on well-drained soils when given ample moisture in the northern part of its range

Botanical name: *Veitchia merrillii* (syn. *Adonidia merrillii*)
Common name: Christmas Palm, Manila Palm
Hardiness range: 10B to 11
Mature size: 15–25 feet tall by 10–15 feet wide
Light requirement: partial shade to full sun
Leaf persistence: evergreen
Flower: white and yellow; inconspicuous in summer
Soil moisture: tolerates some drought
Soil pH tolerance: acid to slightly alkaline
Uses: containers; street tree; specimen
Attributes: attractive fruit
Native: Palawan Island
Notes: very susceptible to lethal yellowing disease; grows well indoors

Botanical name: *Washingtonia filifera*
Common name: Desert Fan Palm, California Washingtonia Palm, Petticoat Palm
Hardiness range: 9A to 11
Mature size: 40–60 feet tall by 10–15 feet wide
Light requirement: full sun
Leaf persistence: evergreen
Flower: white and yellow; inconspicuous in spring
Soil moisture: tolerates drought
Soil pH tolerance: acid to alkaline
Uses: street tree; specimen
Attributes: pest tolerant; attracts birds
Native: southern California, southwestern Arizona, northwestern Mexico
Notes: grows fast in any region within its hardiness range; it looks better than *W. robusta* because the trunk is considerably thicker

Botanical name: *Washingtonia robusta*
Common name: Mexican Washington Palm, Washington Palm
Hardiness range: 8B to 11
Mature size: 50–75 feet tall by 10–15 feet wide
Light requirement: partial shade to full sun
Leaf persistence: evergreen
Flower: white; showy in summer
Soil moisture: tolerates drought and occasional wetness
Soil pH tolerance: acid to alkaline
Uses: specimen
Attributes: pest tolerant
Native: Mexico
Notes: tolerates poor soil and drought and is hardy to about 20 degrees F; however, foliage turns brown with temperatures in the mid-to-low twenties

Botanical name: *Wodyetia bifurcata*
Common name: Foxtail Palm
Hardiness range: 10A to 11
Mature size: 25–30 feet tall by 15–20 feet wide
Light requirement: partial shade to full sun
Leaf persistence: evergreen
Flower: white; inconspicuous in spring
Soil moisture: tolerates some drought
Soil pH tolerance: acid to alkaline
Uses: border; street tree; specimen
Attributes: no major pest problems; attractive foliage
Native: northern Australia
Notes: responds to irrigation and good fertility with rapid growth and bright green foliage; tolerates only a light frost and should only be planted where temperatures remain above freezing

Selected References

Barnett, M. R., and D. W. Crewz. 1997. *Common Coastal Plants in Florida.* Gainesville: University Press of Florida.

Barrick, W. E. 1978. Salt Tolerant Plants for Florida Landscapes. *Proc. Fla. State Hort. Soc.* 91:82–84.

Barrick, W. E. 1979. *Salt Tolerant Plants for Florida Landscapes.* Report 28. Marine Advisory Program, University of Florida, Gainesville.

Bernstein, L., L. E. Francois, and R. A. Clark. 1972. Salt Tolerance of Ornamental Shrubs and Ground Covers. *J. Amer. Soc. Hort. Sci.* 97 (4): 550–56.

Black, R. J., and K. C. Ruppert, eds. 1998. *Your Florida Landscape: A Complete Guide to Planting and Maintenance.* Gainesville: University Press of Florida.

Brandies, M. M. 1994. *Xeriscaping for Florida Homes.* St. Petersburg, Fla: Great Outdoors.

Carrow, R. N., and R. R. Duncan. 1998. *Salt-Affected Turfgrass Sites: Assessment and Management.* Chelsea, Mich.: Ann Arbor Press.

Craig, R. M. 1975. Woody Vegetation for Coastal Dune Areas. *Proc. Fla. Hort. Soc.* 88:428–34.

Dehgan B. 1998. *Landscape Plants for Subtropical Climates.* Gainesville: University Press of Florida.

Ferguson, C. R. 1952. Salt Tolerant Plants for South Florida. *Proc. Fla. State Hort. Soc.* 65:306–13.

Francois, L. E. 1982. Salt Tolerance of Eight Ornamental Tree Species. *J. Amer. Soc. Hort. Sci.* 107 (1): 66–68.

Francois, L. E., and R. A. Clark. 1978. Salt Tolerance of Ornamental Shrubs, Trees, and Iceplant. *J. Amer. Soc. Hort. Sci.* 103 (2): 280–83.

Gilman, E. F. 2000. *Horticopia Professional.* Purcellville, Va.: Horticopia.

Gilman, E. F. 2002. *An Illustrated Guide to Pruning.* 2d ed. Albany, N.Y.: Thomson Learning, Delmar.

Gilman, E. F., and R. J. Black. 1990. *Pruning Landscape Trees and Shrubs.* Department of Environmental Horticulture Circular 853. University of Florida/IFAS, Gainesville.

Gilman, E. F., and R. J. Black. 1999. *Your Florida Guide to Shrubs: Selection, Establishment, and Maintenance.* Gainesville: University Press of Florida.

Gilman, E. F., and S. J. Lilly. 2002. *Best Management Practices: Tree Pruning.* Champaign, Ill.: International Society of Arboriculture.

Haehle, R. G., and J. Brookwell. 1999. *Native Florida Plants.* Houston, Tex.: Gulf Publishing.

Hanlon, E. A., B. L. McNeal, and G. Kidder. 1998. *Soil and Container Media Electrical Conductivity Interpretations.* Soil and Water Sciences Department Circular 1092. University of Florida/IFAS, Gainesville.

Johnson, C. R., and R. J. Black. 1976. *Salt Tolerant Plants for Florida.* Department of Environmental Horticulture Fact Sheet 26. University of Florida/IFAS, Gainesville.

Knox, G. W., and R. J. Black. 1987. *Salt Tolerance of Landscape Plants for South Florida.* Department of Environmental Horticulture Circular 756. University of Florida/IFAS, Gainesville.

Knox, G. W., and R. J. Black. 1987. *Salt Tolerance of Landscape Plants for Central Florida.* Department of Environmental Horticulture Circular 757. University of Florida/IFAS, Gainesville.

Knox, G. W., and R. J. Black. 1987. *Salt Tolerance of Landscape Plants for North Florida.* Department of Environmental Horticulture Circular 758. University of Florida/IFAS, Gainesville.

Knox G. W., T. K. Broschat, and G. Kidder. 2002. *Fertilizer Recommendations for Landscape Plants.* Department of Environmental Horticulture Fact Sheet 858. University of Florida/IFAS, Gainesville.

Langeland, K. L. 1999. *Help Protect Florida's Natural Areas from Non-native Invasive Plants.* Agronomy Department Circular 1204. University of Florida/IFAS, Gainesville.

Meerow, A. W. 1999. *Guide to Landscape Palms.* Hollywood, Fla.: Betrock Information Systems.

Menninger, E. A. 1964. *Seaside Plants of the World.* Great Neck, N.Y.: Hearthside Press.

Nellis, D. W. 1994. *Seashore Plants of South Florida and the Caribbean.* Sarasota, Fla.: Pineapple Press.

Nelson, G. 1994. *The Trees of Florida.* Sarasota, Fla.: Pineapple Press.

Tanji, K. K., ed. 1996. *Agricultural Salinity Assessment and Management.* ASCE Manuals on Engineering Practice 71. New York: American Society of Civil Engineers.

U.S. Salinity Laboratory Staff. 1954. *Diagnosis and Improvement of Saline and Alkali Soils.* Handbook 60. Washington, D.C.: U.S. Government Printing Office.

Waters, W. E.; J. E. Hesmith, C. M. Geraldson and S. S. Woltz, 1972. The interpretations of soluble salt tests and soil analysis by different procedures. Bradenton AREC Mimeo Report GC-1972-4.

Watkins, J. V., and T. J. Sheehan. 1975. *Florida Landscape Plants.* Gainesville: University Press of Florida.

Westcot, D. W., and R. S. Ayers. 1985. Irrigation Water Quality. In *Irrigation with Reclaimed Municipal Wastewater: A Guidance Manual,* by G. S. Pettygrove and T. Asano. Boca Raton, Fla.: Lewis Publishers.

Robert Black is currently professor emeritus in the Department of Environmental Horticulture at the University of Florida. He is the author of numerous extension publications, coauthor of *Your Florida Guide to Bedding Plants,* and coeditor of *Your Florida Landscape: A Complete Guide to Planting and Maintenance,* and *The Florida Lawn Handbook.*

Edward F. Gilman is currently professor in the Department of Environmental Horticulture at the University of Florida. He has authored hundreds of IFAS extension publications and five landscape books, including coauthoring *Your Florida Guide to Bedding Plants* and *Your Florida Guide to Shrubs.*

Related-interest titles from University Press of Florida

Florida's Best Native Landscape Plants
200 Readily Available Species for Homeowners and Professionals
Gil Nelson

A Gardener's Guide to Florida's Native Plants
Rufino Osorio

Common Coastal Plants in Florida
A Guide to Planting and Maintenance
Michael R. Barnett

Florida Gardening by the Sea
Mary Jane McSwain

Florida Wildflowers in Their Natural Communities
Walter Kingsley Taylor

Landscape Plants for Subtropical Climates
Bijan Dehgan

Ornamental Palm Horticulture
Timothy K. Broschat and Alan W. Meerow

Florida Butterfly Gardening
A Complete Guide to Attracting, Identifying, and Enjoying Butterflies of the Lower South
Marc C. Minno and Maria F. Minno

Landscaping for Florida's Wildlife
Re-creating Native Ecosystems in Your Yard
Joe Schaefer and George Tanner

Gardening With Carnivores
Sarracenia Pitcher Plants in Cultivation and the Wild
Nick Romanowski

My Weeds
A Gardener's Botany
Sara B. Stein

For more information or to order these and other books, visit our website at www.upf.com.